CHRISTIANS
HAVE
CRISIS?

UNDERSTANDING CRISIS
AND THE AFTERMATH

JUDITH ISAACS-HERRIG, M.ED, QIDP

ISBN 978-1-64114-461-2 (paperback)
ISBN 978-1-64114-462-9 (digital)

Christian Faith Publishing, Inc.
832 Park Avenue
Meadville, PA 16335
www.christianfaithpublishing.com

Printed in the United States of America

"Consider it pure joy when you face trials
because you know that the testing of your faith
produces perseverance"
(James 1:2).

CONTENTS

INTRODUCTION

Although this book is geared toward Christian families and caregivers, it is directed as a teaching tool for those who are leaders and counselors in ministry.

I am a fact-finder! With each topic, I present researched facts. Some of these facts may come off as being liberal. For some, it will come off as too conservative. I share personal experience and understanding of the topics. I also present what the Bible says about each topic. Scripture is my rule of practice. This has been a long, hard study for me I studied with great diligence to verify each and every scriptural verse, and its placement. It is my intention to ensure it is written it the right context and to not mislead anyone.

It is my prayer that this book will spread throughout the country helping those who are experiencing the pain and uncertainty in life's journey.

It is my prayer that this book will shed light on those who are in managerial, pastoral, or caregiver positions to gain understanding of what a person in a crisis may be experiencing. To open people's minds and their hearts.

My ministry is to find answers and healing for those in crisis and to teach people compassion and understanding for those in need.

What brought me to write this book?

The answer boils down to training and education, life experiences, compassion for the misunderstood, and the love and forgiveness of Christ.

Man is born broken. He lives by mending.
The grace of God is glue.
–Eugene O'Neill

MISSION STATEMENT

My interest in teaching Christians about crisis survival and mental illness is derived from my own experience as a Christian, a parent, from my employment and from my college education. It is derived from my love of learning and sharing those experiences with others.

It is my personal goal to create a supportive, loving environment for couples and families. One way to achieve that is for the readers to have an open mind and a sincere heart.

I believe my passion for teaching crisis survival and mental illness will encourage motivation, problem solving, and healing by seeking God through prayer and biblical knowledge.

I will teach from my heart for practical experience and biblical understanding. I will use variations of the King James Bible to teach biblical principles. I will use my formal education for researching facts and findings, and other educational purposes for validation.

Last and foremost, it is my prayer that my teaching will meet the objectives for writing this book.

> Be careful how you live; You will be the
> only Bible some people ever read.
> –William J. Toms

WITH APPRECIATION

I cannot express the gratitude I have for my husband whom has supported me throughout this entire journey. It was a huge learning curve and he was there for me 110%! This beautiful man has been married to this crazy entrepreneurial spirit since 1981 and two spirited daughters followed. He has shared my love and compassion for people and animals. As they say down here in the south; "Bless his heart!"

I want to thank those very special people in my life who have prayed for me and supported me through some of those trying times. The ones who have helped me to stay on track and the people who have been my teachers and mentored me through this learning process. You know who you are! I appreciate each and every one of you!

To the sweetest of memories of my daddy and my grandma who would be so very proud.

CHAPTER ONE

SUPPORT FOR LOVED ONES
AFFECTED BY MENTAL ILLNESS

Mental illness is a part of all of our lives in one way or another–
It shouldn't have to be a secret.
–NAMI

We must be more aware of mental illness in the church because 26%, YES – that is 1 in every 4 adults in the U.S. suffers with mental illness. That means it is relevant to everyone. Of the 26% of the adults with mental illness, more than 22% of those cases are severe. At least

50% of all adults will develop depression, anxiety, self-harm, eating disorders, bipolar disorder, PTSD, borderline personality disorder, schizophrenia, or some other mental illness in their lifetime. And with homelessness, 40% are mentally ill with 20–25% have serious mental illness.

Some people do not believe that mental health is real or at least considered a medical illness. But with head scans, medical researchers have found that there are actual differences in the brain of those with and without mental illness. There is biological evidence, therefore it is a medical illness.

Mental illness is common, it is real, and affects all of us. It is nobody's fault, it is not a spiritual problem, and it is treatable—not curable.

Because there is more than one in four people who suffer with mental illness in the U.S., there is a strong need for educating the community in helping them through mental health and disability issues. It is proven that the church can be a great asset to a spiritual life and offers a higher chance of recovery for those with mental illness. The church can provide support for their caretakers and/or family members. The church can be a safe harbor for everyone!

AS A CHURCH

No one is untouched by mental illness. As a church, we need to acknowledge and be more accepting of our own brokenness to be more effective.

Some Christian theologians teach our brokenness is caused by sin. Sin has caused all creation to fall from the perfect state in which God intended it. The world is in bondage to death and decay so that it cannot fulfill its intended purpose. One day, the world will be liberated and transformed. Until then, Christians are to go with Christ into the world where they heal people's bodies and souls and fight the evil effects of sin in the world (Rom. 8:19–23).

Loving others unconditionally is a response to forgiveness and grace. Those who understand the depth of their sin can understand the depth of forgiveness and mercy God gives us. He rescues believers from eternal death (Luke 7:47).

Talk about brokenness in your teaching and sermons. We are all affected by our own brokenness in one way or another. It is often said that the church is the guiding light for those who feel lost and a hospital for those who are broken. It is important that we remember we are *all* broken.

There are some people that seem to attract those who need help or guidance. It may feel like a burden when it truly is a spiritual gift. When you understand what your spiritual gifts are, they can be very powerful tools.

SPIRITUAL GIFTS

To operate effectively, the church has many roles to fill; from maintenance and bus drivers to musicians, sound system technicians, teachers, leaders, and office staff. God gave every person spiritual gifts and wants them used for His purpose.

Some churches provide training to learn what each person's spiritual gifts are. Knowing your spiritual gifts will provide spiritual direction. God has given each of you a gift from His great variety of spiritual gifts. Use them well to serve one another (1 Pet. 4:10).

Lead a life worthy of your calling for you have been called by God. Always be humble and gentle. Be patient with each other, making allowances for each other's faults because of your love. Make every effort to keep yourselves united in the Spirit, binding yourselves together with peace (Eph. 4:1–3).

What if your spiritual gift is leadership yet you do not feel you have the knowledge to take on such role? In Ephesians 4:11–13, Paul writes: These gifts God gave to the church; the apostles, the prophets, the evangelists, pastors and teachers. Their responsibility is to equip God's people to do his work and build up the church, the body of Christ. This will continue until we all come to such unity in our faith and knowledge of God's Son that we will mature in the Lord, measuring up to the full and complete standard of Christ.

AS A LEADER

Throughout the Bible, there is scripture that pertains to the expectations of leadership roles.

Any leader who expects to lift the spirits of others must start with purification. To minister to other people, our hearts must be clean before God (Neh. 12:30).

Christians are not immune from suffering. As a leader, you first need to relate to your own suffering. When we suffer, we often feel as though our pain will never end. But God promises after you have suffered for a time, He will restore, support and strengthen you and place you on a firm foundation. (1 John 5:10).

Good, strong leaders come from overcoming!

God will equip you to speak the truth with love (Eph. 4:14–15).

God takes His stand in His own congregation; He judges in the midst of the rulers. Vindicate the weak and the fatherless; do justice to the afflicted and the destitute. Rescue the weak and needy; deliver them out of the hand of the wicked (Psalms 82:1–4).

Ecclesiastes 8:1–5, Solomon reminds us of our personal accountability to our job as a leader and to God.

In all the years I have been a Christian, I have been afflicted by so many people with their misguided comments and judgment. People can be totally turned off by well-meaning, overbearing Christians. Leaders need to treat people like they would want to be treated if they are in the same situation! As a leader, you are accountable to God for your use of authority. Ephesians 4:11 and Hebrews 13:17. Your authority is a gift from God. You can make many plans, but the Lord's purpose will prevail (Prov. 19:21).

No matter what the differences, everyone has suffered or is suffering. Everyone has their own story. Be a friend. Be patient and kind. You may be the one person that can open a new door for someone.

Get past the stigma, be the one to set the example.

Educate others, advocate and volunteer.

Every single leader in the church should receive crisis and mental health training as soon as possible. Don't wait until there is someone in your church going through a major crisis!

The National Institute of Mental Health (NIMH) and National Alliance on Mental Illness (NAMI) are excellent informational resources. If anything is slightly unclear, make sure you ask questions. You will need to understand the physical, emotional, spiritual, and social needs of a person or family in crisis.

Start a support group in your church. Amy Simpson, author of "Troubled Families: Support for Loved Ones Affected by Mental Illness" has the profile of a support group in her book. NAMI can help set up a First Aid for Mental Illness Crisis class for your church to improve response to people who are in crisis.

The church may be a person's first resort or their last. Provide help and support for the family with resources. Your church can be a strong advocate by creating alliances with professionals. This may include Christian family counseling. Be aware of what services are available in the community. Have references readily available. You never know when this information may be life-saving to a person. If possible, engage with family members through the process. Try to prevent misinterpretation of exclusion.

If you feel the need to share your own personal story when speaking with someone, talk openly and appropriately about your own family, but don't make the conversation about you. Quickly get the focus back on the other person by asking an open question. Always be honest, never exaggerate. Remember that God is working through you. Never use a tone that can be taken as demeaning. Speak with integrity (Prov. 16:13).

Create and enforce good boundaries! Keep comments, hands, and hugs appropriate. As a leader, it is important to protect the church from legal ramifications.

If you are ministering a person in a crisis, encourage them to get professional help. Make sure treatment information is readily available. Refer people to counselors and mental health professionals. Assist them with a written plan and support system. Don't abandon them. If you are actively involved in their therapy, sign release of information forms and privacy forms.

Some people mistakenly believe that because they are not licensed therapists, they are exempted from this law!

Have realistic expectations. Recovery is not a one-time deal, it is a process that continues throughout their lifetime. There will be ups and downs—often in extremes.

As a Christian, we need to be understanding and empathetic to their issues. If you don't know what to do for a person in trouble, go to someone who does.

It is often said that as a Christian, we may be the only Bible a person ever sees. That is a profound statement!

AS A CHRISTIAN

I am mortified by the number of people who are turned off from the church because they have endured judgment, hypocrisy, and forceful Christians. We are *all* humans needing grace from sin. As a Christian, show mercy and help to carry each other's burdens.

Even if we don't like a person, we are to stop and help them (Exod. 23:5).

You can make an impact on your community by doing kind things for others as Tabitha did in (Acts 9:36).

Consider how we may spur one another on toward love and good deeds (Heb. 10:22–24).

In James 5:16, we are reminded that confessing our sins to each other is important to the life of the church. As it would be important to any relationship. When we sin against someone, we need to ask that person for forgiveness. And we need to forgive others (Matt. 6:14–15).

Romans 12:13: When God's people are in need, be ready to help them. Always be eager to practice hospitality. This does not mean your home needs to be spotless and offer a ten-course meal. It only means to offer a place to stay, nourishment, and/or a listening ear.

In 1 Corinthians 12:25–26, Paul teaches to share happiness with those who are happy and share their sorrow when others are sad. We should be involved in the lives of others and not just enjoy our own relationship with God.

In 1 Peter 4:11, Peter teaches us that our abilities should be used in serving others not to fulfill our own egos. He assures us that we *all* have gifts that God can use. In Matthew 6:1–8, we are reminded to do the right thing for the right reason—whether you have been a Christian for many years, or new to Christianity.

NEW CHRISTIANS

You probably attend a church for the same reason you would want to read this book. Because you need uplifting. You might be looking for answers to questions you cannot even describe. Do you need a promise that everything will be okay, or to fill an empty space in your heart?

Whatever the reason, you somehow know that God is going to help you through it. And He will. God promises it! (Mark 1:2–3). God is faithful (Mark 9:50).

STUDY

- The book of Proverbs to learn about godly living.
- The Beatitudes in Matthew 5:3–12 is a standard of conduct for all believers

Find a mentor to guide you when you have questions and concerns. Make sure the person you choose is well versed with the Bible and biblical principles.

ALL CHRISTIANS

The best practices for Christians to follow are written throughout the Bible. Attend Bible studies so you learn the Bible and gain a deep relationship with Christ. The more you learn about the Bible, the more you will be motivated to learn more.

Submit to the word of God. Read your Bible daily (Neh. 10:1–30).

Let each day's first words be praise to God (Psalm 51:15).

Listen to your spiritual leaders, do what they say because their work is to watch over your souls and are accountable to God. Give them a reason to do this with joy (Heb. 13:17).

Support the House of God, tithe faithfully (Nehemiah 10:32–39, Matthew 23:23, and Luke 11:42).

Remember that God will supply all your needs (Phil. 4:19).

When you focus correctly, you can smile, sing and rejoice. Sing songs of praise and thanksgiving unto God (Neh. 12:46).

MOST IMPORTANT! Find hope in Christ (Psalm 42:5). I have come to bring you a future and hope (Jer. 29:13).

Some people are hurting so bad
you have to do more than preach a message to them.
You have to BE a message to them.
–Spiritual Inspiration

READING RESOURCES:

A Tale of Three Kings
By Gene Edwards

Cape Approach: A Compassionate Method to Christian Counseling;
Crisis Hotlines and Soul Care
By Judith A. Justiniano-Houts

Christian Counseling: A Comprehensive Guide
By Gary R. Collins, Ph.D.

The Complete Guide to Crisis and Trauma Counseling:
What to Do and Say When it Matters Most
By Dr. H. Norman Wright

Crisis Ministry: A Handbook
By Daniel G. Bagby

God's Answers to Life's Difficult Questions
By Rick Warren

What to Say When You Don't Know What to Say: In Times of Grief,
Heartache and Crisis
By H. Norman Wright

Women Reaching Women in Crisis: Ministry Handbook
By Chris Adams

Working with Families of the Poor
By Patricia Minuchin, Jorge Colapinto, and Salvador Minuchin

QUESTIONS TO PONDER:

1. Church is the guiding light for those who feel lost and a hospital for those who are broken.
   Do you agree with that statement?
   Does your church resonate with that statement?

2. Spiritual Gifts:
   Do you know what talents God has gifted you with?
   Do you use your gifts to benefit others?

3. Leadership:
   What attributes do you possess that makes you a good leader?
   What have you experienced to make you a good leader?

4. Do you love others unconditionally?
   No matter what?
   Do you have limits? If yes, what are they and why?

5. Do you know someone that has been rejected from a church?
   What was the situation?
   How do you feel about it?

6. Have you experienced a situation in which a well-meaning Christian hurt you or someone you love?
   What was the situation?
   How do you feel about it?

7. Was any part of this chapter eye-opening for you?
   Does it motivate you to change anything?

8. What verse or verses are important to you?

CHAPTER TWO

MENTAL HEALTH AND THE CHURCH

There are many different types of mental health issues church leaders should not only be aware of, but have an understanding of how to recognize it. The symptoms vary in degree from unnoticed to severe. This chapter is not meant for a layperson to diagnose anyone. It is literally basic information to help understand how these diagnoses can affect each person, their family, their vulnerabilities, their choices, and their spirituality.

Behind every person is a family that has been changed by mental illness. Mental illness creates suffering in families. There are psychological and emotional symptoms. A family may go into crisis from not only the chaos but how mental illness monopolizes family resources. There are financial hardships due to job loss, hospitalizations, treatment, residential care, and alternative schools. Unfortunately, health insurance often doesn't adequately cover mental illness treatment. Insurance will delay care as insurance tends to limit the amount of time used for a person in crisis. Generally, insurance will only allow enough time to get medically stabilized. It often takes two to six weeks for psychiatric medications to be effective when they are only admitted for twenty-four to forty-eight hours. There is a tendency to have a long waiting list to admit a person in crisis into a mental health facility for extended care. Psychiatric clinics tend to be overbooked. Laws or rules and regulations will often work against families trying to get help.

Generally, police tend to be the frontline resource to get the families immediate help. The officer may or may not have an understanding of mental illness. This can increase safety risk for all people involved. Ryker's Island and LA County Jail treat more mentally ill people than any psychiatric hospital in this country. Often, a person needs to be incarcerated to receive appropriate mental health care. Generally incarceration is due to extreme behavior that puts them and others at risk.

It is hard for a family to witness incarcerating a loved one to get help. However, there is something to be said for team cooperation. I worked with a young man whom had a very athletic stature. This large, muscular young man displayed dangerous, raging behaviors. He needed psychiatric medications but his family refused the use of medications insisting the young man to go through counseling and behavior monitoring—against the advice of his entire professional team. This young man became more and more intense, his aggression progressed with fits of raging anger. His verbal threats increased with intense yelling, slamming doors to the point of breaking them, and hitting his fist on things. The grand finale was when he used his baseball bat to threaten his housemates and staff in his home, he demolished his bedroom furniture, walls, and doors. The police were able to contain him; however, because his behavior was extremely aggressive, the hospitals would not admit him. He was admitted to a correctional facility to protect himself and others. He was beyond the help his residential facility and social services could offer him. An incident of this magnitude could have been prevented had prescribed medications been administered to him.

WHAT IS NORMAL?

Because we all come with different personalities, beliefs, lifestyles, backgrounds, and experiences, normal differs from one person to another. Basically, normal does not interfere with healthy functioning or setting short or long-term goals. In other words, abnormal interferes with daily living and goal setting.

Experiencing day-to-day life with mental illness can be used as an opportunity to use as a teaching tool. A person with mental illness can teach others about mental illness and coping strategies. They can inspire others who are suffering or living with someone that suffers with mental illness.

STIGMA

The greatest problem with mental health is the collective stigmas.

Stigma defined: People who views mental illness in a negative way (stereotype). Others' judgments is the result from those who lack understanding rather than information based on the facts. Most people have knowledge of particular stereotypes because they develop from societal means such as media.

Negative attitudes and beliefs about mental health is common and can lead to discrimination. Discrimination can be blatant negative comments. It may also be subtle just by avoiding a person. Some people assume that a person with mental illness may be unstable, violent, or dangerous. Discrimination causes fewer opportunities for work, school, or social activities and housing. People who are discriminated against tends to be bullied and harassed.

Fear of discrimination can cause a person to avoid seeking help or treatment. There may be a lack understanding by their family, friends, co-workers, and other people they associate with. The belief is that they may be dangerous or incompetent. Those beliefs can be harmful to a person living with mental illness.

When we acknowledge the role of social beliefs and internalization, the behavioral processes can lead to social isolation and ostracism. Individuals who live with mental illness are vulnerable to endorsing these stereotypes about themselves (self-stigma). The effect of self-stigma is low self- esteem and poor self-efficacy inadvertently causing unemployment and homelessness. Some perceive their mental issues is a sign of personal weakness or they feel they should be able to control the symptoms on their own. As self-stigma manifests itself, it will ultimately cause poor health outcomes and a poor quality of life.

According to a study shared by the National Institute of Health (NIH.gov), "Empowering individuals seems to be an effective way of reducing self-stigmatization, encourage people to believe they can achieve their life goals, and circumvent further negative consequences."

"Empowerment is the opposite of stigma; involving power, control, self-advocating, activism, righteous indignation, and optimism. When shown empowerment, people gain better self-esteem, better quality of life, increased social support, and increased satisfaction with mutual-help programs."

DO'S AND DON'TS?

First and foremost, educate yourself. Speak out against stigma and mental health. Consider expressing your opinions at events in letters to the editor and online blogging. It can encourage others facing similar challenges and educate the public about stigma and mental illness.

If *you* are living with mental illness:

Get treatment. Don't let the fear of being labeled prevent you from getting the help you need. Treatment can provide relief by identifying your needs and reduce the symptoms that interfere with your work and personal life.

Medications and Appointments: Never mix over the counter medications without consulting your pharmacist or physician.

Never use drugs not prescribed to you, street drugs or alcohol! It exacerbates mental illness symptoms and can be fatal.

Make sure appointments are kept and follow through with recommendations of other treatments and/or counseling. Don't stop going to appointments or taking medications because things seem better. Your medications are the reason you feel better.

Don't let stigma instill self-doubt and shame. Seek psychological counseling—find one that you are comfortable with. Educate yourself about your condition. Share your knowledge with your spouse. Connect with others with mental illness through support groups. They can help you gain self-esteem and overcome destructive self-judgment.

Don't become your illness. Your illness is not your identity and your chemistry is not your character. You are not bipolar; you are a person with bipolar disorder.

Don't allow yourself to become isolated from others. If you have a mental illness, you may be reluctant to tell people about it. Your family, friends, pastor/minister, or members of your community can offer you support if they know about your mental illness. Reach out to people you trust for the compassion, support, and understanding you need.

If you or your child has a mental illness that affects their learning, find out what plans and programs the school can help you with. It is against the law to discriminate against a person with a mental health condition. They are required to accommodate students. Talk to teachers, professors, or administrators about the best approach and their resources. Remember that if a teacher or educator is unaware of a student's disability, it can inadvertently lead to discrimination, barriers to learning and poor grades.

When there are invisible wounds, people are not able to offer sympathy. But with actual physical issues, people are more willing to reach out. We have to remember to create an environment of warmth for everyone (2 Cor. 4:7).

LABELING

One of the major issues with mental health is what is known as Iatrogenic Labeling. Often, a person given labels will believe there is something wrong with them which will contribute to negative treatment effects. If the client is told that their problem cannot be resolved or may get worse without treatment, the client may live up to the label(s) justifying their behavior. They act out the role assumed by the diagnosis.

> "Labels are for soup cans."
> –President George W. Bush

The therapist may see more disorder than what is actually present and persuade the client with the same belief. The therapist has bias judgment.

Labeling a person can create more damage than the actual diagnoses can cause. Psychiatric labels can contribute to negative self-perceptions and social stigma.

BLAME GAME

Don't allow yourself to fall into the blame game. Mental illness is a part of human nature. I have heard people blame their upbringing as a reason for their child's mental illness. Some want to blame doctors because of their beliefs that "doctors all push vaccines and toxic medications." I have seen many people blame the sufferer because they are seeking self-pity, they have a lack of faith, choose to be depressed or that it is from a lifetime of not taking care of themselves.

Be careful of judgment as you do not walk in their shoes.

Do not judge others, and you will not be judged. For you will be treated as you treat others. The standard that you use in judging is the standard by which you will be judged (Matt. 7:1–2).

Forgive them-even if they are not sorry (Col. 3:13).

WHAT DOES THE BIBLE SAY ABOUT MENTAL ILLNESS?

There is no admission in the Bible, but a representation of mental health. Mental health is the product of a post-fallen world. There is no record of mental illness in Eden, but with sin, it has altered the world.

Some people believe that mental illness is a spiritual problem allowing Satan control of your mind. Some believe psychiatry is evil because of the Darwinian Evolutionists. "The devil loves the mental health industry" (www.bible.ca)

SCRIPTURE ON MENTAL HEALTH:

And his fame went throughout all Syria: and they brought unto him all sick people that were taken with diverse diseases and torments, and those which were possessed with devils, and those which were lunatic, and those that had the palsy; and he healed them (Matt. 4:24).

At the foot of the mountain, a large crowd was waiting for them. A man came and knelt before Jesus and said, "Lord, have mercy on my son. He has seizures and suffers terribly. He often falls into the fire or into the water. So I brought him to your disciples, but they couldn't heal him." Jesus said, "You faithless and corrupt people! How long must I be with you? How long must I put up with you? Bring the boy here to me." Then Jesus rebuked the demon in the boy, and it left him. From that moment, the boy was well. Afterward, the disciples asked Jesus privately, "Why couldn't we cast out that demon?" "You don't have enough faith," Jesus told them. "I tell you the truth, if you had faith even as small as a mustard seed, you could say to this mountain, 'Move from here to there,' and it would move. Nothing would be impossible." (Matt. 17:14–20)

Sin is described as a virus of self-centered blindness to the truth and glory of God. It has twisted and broken every aspect of human nature from the clarity of our mental processes to the bio-chemical make-up of our brains. It affects the human race from generation to generation. But remember that God paid a ransom to save you from the empty life you inherited from your ancestors (1 Pet. 1:18).

CAN JESUS HEAL MENTAL HEALTH?

Psalm Chapter 107 reminds us we are to cry (pray) unto the Lord about our troubles and to be saved from our distress. Some people want to pray away a disability or a disorder and then get angry at God because it didn't go away. This is where we have to be cautious when using verses that can cause people to feel it is their lack of faith or that God does not love them enough to heal them.

Mental illness is not a spiritual problem. It is not a lack of faith or the result of sin. Nor is it a punishment from God. And it is most certainly not disloyal to God to seek mental health treatment.

Integrating faith-based therapy with medications can be helpful for someone in a mental health crisis. As Christian leaders, you have credibility. You can help remove the stigma against taking medications. Yes, there are risks and benefits as well as complicating side effects. But for some people, stopping their medications can be fatal.

In James 5:15, we are reminded that prayer of faith will save the sick and the Lord will raise him up. And Isaiah 53:4 says that He has lifted up our suffering and sorrows.

We have to remember that God does things in His time and we need to be constant in prayer and faith. I cannot count how many times I wanted something so bad—but God said no. Not now. And I was provided with a much better answer later (Psalm 56:3).

Isaiah 26:3 reminds us that God will keep us in perfect and constant peace when our minds are stayed on Him. In 1 Peter 5:10, it says that after you have suffered awhile, God of all grace will restore, confirm, strengthen and establish you. And in Ecclesiastes

3:1, Solomon reminds us that for everything there is a season; a time to heal, a time to weep, a time to mourn.

In John 5:8, Jesus said to rise up from the bed and walk. We need to encourage each other to get up and walk. That is not the same as people telling a person to "get over it." Sometimes, you need to "stand up and get moving" for recovery to take place. As you work for healing, the healing will come.

As discussed, we are all broken people. For some people, they need to seek a mental health professional to get stabilized (get through the roughest times). It doesn't mean you are a bad person or weak in your faith!

> "The primary cause of unhappiness is never the situation but your thoughts about it."
> –Eckhart Tolle

Some people need to go through repentance to release their guilt and shame. Recognize your mistakes, make restitution if necessary and move forward. Repentance will make room for healing.

Forgiving yourself and forgiving others who have offended you is an opportunity for healing. Tears are prayers that travel to God (Psalm 56:8).

BASIC OVERVIEW OF COMMON DISORDERS

AUTISM

Autism Society of America (ASA) defines Autism as "a complex developmental disability that typically appears during the first three years of life and is the result of a neurological disorder that affects the normal functioning of the brain. It impacts the development in the areas of social interaction and communication skills. Both children and adults with autism typically show difficulties in verbal and non-verbal communication, social interactions, and leisure or play activities."

As many as one in 68 children are diagnosed with Autism Spectrum Disorder (ASD) found in all races and ethnic groups. It has been recognized as the fasted growing disability showing a 23% increase. It is considered a lifelong disability however can be managed through treatment and therapy. To lead meaningful, productive lives, early intervention is crucial.

WHAT DOES AUTISM LOOK LIKE?

The two notable characteristics of autism is persistent deficits in social communication and interaction as well as repetitive patterns and behaviors. It varies in age of onset and the severity of the symptoms. Even though there are commonalities in the symptoms, each individual's abilities and challenges will differ.

Approximately forty percent of individuals with autism vocalize sounds as they are unable to speak. They may have echolalia, which is the repeating of words or phrases over and over. Many are unable to understand nonverbal messages that include social cues, body language, and vocal qualities (pitch, tone, and volume).

Individuals with autism interact different with others. They often appear to live in their own world leading to isolation. They have difficulty understanding and expressing emotion. They may have difficulty expressing attachment.

As we all are aware of, children learn and grow at different rates. Children with autism often have a different rate of development especially in the areas of communication, social, and cognitive skills. Yet, their motor skills may develop at a typical rate. Children with autism may not play with toys in the same manner as their peers and may become fixated to specific objects. They may get upset if objects in their environment or time schedules change. Persons with autism may be extremely sensitive to sensory stimuli that they see, hear, touch, feel, or taste. And when these senses go on overload, they may overreact.

WHAT TO DO IF YOU THINK YOUR CHILD HAS AUTISM?

- Get a diagnosis. If you are concerned or believe a person has autism, see a doctor who's familiar with ASD. Don't assume the child will catch up.
- Get help. Early intervention including special schooling and speech therapy are critical. Check resources below for services or assistance locating service providers in your area.
- Know your rights. There are government mandated services available. Contact the National Information Center for Children and Youth with Disabilities for more information.

Perhaps you're not sure your child or loved one has autism and want to learn more about it. Even though autism is not considered a mental health issue such as depression, the National Alliance on Mental Illness (NAMI) is an excellent resource for education and support for family members of those suffering from mental illness.

RESOURCES:

Autism Society of America
Autism Research Institute
Autism Speaks
Centers for Disease Control
Behavior Frontiers
Easter Seals: MaketheFirstFiveCount.org
American Academy of Pediatrics
National Information Center for Children and Youth With Disabilities

DEPRESSION

WHAT DOES DEPRESSION LOOK LIKE?

- Significant weight changes including weight loss or weight gain of more than 5% body weight in a month.
- Significant increase or decrease in appetite
- Excessive sleepiness or insomnia including fatigue or loss of energy nearly every day
- Diminished thinking ability. Difficulty concentrating and/or making decisions.
- Agitation, restlessness
- Recurring thoughts of death or suicide

Understand that people have ups and downs. Yes, even Christians! This does not mean you are depressed. So what can you do to work your way through it?

Depression is multifaceted. It affects our emotions, cognition, perceptions, physical health, sleep patterns and appetites.

THE CAUSES ARE:

1. Biological—genetics or pre-disposed.
2. Psychological—attachment factors, loss and relationships. They will feel worthless, struggle at school or work, they may have morbid thoughts.
3. Social, economic, and cultural factors
4. Behavioral patterns—withdrawal, drained of effort

Treatment for depression may include one or more of these therapies: psychotherapy, cognitive therapy, medication, group therapy, hormonal therapy, spiritual support, prayer, and meditation, forgiveness, diet, and exercise.

People who have not experienced depression cannot clearly understand the problem. Depression can be profoundly debilitating with intense suffering.

In 2003 Pope John Paul II said, "Depression is always a spiritual trial" recognizing that depression can affect your spiritual being, putting a person into a spiritual crisis. If failing relief spiritually, the person will feel God has turned on them. They will lose hope in prayer.

Spiritual counsel should provide confidentiality, structure, curriculum and/or resources. Spiritual counsel can offer a person the ability to rediscover their self-esteem, healing, restore hope, giving the person a reason to live. They will perceive the tenderness of God, to love and to be loved.

FEAR

Fear can be healthy when it is appropriate. But irrational fear in general is unhealthy and can emotionally paralyze a person. I have an irrational fear of storms, electricity, and fire for a number of reasons. When I look back over the years, my mother was afraid of fire and electrical wiring. We were always checking things to make sure they were unplugged and/or off. And the fear has grown with experience; my aunt's house was burned down because a curling iron was left on. Also, lightning caused one of our window fans to catch fire. It helps me to understand why I have these fears, but it doesn't take it away.

While fear is natural and we all have experienced it, it can be sinful because fear takes our minds from what we know is good and right. It can hinder praise in that we focus on ourselves or our circumstances. We become angry, we worry; we are ungrateful, hopeless, and complain to everyone. We allow our imaginations to soar with negative thoughts. How can one be prayerful and sing praises in that frame of mind?

I cannot avoid the fear because electricity is in our daily lives. I cannot fix the fear because a wiring fire could actually happen. And I cannot stop a storm from scaring me. But I can work on my trust on the promises of God. The cure for fear is faith in God versus our faith in what is happening around us, our emotions and our imagination.

I sought the Lord and he answered me and delivered me from all my fears (Psalm 34:4).

"Do not fear" is written in the Bible 365 times. That is a daily reminder. Don't worry about anything; instead pray about everything (Phil. 4:6).

Fear not, for I am with you; be not dismayed, for I am your God; I will strengthen you, I will help you, I will uphold you with my righteous right hand (Is. 41:10).

Behold, God is my salvation; I will trust, and will not be afraid; for the Lord God is my strength and my song, and he has become my salvation (Isa. 12:2).

Every word of God is pure. He is a shield unto them that put their trust in Him (Prov. 30:5).

ALZHEIMER'S AND DEMENTIA

What is the difference between Alzheimer's and Dementia?

Alzheimer's disease and dementia are often used interchangeably as many people believe they are the same. The difference between the two diseases often causes confusion, while related, they are remarkably different.

According to the National Institute on Aging (NIA), Dementia is a brain disorder that affects communication and performance and Alzheimer's disease is a form of dementia that specifically affects parts of the brain that controls thought, memory and language.

Because there is so much more to learn about Alzheimer's and Dementia, there is still a lot of scientific research needed. Public awareness of these worldwide epidemics are in dire need.

Dementia has a set of symptoms including impaired thinking and memory. It is often associated with the cognitive decline of aging. There are issues other than Alzheimer's that can cause dementia.

According to the Center for Disease Control, Alzheimer's disease is a very specific form of dementia. Symptoms of Alzheimer's include impaired thought, impaired speech, and confusion. There are a variety of screenings to determine the cause of dementia.

How are they different?

Alzheimer's is not a reversible disease. It is degenerative and incurable at this time. Some forms of dementia, such as a drug interaction or a vitamin deficiency, are actually reversible or temporary. Once a cause of dementia is found appropriate treatment and counseling can begin.

2015 ALZHEIMER'S STATISTICS

- Worldwide, nearly forty-four million people have Alzheimer's or a related dementia. (Alzheimer's Disease International)
- Proportion of People With Alzheimer's Disease in the United States by Age: (Alzheimer's Association) 85+ years, 38%, 75–84 years, 44%, 65–74 years, 15%, <65 years, 4%
- Only one in four people with Alzheimer's disease have been diagnosed. (Alzheimer's Disease International)
- Alzheimer's and other dementias are the top cause for disabilities in later life. (Alzheimer's Disease International)
- One in three seniors die with Alzheimer's or another kind of dementia. (Centers for Disease Control)
- Typical life expectancy after an Alzheimer's diagnosis is four to eight years. (Alzheimer's Association)

WHO GETS ALZHEIMER'S DISEASE?

- Two in three people with Alzheimer's are women. (Alzheimer's Association)
- African American and Hispanic Americans are more likely to develop Alzheimer's than white Americans. (Alzheimer's Association)
- North Dakota has a higher rate of Alzheimer's mortality than any other state (Fifty-four Alzheimer's deaths a year per 100,000 residents)

- Alzheimer's mortality is lowest in Nevada (Eleven Alzheimer's deaths a year per each 100,000 residents) (Alzheimer's Association)
- Thirty percent of people with Alzheimer's also have heart disease, and twenty-nine percent also have diabetes. (Alzheimer's Association)

CAREGIVERS

- More than forty percent of family caregivers report that the emotional stress of their role is high or very high. (Alzheimer's Disease International)
- In 2014, Alzheimer's and dementia caregivers had $9.7 billion in additional health care costs of their own. (Alzheimer's Association)
- In the 2009 NAC/AARP survey, caregivers most likely to indicate stress were women, older, residing with the care recipient, and white or Hispanic. In addition, these caregivers often believed there was no choice in taking on the role of caregiver. (Alzheimer's Association)
- People with Alzheimer's disease are hospitalized three times more often than seniors without Alzheimer's. (Alzheimer's Association)
- Seventy-four percent of caregivers of people with Alzheimer's disease and other dementias reported that they were somewhat concerned to very concerned about maintaining their own health since becoming a caregiver. (Alzheimer's Association)
- More than fifteen million Americans provide unpaid care for people with Alzheimer's disease and other dementias. (Alzheimer's Association)

TRAUMATIC BRAIN INJURY (TBI)

Injuries can happen to your brain in many ways. They could be brought on by medical problems like a stroke or tumor. These are called acquired brain injuries (ABIs). But most often, brain injuries are due to a violent blow or jolt to the head. These are called traumatic brain injuries (TBIs). WebMD

Some people suffer with comorbidity (the presence of more than one diagnosis). This is commonly found in soldiers who suffer with a combination of Post Traumatic Syndrome Disorder (PTSD) and Traumatic Brain Injury (TBI). With either of those diagnoses, the affects promotes a cycle of mental health issues—such as anxiety and depression—which exacerbates the effects of the diagnoses.

Those who suffer with TBI may be confused and disoriented immediately after their injury, but once they understand the extent and severity of their condition, they will likely suffer a tremendous sense of loss and depression. Similarly, families and loved ones of those disabled by traumatic brain injury will also likely suffer grief and a sense of loss when they realize how people with TBI will be permanently impaired.

As a result, those with TBI and their families can benefit from understanding the emotional stages of recovery. The better patients and families understand the nature of TBI and how it affects their lives, the faster they will be able to accept the prognosis, get through their grief process, and achieve strength from it.

GRIEVING

The feelings of grief are usually brought on by situations in which we have no control. A grieving person may suffer from any combination of anxiety, depression, fear, guilt, insomnia, rage, stress, and shock. Different people will grieve differently, depending on their individual personalities and triggers of grief.

According to Kübler-Ross, "On Death and Dying," the emotional stages of recovery as follows:

- Denial: Most people experience denial as their first emotional stage in recovery. In denial, they may be anxious, afraid, in shock, or in disbelief about their condition.

- Anger: While brain damage may directly cause anger, others may become enraged when they realize the extent of their loss. In this emotional stage of recovery, the grieving person may blame others, throw tantrums, yell or become extremely frustrated.
- Bargaining: When people make statements like "I would pay anything to get better" or "I promise something if I can get better." They are in the bargaining stage of emotional recovery. Although this stage appears to show a degree of acceptance of the condition, it also reveals persisting traces of denial that needs to be worked through.
- Depression: As soon as the grieving person starts to accept the nature of their condition and resulting disabilities, they will likely become overwhelmingly sad, suffering from depression. In general, depression is the hardest emotional stage of recovery to work through. They will feel incapable and hopeless, decreasing the chances they will follow through for help.
- Acceptance: When the grieving person develops a healthy acceptance of their condition, they will enjoy higher self-esteem, a positive attitude and a sense of hope for their future.

Going to therapy for both individual and family therapy can help people experiencing grief to understand their feelings and appropriately work through them. Some may even benefit from going to support groups or a local church group where they can find strength, comfort, and support from others enduring the long, hard road to recovery.

Emptiness and loneliness is an emotion that can be reduced with prayer, meditation, journaling, exercise, and getting out to meet with family and friends. Emptiness and loneliness may be a symptom of depression. If you are experiencing these feelings, tell somebody you trust will be honest with you and will seek professional help if you need it. If it is serious (you feel you may hurt yourself or someone else), call your doctor. If it is after hours, go to the emergency room to determine what you need to get through this time quickly and safely.

BIPOLAR DISORDER

Dr. Tom Okamoto, Psychiatrist gave a lecture "Living with Bipolar Disorder" at the "Mental Health and the Church" seminar. It was explained Bipolar Disorder was considered to be extreme moods of ups and downs, but that it is much more complex than that. It is mood that doesn't regulate (rapid cycling of depression, mania and hypermania). It may be made up from biological (including hormones), environmental/stress, brain damage, and/or genetics (DNA).

A person with bipolar disorder may be a sharp, productive person, yet they are self-destructive. They often run into legal issues. With the stigma of bipolar disorder, it may force people into early retirement or becoming completely reliant on human services.

FACTS:

- 2.6% of the general population are diagnosed with Bipolar Disorder. 5% to 7% in other countries. That's six million adults.
- The average age of onset diagnosis is twenty-five years old.
- Fourteen to eighteen years diagnosed with depression (actually Bipolar)
- On an average, it takes ten years to be correctly diagnosed.
- Famous people: Jane Pauley, Demi Lovato and Jean-Claude Van Damme
- Sixth cause of disability due to loss of work and relationships.

Society doesn't really accept or understand the significance of bipolar disorder. It can be very serious. It is not a character defect or a lack of faith. It is not being possessed. Years ago, people were restrained and chained. People believed it would be relieved by having their blood released. It was in the 1850s that there were more diagnostics. Psychiatric doctors would give their patients a lobotomy or shock treatments to make them forget their problems. There is Lithium, Depikote, and other psychotropic medications that are available to help stabilize the moods. Economics and politics effects the development of new medications.

Bipolar Disorder is treatable.

WHAT DOES BIPOLAR DISORDER LOOK LIKE?

MANIA AND HYPERMANIA:

- Grandiosity, out of character, out of control, extreme and out of bounds
- Need less sleep
- Paranoid
- Agitated, aggressive, and raging
- Risky behavior, hyper-sexuality, impulsive
- Poor decision-making

DEPRESSION:

- Lack of energy, sleeping excessively
- Isolation
- Suicidal thoughts
- Catastrophic

CHILDREN:

- Hear voices
- Extreme silliness
- Grandiosity
- Suicidal

- Raging
- Homicidal
- Sleepless
- Catastrophic (fear and terror)

When working with people that are dual diagnosed with bipolar disorder and intellectually challenged, I found that they would display symptoms from all three of these categories including those with less challenges.

COMMON DIAGNOSIS WITH BIPOLAR DISORDER:

- ADD/ADHD (cannot tolerate Ritalyn when Bipolar)
- OCD (Obsessive Compulsive Disorder)
- Anxiety
- Panic Attacks
- Addictions
- Mood Disorders
- Eating Disorders
- Post-Traumatic Stress Disorder (PTSD)

When a person has not been properly diagnosed, they are at the mercy of people's judgment. They often are given medications that are counter-productive. They live with turmoil, moodiness, and will suffer consequences of their actions. Bad things happen!

Imagine a person with bipolar disorder as being a boiling pot. As each issue or negative event occurs, it turns the fire up making the pot hotter and hotter. Because the process is collective, it could be one simple thing that builds enough pressure for the pot to boil over.

The person may be unable to decipher good from bad; only to react without considering the consequences. I have been told by those with bipolar disorder that "When it takes over, it just takes over." When they are experiencing psychosis or are delusional, it is advised to offer a reality check with careful feedback. You probably won't convince them that their hallucinations or delusional experience is not reality. It is very real to them.

PSYCHOTHERAPY:

- CBT, Cognitive Behavior Therapy which is primarily to identify negative behaviors and their triggers. To learn how to replace negative thoughts to positive thoughts.
- FFT, Family Focus Therapy provides support and education for the entire family to be a more cohesive, and supportive system.
- PSRT, Personal Social Rhythm Therapy; by tracking moods and routines to stabilize their circadian rhythms, often results in better and healthier interpersonal relationships and skills.
- PE, Psychoeducation is to educate patients and family members about bipolar disorder and how to improve their long-term outcome working collaboratively with a clinical team.

HOW CAN I HELP?

For those recovering with bipolar disorder, life becomes hard work. But the church can help through bleak times for additional support. Some people need help to find direction. Spiritual healing can be extremely important to their emotional well-being.

Get educated! There are great resources listed in the back of this book.

Understand that recurrence rates are very high. Bipolar disorder doesn't get better and go away. It has highs and lows and it is hard work to maintain emotional stability.

Compliance means staying on prescribed medications. Common complaints while taking medications is that they don't feel good when they take them, they feel sedated or lethargic, or the medications cost too much. Often, a person will go off of them because they feel better and believe they are not necessary.

***When a person goes off their medications without appropriate titration, it is harder to recover the next time. Going off the medications can cause more effects and more damage including seizures. The ideal full remission is to stay on medications for maintenance.

CUTTING AND SELF-INJURY

Non-suicidal self-injury is the act of deliberately harming the surface of your own body such as cutting or burning yourself. It's typically not meant as a suicide attempt. Rather, this type of self- injury is an unhealthy way to cope with emotional pain, intense anger, and frustration. It is usually followed by guilt and shame and the return of painful emotions. Although life-threatening injuries are usually not intended, with self-injury comes the possibility of more serious and even fatal self-aggressive actions. Getting appropriate treatment can help learn healthier ways to cope.

FORMS OF SELF-INJURY

Self-injury usually occurs in private and is done in a controlled or ritualistic manner that often leaves a pattern on the skin. Examples of self-harm include:

- Cutting (cuts or severe scratches with a sharp object)
- Scratching
- Burning (with lit matches, cigarettes or hot, sharp objects like knives)
- Carving words or symbols on the skin
- Hitting or punching
- Piercing the skin with sharp objects
- Pulling out hair
- Persistently picking at or interfering with wound healing

Most frequently, the arms, legs and front of the torso are the major areas of self-injury. People who self-injure may use more than one method to harm themselves. Becoming upset can trigger an urge to self-injure. Many people self-injure only a few times and then stop. But for others, self-injury can become a long-term, repetitive behavior.

Some people will self-injure in public or in groups to bond or to show others that they have experienced pain.

If you are injuring yourself or have thoughts of harming yourself, ask for help. Any form of self- injury is a sign of bigger issues that need to be addressed.

Talk to someone you trust; such as a friend, loved one, health care provider, spiritual leader or a school official who can help you take the first steps to successful treatment. While you may feel ashamed and embarrassed about your behavior, you can find supportive, caring, and nonjudgmental help.

WHEN A FRIEND OR LOVED ONE SELF-INJURES

If you have a friend or loved one who is self-injuring, you may be shocked and scared. Take all talk of self-injury seriously. Do not worry about betraying a confidence. Self-injury is too big a problem to ignore or to deal with alone.

If your child is involved in any form of self-injury, consult your pediatrician or other health care professional who can provide an initial evaluation or a referral to a mental health specialist. Do not raise your voice or punish your child or make threats or accusations. Show compassion and express concern.

If a teenage friend is involved in self-injury, suggest that your friend talk to parents, a teacher, a school counselor or another trusted adult.

If your friend is an adult, gently encourage the person to seek medical and mental health treatment.

According to Mayo Clinic, "Although self-injury is not usually a suicide attempt, it can increase the risk of suicide because of the emotional problems that trigger self-injury. And the pattern of damaging the body in times of distress can make suicide more likely."

SUICIDE AND PREVENTION (ALSO SEE TEEN SUICIDE IN CHAPTER 9)

Suicide is a very personal subject. It may be a struggle that you are personally fighting, or someone you know. We know many famous people—from all walks of life that committed suicide.

- Robin Williams; comedian, actor
- Richard Jeni; comedian, actor
- Brian Keith; actor
- Don Lapre; television pitchman
- Gia Alleman; model, actress
- Whitney Houston; singer/actress
- Whitney Houston's twenty-two-year-old daughter, Bobbi Kristina Brown; singer, actress
- Simone Battle; musician, singer of girl group G.R.L, actress
- Capital Steez; Hip-Hop artist
- Marie Osmond's eighteen-year-old son, Michael Blosil
- Joseph Brooks;s screenwriter, director, producer, composer
- Michael Alfonso aka Mike Awesome; wrestler
- Jeff Alm; Houston Oilers football player
- Jovan Belcher; Kansas City Chiefs football player
- Mark Green; record-setting minor league hockey star
- Vince Foster; Deputy White House Counsel to Bill Clinton
- James D. Ford; Chaplain of the U.S. House of Representatives for two decades
- Marshall Applewhite; leader of Heaven's Gate religious cult
- Adolf Hitler; Nazi Germany leader
- Bruno Bettleheim; psychologist, writer
- Iris Chang; historian, author
- Jeremy Blake; artist
- Finn M. W. Capersen; financier, philanthropist
- Jeremy Michael Boorda; Chief of Naval Operations, U.S. Navy

SUICIDE PREVENTION

Twenty years ago, suicide prevention was not mentioned in congressional records because it was not considered a public health problem. It was private between patients and their healthcare providers. Clinical training in suicide assessment and effective treatments was rare. There was little prevention capacity and infrastructure because there was little to no funding for suicide prevention.

Jessica Vander Stad of NAMI and Dr. Jerry Reed, Director of Center for Study and Prevention of Injury, Violence, and Suicide provided information that will help to equip us with skills to use as an opportunity to help others. The statistics are alarming to me. It helps to know the statistics because it shows that you are NOT alone!

FACTS:

- 40,000+ Americans die every year from suicide. That is 1 person in every 14 minutes.
- It is the 2nd leading cause of death for college students.
- It is the 2nd leading cause of death for people ages 25 to 34.
- It is the 3rd leading cause of death for the ages 10 to 24!
- If a parent has committed suicide, it is 60% more likely their child will attempt suicide.
- Twenty percent of the general population has had a family member commit suicide.
- Sixty percent of the general population personally knows someone that has committed suicide.
- Eighty percent will give signs before they commit suicide.

WHAT ARE THE WARNING SIGNS?

- Change in behavior including dramatic mood swings, appearance, going from outgoing to withdrawn or well-behaved to rebellious
- Self-destructive behavior

- Talking about killing or harming themselves
- Writing a lot about death or dying
- Seeking things to use to commit suicide; weapons, street, and prescription drugs,
- Loss of interest of things that matter to them
- Hopelessness

YOU SHOULD ALWAYS TAKE A THREAT SERIOUSLY.

Myth: People who talk about it won't really do it. Fact: Eight out of ten people will leave some sort of clue(s).

Myth: Some people think that once the decision has been made there is nothing you can do to stop them from committing suicide. Fact: most people who are considering suicide don't really want to end their life. They want to end their pain.

Myth: People who attempt suicide and survive will not attempt suicide again. Fact: 80% of people who die from suicide has made prior attempts of suicide.

Myth: Discussing suicide with someone considering suicide might plant the seed to end their life. Fact: An open discussion may actually be the best thing you can do to help the person. It allows them an opportunity to sort through their problems offering some relief and understanding.

Is suicide a sin? Only if having mental illness is a sin. People who consider suicide are experiencing a mental health crisis. Suicide is an act that occurs when suffering with mental illness. Sadly, there are many Christians that believe people who commit suicide will go to hell because they have committed murder. But educated Christians understand that even a murderer with life in prison can be saved. John 3:16 is one of many verses that will back that up!

AS A CHURCH, HOW CAN WE HELP?

Start educating frontline people so you can have an immediate response person. Your receptionist should be able to access a person immediately. She too should be a part of the team as she may need to triage calls.

In 2013, middle aged men had the greatest increase of suicide. They are vulnerable when struggling with employment and financial crisis, divorce, children in their teens and college years, family, and health issues. Transitions are difficult for any person being head of household. Create ministries for men in their mid-years to teach coping skills and strategies as well as having a strong support system.

Always offer compassion and comfort to the loved ones of suicide victims. They are feeling the excruciating pain of loss, shame from gossip and stigma, and the burdens that were left behind. Some have left behind financial burdens, children, and animals to be cared for, personal things to go through, a house to prepare to sell or apartment to clean and remove things from.

These may all require legal and court issues. The list of sudden responsibilities and loss may be extremely overwhelming. They are going to need help getting through this turmoil along with finding their new normal.

Teach children and young adults early the coping skills and strategies. A person may not be able to choose how they feel, but they can choose how they cope.

WHAT IF I AM THE PERSON?

"What would you do if I killed myself?" What do you do if someone you are ministering to asks you that question? What would you do if someone in your family asked you that question?

If you happen to be the person at the right place at the right time, you need to know what to do. You do not have to be afraid to talk about their feelings. You will not give them the idea, it will not push them over the edge. It will most likely open a door to communicate with you.

- Be direct, but non-confrontational. You may need to ask the same questions in different ways to get an answer. Remember that the word *harm* is not the same as the word *suicide*.
- Listen to what is being said. Engage with the person and reflect what you are hearing. Always use age appropriate language. Be genuine and show that you care.

- Remind them that they are not alone!
- Ask them to look for a doctor that can help them. They may have to keep looking until they find the right doctor for them.
- If they don't want to see a doctor because they are embarrassed and afraid, they need to keep it a secret, you ask them, "Would you see a doctor if you had cancer or diabetes?"
- Remind them, "The world is better with you here."

***If you are challenged with a person that has a borderline personality disorder, bipolar disorder or schizophrenia, there is a different distinction in how to deal with suicide.

Listen to their reasons. Allow them to express how they are feeling. Don't make a trite statement like, "You have so much to live for." This person with mental illness and in crisis is not going to feel that way. They will shut the communication off.

If you are worried about a person attempting suicide, trust your gut! Don't leave them alone—even if it is to talk on the phone. Text if you must. Try to strengthen positive reasons for living.

Know your referral system both online and in the community. Some counties have a twenty-four-hour crisis team.

You do not have to be the person in crisis to call a suicide prevention line. There are wonderful places online to talk: Teen Crisis Chat. With an acute crisis, call 9-1-1.

Try to get a safety plan in place. You may need to engage the person to get help. Make sure the person in crisis has a network. How long can the person stay safe until they receive appropriate services?

Recovery is a process. It is a healing process, it does not happen in a single visit. Try to get a commitment from the person that they will do what they need to do to stay safe. You may need to remove dangerous items from their possession.

Again, if it becomes an acute crisis, hang up and call 9-1-1.

EATING DISORDERS AND BODY DYSMORPHIA

As described on webMD, "An eating disorder is an illness that leads people to overeat, starve themselves, or adopt other unhealthy behaviors surrounding food and body weight. These disorders- binge eating, anorexia nervosa and bulimia are not simply bad habits. They interfere with daily life and without proper treatment they can cause serious health problems."

Eating disorders frequently appear during the teen years or young adulthood but may also develop during childhood or later in life. These disorders affect both genders, although rates among women are two-and-a-half times greater than among men. Researchers found that eating disorders tend to run in families.

BINGING, PURGING, ANOREXIA AND BULIMIA:

Eating disorders are of the highest mortality rate among mental illness. The dangers of these eating disorders is that the acid in the stomach deteriorates the throat and mouth. It causes deterioration of the teeth and throat burn. Their vitamins are depleted, and suffer with the effects of low potassium. Having low potassium affects the muscle function and the heart causing heart attacks. They also have problems with Osteomelasia, which is a bone disorder.

With media making people look like Barbie and Ken, this subject needs to be taken seriously. Many people have face lifts, hair transplants, breast implants, and tummy tucks. Extremists distort their faces with mutilating holes, slicing their tongues, and radical tattoos. Some consider that practice as eccentric or eclectic, a means of rebellious self-expression.

I have seen men have muscle implants to appear brawny. Some people will go as far as having ribs removed to have a smaller waist. This is considered Body Dysmorphic Disorder (BDD).

Body Dysmorphic Disorder is a mental disorder characterized by a preoccupation with a perceived defect in the person's physical appearance. They can spend the majority of their day scrutinizing themselves in the mirror. Their concern is markedly excessive causing significant distress or impairment in social, occupational, or other areas of functioning. They are preoccupied with their "defective body parts," their complaints tend to be specific (too big, too small, too round, too narrow, too dark, too light, uneven, etc.). In addition to holding negative thoughts about themselves, people with BDD assume that others view them negatively. Feelings of self-consciousness about their "defect" often leads to avoidance of work or public situations literally debilitating them.

Some people view body dysmorphic disorder (BDD) as vanity; others believe it's a rare and extreme condition. BDD is a real, fairly common body image disorder. Clinical settings have suggested BDD affects about 0.7 percent to 3 percent of the population, however, research suggests in medical settings that it is actually a much higher rate. It affects men and women equally and has levels of severity. Body dysmorphic disorder (BDD) sufferers often have secondary conditions, including major depression, social anxiety, and substance abuse.

Seventy-five percent of individuals with BDD will experience major depressive disorder in their lifetime, and the suicide rate among people with BDD is substantially higher than that among other psychiatric populations—including eating disorders, major depression and bipolar disorder. Forty-five to seventy-one percent experience suicidal ideation due to BDD and twenty-four to twenty-eight percent have attempted suicide.

Treatment plans for BDD may include one or more of the following:

- Individual, group, and/or family psychotherapy
- Medical care and monitoring
- Nutritional counseling
- Medications

SELF-PITY

It is normal to suffer with self-pity when a person is going through some extreme hardships, but when it takes over the center of your existence, your self-pity has become excessive. Self-pity can be a form of self-indulgence. Does it bring you attention? What is your reward for your behavior?

Figure out if you are bringing on your own disasters. Are you too demanding? Is your complaining driving others away?

Use your discomfort to motivate you. Do things that make you happy. Are you neglecting hobbies you enjoy? Take a dance or art class. Volunteering is fulfilling.

Huffington Post reports that exercise will reduce stress, increase happy chemicals in your brain, improve self-confidence, and alleviate anxiety.

MUNCHAUSEN SYNDROME AND MUNCHAUSEN BY PROXY

According to webMD, Munchausen Sydrome is "a mental disorder in which a person repeatedly and deliberately acts as if he or she has a physical or mental illness when he or she is not really sick. Munchausen syndrome is considered a mental illness because it is associated with severe emotional difficulties. People with Munchausen Syndrome deliberately produce or exaggerate symptoms in several ways. They frequent emergency rooms and seeks unnecessary procedures and surgeries. They may lie about or fake symptoms, hurt themselves to bring on symptoms, or alter tests such as contaminating a urine sample."

Munchausen Syndrome is more common in males than females. The cause of Munchausen Syndrome is unknown, however, theories suggest a link to personality disorders, a history of childhood neglect and abuse or multiple hospitalizations as a child.

According to KidsHealth.org, Munchausen Syndrome by Proxy (MSBP) is a relatively rare form of child abuse that involves the exaggeration or fabrication of illnesses or symptoms by a primary caretaker. Also known as *medical child abuse.* In MSBP, usually a parent or caregiver causes or fabricates symptoms in a child. The adult deliberately misleads others (particularly medical professionals), and may go as far as to actually cause symptoms in the child through poisoning, medication, or even suffocation. In most cases (85%), the mother is responsible for causing the illness or symptoms.

Often, the cause is to seek attention and sympathy from others. Some experts believe that it's not only the attention that's gained from the illness of the child that drives the perpetrator, but also the satisfaction in deceiving people they consider to be more important and powerful than themselves.

MSBP is considered a psychiatric condition. It has been found the perpetrators were neglected as well as abused physically and/or sexually as children. Being sick may have been a way to be cared for or to receive love.

PERFECTIONISM

Obsessive Compulsive Disorder (OCD). I saw on a shirt; "Some people prefer to call it CDO, which is OCD in the correct order."

How many of you know someone that calls themselves a "Micro-Manager of the Household?" She goes around perfecting the house? Does she do a partner inventory? Nobody makes beds, does laundry, goes grocery shopping, or loads the dishwasher right?

With such perfectionism, their spouse and children will feel they can't measure up. They will simply give up on mom because whatever they do won't be good enough for her anyway. There is a difference between running a household effectively versus being overbearing and demeaning. When a person keeps inventory of their spouse, their marriage becomes a parent/child relationship.

NARCISSISM

It is believed that Narcissism in adults is related to defenses against shame. Narcissistic Personality Disorder (NPD) is connected to shame as well. Psychiatrist Glen Gabbard suggested that NPD could be broken down into two subtypes, a grandiose, arrogant, thick-skinned "oblivious" subtype and an easily hurt, oversensitive, ashamed "hypervigilant" subtype. The oblivious subtype demands admiration and envy, and a grandiose self - contrary to the weak internalized self which hides in shame. The hypervigilant subtype neutralizes their devaluation by seeing others as unjust abusers.

According to Dictionary.com, a narcissist is defined as "a person who is overly self-involved, and often vain and selfish."

Ask yourself, "Is everything always all about him or her?" The world revolves around them? Are your thoughts and opinions completely rejected or ignored?

Generally, when you first meet a narcissist, you are amazed by them. They will sweep you off your feet. This person is outgoing and charming—until you get to know them—when their true colors show.

Narcissists often put others down to boost their ego.

WHAT ARE THE SIGNS OF A NARCISSIST?

1. Self-centered—they talk about themselves. They seek attention by trying to impress others. They brag or exaggerate their wealth, their world experiences, and how they are needed and adored by everyone. You don't need to pat them on the back for things they do as they exemplify themselves.

2. Disinterested in what others have to say. They interrupt you in conversation because they are not listening to a word you are saying.

3. Entitlement. Narcissists are likely to expect preferential treatment. They tend to be rude to service providers such as a waitress or waiter, baristas, valet workers, etc.

4. Narcissists often put others down to boost their oversized ego.

5. Conceited. They believe others are jealous of them. They are the best at everything.

6. Center of Attention. Narcissists literally thrive when all eyes are on them. They do not like to share the spotlight—which makes them unable to be a good team player.

7. Has to get their own way. They are not fun to play games with as they are sore losers. They are right fighters (always have to be right), and generally loud and demeaning in their argument.

8. Never able to accept criticism, they are always right. Narcissists are hypersensitive to any perceived critique, they have an excessive need for praise and admiration. When offered any sort of criticism, they feel rejected and hurt. Their reaction may cause them to display extreme defensiveness, argumentative, and belligerent.

9. They lack long-term friends. To determine a narcissist, observe the types of friendships they have. If the person is unable to maintain long-term friends and is more of a casual friendships kind, it is a sign of narcissism.

10. A narcissist thrives by controlling others. Narcissists have a high need for control, even arrange events and manipulate people and situations to orchestrate the outcomes they desire. Be aware when you feel anxious about expressing your preferences as narcissists tend to enforce their own preferences and views.

Being aware of some of these signs could guide you to determine whether or not a relationship is worth maintaining. Love yourself enough to not live in the contempt of a narcissist!

IS NARCISSISTIC BEHAVIOR A SIN?

As in the definition "a person who is overly self-involved, and often vain and selfish." Yes, that is a sin! The Bible has plenty to say about it!

The Lord hates evil; I hate pride and arrogance (Prov. 8:13).

An unfriendly person pursues selfish ends and against all sound judgment starts quarrels (Prov. 18:1).

Haughty eyes and a proud heart-the unplowed field of the wicked-produce sin (Prov. 21:4).

In his pride the wicked man does not seek him; in all his thoughts there is no room for God (Psalm 10:4).

Let their lying lips be silenced, for with pride and contempt they speak arrogantly against the righteous (Psalm 31:18).

Whoever slanders their neighbor in secret, I will put to silence; whoever has haughty eyes and a proud heart, I will not tolerate (Psalm 101:5).

For I am afraid that when I come I may not find you as I want you to be, and you may not find me as you want me to be. I fear that there may be discord, jealousy, fits of rage, selfish ambition, slander, gossip, arrogance and disorder (2 Cor. 12:20).

Do nothing out of selfish ambition or vain conceit. Rather, in humility value others above yourselves (Phil. 2:3).

For where you have envy and selfish ambition, there you find disorder and every evil practice (James 3:16).

The arrogance of man will be brought low and human pride humbled; the Lord alone will be exalted in that day (Isa. 2:17).

I will put an end to the arrogance of the haughty and will humble the pride of the ruthless (Isa. 13:11).

SOCIOPATHIC BEHAVIOR

A lot of people like to loosely latch this label onto people. Be careful about labeling others. It can be harmful socially and emotionally.

Sociopathic behavior often starts early in childhood. The child tends to have conduct issues, fighting, bed-wetting, pyromania, and cruelty to animals. They may display a total lack of empathy and disregard other people's well-being or rights—unless there is a personal gain to themselves. They will lie, cheat, and steal to gain what they want. If they want it bad enough, they will not allow anyone to get in their way.

A classic example of a sociopath is Ted Bundy who would put his arm in a sling to seek sympathy.

A sociopath tends to exaggerate, are narcissistic, and have a false sense of abilities that set themselves up to fail by setting unrealistic long-range goals. Some will brag about committing crimes as they are proud of outsmarting the law.

An interesting book I read about sociopaths is called "The Sociopath Next Door" by Martha Stout listed in the reading resources section (end of this chapter). It is incredibly accurate.

BULLYING IN ADULTS

Bullying is a relentless form of abuse. Bullying includes repeated, intentional acts over time designed to enforce power over another specifically by intimidating, hurting, or ostracizing another person or group. Bullying behaviors include verbal comments, physical harm, coercion, emotional abuse, or threats. Bullying can be physical, emotional, or verbal, depending on what means the bully uses to attack you. It includes behaviors intended to exclude or alienate another individual. This can be started with rumors, talking negatively, condescending comments, or finding ways to isolate the individuals.

A person may experience bullying anywhere-in their neighborhood, community, church, work, and anywhere else in which you interact with other people.

WHY DO PEOPLE BECOME BULLIES?

Some consider bullying to be purposeful attempts to control others. Here are some reasons why people are bullies:

- Home, school, or the workplace—does not have high standards for the way people treat each other.
- When one gets more social recognition for negative behaviors than for positive ones
- Dysfunctional families
  - o discipline and monitoring are inconsistent
  - o punitive atmosphere
  - o families that are not warm and loving
  - o feelings are not shared
- Jealousy or envy
- Intolerance of others' differences
- Lack of personal and social skills
  - o Those who experience social rejection
  - o Academic failure
- The high rate of domestic violence means that many young people grow up expecting that violence is an acceptable way to get what one wants.
- Having power makes some people wield it.

Cyberbullying is another form of bullying in which the internet and cell phones are used to harm another individual. This includes threatening emails, text messages, instant messaging, berating someone on a chat room, or otherwise using technology to harm, upset, threaten, or intimidate others.

Bullying should never be permitted. Never allow violence because violence will escalate. If you are in a violent situation, seek help immediately.

You do not have to be strong and "deal with it." Speak up and ask for help. Remember, if you are being bullied, someone else is likely being bullied by that person as well. NOBODY deserves to be bullied!

Does this behavior sound like something you do? Are YOU a bully? Does this behavior align with your moral and Christian values?

SELF-INDULGENCE

Whether eating, drinking, making purchases that sacrifices your budget, gambling, etc., self- indulgence is not favored by our Lord (1 Cor. 5: 6–11). God wants us to live in moderation (Prov. 27:7)

Self-indulgence is used to sedate what is broken on the inside. Psychiatrists say that extreme self- indulgence can be considered sociopathic behavior. Their goal is to satisfy themselves as they impress others.

For many, people who indulge themselves desire luxury and riches. They want to have things that the world desires—envy of what others have. The internet social sites like Facebook give people access to fleshly desires. Want, want, want (Prov. 23:3 and 23:17)!

READING RESOURCES:

Beyond the Shadows: Discover Hope for Overcoming Depression
By Ramon Presson

Hope Prevails
By Dr. Michelle Bengston

I Am Not Sick, I Don't Need Help! How to Help Someone with
Mental Illness Accept Treatment
By Xavier Amador

Luckiest Man on Earth; Surviving Long-Term Depression
By Robert L. Hamlett

Mending Your Heart in a Broken World
By Patsy Clairmont

Overwhelmed: Winning the War against Worry
By Perry Noble

The Sociopath Next Door
By Martha Stout

Troubled Minds; Mental Illness and the Church's Mission
By Amy Simpson, MBA

HOTLINES:
National Suicide Hotline: 1-800-273-TALK (8255)
National Domestic Abuse Hotline: 1-800-799-SAFE (7233)
National Child Abuse Hotline: 1-800-4-A-CHILD (422-4453)
NAMI, National Alliance on Mental Illness, nami.org: 1-800-950-6264

QUESTIONS TO PONDER:

1. What is your definition of normal?
2. What would you do if you believe someone was being inflicted by stigma?
3. How might the blame game affect the person living with mental illness?
4. Do you or anyone close to you have symptoms or an actual mental health diagnosis? What are the behaviors you recognize?
   How do you feel around them when you see the behaviors?
   How do you react to the behaviors?
   What can YOU do to handle the situation better?
   Do you have a reliable support system?
   Who do you know that is experienced that you can talk to?
   How often should you talk to someone who gets it?
   Who are your spiritual supports?

5. Did someone close to you attempt or commit suicide?
   How did that affect their loved ones?
   How did YOU feel about it?
   What would you do if YOU were the safe person they called on?

6. Do you believe mental illness is a spiritual problem?
   What is the one thing that frightens you most?
   Is it an unhealthy fear?
   Does it get in the way of your daily life?

7. Do you or someone you know indulge in self-pity?
   Are you self-indulgent in any way?
   What can you do to change that problem?

8. Have you bullied or have been bullied by another adult?
   Describe how you feel about that experience?

9. Does this chapter entice you to learn more about mental health?
What can you do to collect information about mental health?

10. Was any part of this chapter eye-opening for you?
Does it motivate you to change anything?
What verse or verses are important to you?

CHAPTER THREE

DISABILITY AND CHRONIC ILLNESS

As an aging person with chronic pain, I can't speak for everyone with disabilities and chronic illness, but I think I can speak for most. I have years of experience to share with you. Now that I am older (gray haired and granny plump), I find it frustrating what people assume!

My illness is invisible. I physically appear to be fine so others often ask, "What do you do for a living?" or "Where do you work?" This is a loaded question for me! With Lupus and Fibromyalgia, I have a difficult time working. I have been in management since I was seventeen years old and upper management since my thirties. I had been the bread winner for a number of years.

I live with a debilitating invisible disease that is painful emotionally as well as physically. Stress instigates pain and intensifies existing pain. At times, I am extremely fatigued, I lack stamina to the point of having difficulty driving. Especially when I work AND drive. Due to Fibromyalgia, hugs can be painful. Even wearing clothes and shoes can be painful. I am in pain every single day. And yet, I look fine. Every medication I take causes weight gain, which adds to the issues. Sometimes, I feel great anger or depressed.

Bottom line is that I miss the old me. I strongly desire to do things I have always been able to do. I want to contribute to society or at least contribute to my family. I just want to have a normal, quality life—whatever that may be.

Someone like myself may become a bit anti-social, not the jovial person people are used to seeing. This is not the time to try to confront them, nor to make future plans—even if they are simple. And don't take it personally if this person cancels out on an event with you. The person cancelling is most likely angry that they are not well enough to attend! It may be helpful for you to realize that with changes like this, it is generally not only the pain this person is suffering with.

Understand that a person with irregular work is dealing with financial struggles as well. The bills just won't go away yet a person with these health issues cannot find a job that is compatible with their disabilities.

More than a million times, I have heard, "You should do this and try that" and "Don't, don't, don't." Until you've walked a mile in these old tennis shoes, you will not really understand what I (we—this affects my husband too) am going through. Getting advice from healthy people is like getting child rearing advice from a person who has never had children. Honestly, I understand people are compelled to help, but don't assume a suffering person wants advice.

I have a disability card for my car. At times, I receive judgmental looks from people when I am getting in or out of my car. Don't judge! You don't know what I feel.

Understand that sometimes advice comes off as judgment. How many of you that are overweight or have diabetes have had more diet and exercise advice than you can stomach?

"Just get off your butt and do it!" "Get over it!"

"If I were you . . ." "You used to . . ."

Do you feel judged when someone gives you advice? For myself, I have had these health problems for years, and I do my best with years and years of experimenting with medications, exercise and diet, to changing my entire career. I have had to learn what works best and when.

It is extremely difficult emotionally when you have family and close friends who don't understand a newly developed disability—or an invisible disease. My life is changed forever and yet the world keeps going on around me like nothing happened.

One of my best managers is permanently disabled due to a combination of medical errors (a crossover of mistakes made between the local emergency room and the pharmacy she had been using). She was a blessing to have on my team. She is intelligent, articulate, and has the unique ability to discern behavior triggers and methodologies we used while working with persons with intellectual disabilities and chronic mental illness. We truly enjoyed working with each other.

This sudden brain disorder, Hyponatremia, literally almost killed her. After she came out of a coma, she was admitted to a nursing home for twenty-four-hour care and intense therapy.

Sadly, we know that her brain will never be the same. She speaks slower but still has all her faculties. She has the same sarcastic sense of humor. She will admit she has lost the ability to filter what comes out of her mouth. Many of her physical problems resembles Multiple Sclerosis. She has improved immensely, however, she continues to have a lot of issues from this brain disease.

When this tragedy happened, she was very active with two young boys at home. It affected how she was able to interact with her boys, her husband, extended family, friends, and her job. She went from being a mother and a caregiver to needing her children and spouse to be her caregivers. It was life changing in every facet of her being.

Her family was very involved with her while she was going through the healing process and in the nursing home. Unfortunately, there were family members that questioned the severity of the prob-

JUDITH ISAACS-HERRIG, M.ED, QIDP

lem. There are also family members that are estranged since her financial settlement from this life-changing event. She not only suffers her invisible disease, she suffers judgment and isolation.

We are reminded in 1 Samuel 16:7 not to judge a person by their appearance because the Lord doesn't see others the same way that we see others. The Lord looks at the heart.

MY IDENTITY IS LOST WITH THIS ILLNESS

It seems simple until you've been diagnosed with a chronic illness or permanent disability. People like myself that are career oriented and high energy really suffer the challenge of the disability. My career identity changed and my goals were entirely deflated.

So now what?

First of all, make sure you know and understand your disability. The more you know about it, the more you can advocate for yourself.

You CAN make a conscious choice to be happy! Is your cup half full or is it half empty? (2 Tim. 1:7) Are you going to live your life to its fullest, or you going to let it beat you down?

I consider that our present sufferings are not worth comparing with the glory that will be revealed in us (Rom. 8:18).

You have to learn to work around your disabilities and focus on your abilities! Ephesians 3:20 reminds us that God is able through His mighty power at work within us to accomplish infinitely more that we might ask or think.

Over time, I had to make career changes. As a manager of a group home for mentally ill and/or intellectually disabled adults, I decided it was time to earn an associate's degree so that I could become a program manager. With my inconsistent, extreme levels of pain, doing direct care with the clients was difficult. I completed a bachelor's degree to work into a QMRP position (Qualified Mental Retardation Professional—not a politically correct term now). That is basically managing the client programs, coordinate and facilitate team meetings and all the paperwork that comes with it. I was quickly promoted to the Program Director of the company. But the

70

stress and long hours was wearing me down. It was time for another change.

My husband and I opened our own residential facility where we eventually worked together. While it was quite successful, it was a lot of work! With the guidance of a life coach and much prayer, I decided to go back to college for a master's degree. Oh, how God knows my desire to teach!

With the support of my husband and with prayer, God revealed His guidance for my life with this invisible illness. All my experiences were the path to where He wants me today. He's given me opportunities to teach part-time, speak and write.

In Acts 8, Paul writes about Phillip obeying God by leaving his successful preaching ministry to travel to Ethiopia. With this scripture we learn, if the path God is leading seems like a demotion, we need to follow His instruction anyway. We may not understand His instruction, but we will know by the results that His plan is perfect.

Paul reminds us in Romans 12:2 that we are not to follow the behaviors and customs of the world. God will transform you into a new person by changing the way you think. Then you will learn to know God's will for you which is good and pleasing and perfect.

MY CHILD, PARENT OR SPOUSE IS CHRONICALLY ILL OR DISABLED

UNDERSTAND GRIEF AND LOSS

People go through a grief and loss process when faced with an uncontrollable event that requires a caregiver. It is life changing. A person who has become a caregiver due to life's circumstances may experience grief and loss as well. Caregiving can be life consuming!

Loss: Driving, relationships, family, jobs, abilities, and non-obtainable dreams.

1. Grieving—is a painful process of loss and everyone processes it differently.
2. Denial—is behaving as though nothing has happened.
3. Anger—argumentative, agitated, rebellious. Everyone displays anger in different ways
4. Bargaining—with God
5. Depression—looks different with everyone. May include cutting, isolation, silence, suicide threats

Acceptance is different for everyone. Don't make your own judgment as to how long anyone should be allowed to grieve. One of the most damaging statements a person can ever hear when they are grieving is to "Just get over it and move on."

I agree that some people use grieving as a form of attention seeking behavior. However, be careful if YOU believe that is what is happening (emphasis on YOU). Remember that a crisis can bring on the need to process these stages over again.

Behavior doesn't define WHO they are. It is a form of communication.

Offer empathy—not sympathy.

Defined: Both empathy and sympathy are feelings concerning other people.

Empathy is trying to understand by relating to their issue. Sympathy is feeling sorry for someone—or to pity them.

Understand their diagnosis. There are so many variants to a diagnosis. Make sure to read as much as you can about the diagnosis as possible. It is amazing what you can find online.

Avoid judgment of any kind. Don't judge others, and don't allow others to judge you. Obviously you cannot stop a person from judging you, but you can make the choice to not allow others' judgment to affect you.

Consistency: Consistency with meals, medications, and even favorite TV shows will help a confined person to orient themselves with what time of day it is. Keeping a calendar with them and reviewing it will help orient them with the date, upcoming appointments, etc. Communicate when you are changing a meal time or doing something different. You want to do everything you can to keep them informed and active in decision making.

There are five major areas to consider when you are caring for someone:

1. Physical—illness, pain, hungry, thirsty, tired, hot/cold, medication issue
2. Emotional—are they lonely, depressed or anxious?
3. Social—are they able to visit family and friends?
4. Spiritual—are they able to attend church?
5. Environmental—too much stimulation; too loud, too messy, too bright, too dark. Some people are affected by cloudy, rainy days.

Be patient—slow down, you may need to repeat things if necessary. Be careful not to be demeaning in how much you slow down. Don't finish sentences for them.

Understand that just because a person is disabled does not mean they do not understand you. I am amazed at how people will bend over a wheelchair and talk loud and slow. I have seen wheelchair-bound people become irate with that mindset. Until you have knowledge of their disability, don't assume anything. A person with a traumatic brain injury may talk very slow but might understand every bit that is being said to them. As with a person wearing a hearing aid may hear clearly or only help assist with some sound. The words may still be somewhat unintelligible. With some types of hearing loss, lip-reading is necessary. Speaking louder does not help.

Avoid power struggles. Be creative—offer choices.

If a person is agitated, are there distractions? Are they disappointed? Don't solve problems for them, help them work through it.

Be flexible and resilient. Go with the flow.

What kind of energy and interests does the person have?

"I thank Christ Jesus our Lord, who has given me strength, that he considered me faithful, appointing me to his service."
–I Timothy 1:12

CAREGIVER BURNOUT

For some of us caregiving is a 24/7/365 job!

Anyone that has a child, parent or spouse that is chronically ill or disabled is going to need a lot of support and understanding!

Do everything you can do to prevent caregiver burnout.

WHAT ARE THE EFFECTS OF CAREGIVER BURNOUT?

Fatigue—by keeping an inconsistent schedule or having varied work patterns is basically burning the candle at both ends. It is a matter of time before you become burned out.

Sleep Deprivation—never allow yourself to be sleep deprived for long periods of time. One of the best predictors of insomnia later in life is the development of bad habits.

WHAT CAUSES SLEEP DEPRIVATION?

- Having sleep disturbed by young children.
- Twenty-four-hour accessibility to TV.
- Electronic gaming and the internet varied work patterns.
- The medical field often work rotating shifts. There is evidence that shifts exceeding twelve hours in length as well as over-time (four hours per week) increases the risk of errors in care. (Ann Rogers, PhD, RN, professor at Emory University)

If you see any of these changes in the attitude of a caregiver, you are witnessing the effects of caregiver burnout:

- Doesn't seem to care anymore; comes in to work late, leaves early and takes too many breaks.
- Absenteeism
- Not present in the moment.
- Negative attitude.
- Lack of self-care.
- Over-eating for comfort or skipping meals from stress.
- Not taking the time to exercise. Exercise allows for better relaxation.
- Skipping medical care.
- Not engaging in a personal or social life.

CAREGIVER BURNOUT RISKS:

Poor Health.

People who are burned out tend to be suffering with hypertension, anxiety, depression, and other stress-related illnesses.

You risk the safety of the person you care for:

People who are burned out become less connected, become cranky and impatient. They have a lack of insight, they lose their ability to read between the lines. And they are not as eager to go the extra mile. It is hard to be interested in someone's person-centered plan when all you want to do is be done.

People who are burned out may be driving while they are overtired. Researchers found that seventeen hours of sustained wakefulness leads to a decrease in performance equivalent to a blood alcohol-level of 0.05%. The NRMA Research Center estimates fatigue is involved in one in six fatal road accidents.

HOW DOES THAT EFFECT YOUR JOB?

- Medication and documentation errors
- Make more mistakes
- Negative job attitude
- Feeling overworked and unappreciated

CAREGIVER BURNOUT PREVENTION:

- Strive for balance in your life.
- Make time for activities and people you enjoy.

ASK YOURSELF THESE QUESTIONS:

- What is your caregiver role?
- Is your caregiver role your choice?
- What makes you angry?
- How do you know when you are angry?

What about you? Are all (if any) of your needs being met? People have no idea how difficult it is to care for someone else until they have experienced it themselves. If you are in need of help, ask for help.

ASK FOR HELP!

ARE YOU ONE OF THESE CAREGIVERS?

"I can't ask because they're just too busy. I don't want to bother them."

"I don't want people to think I can't handle this."

Sorry . . . but you are not indispensable. OTHER people CAN help you. If you have a hard time with letting go, start small. Use your support system. Start by having someone help so you can go pick up groceries, see a doctor or go to the hairdresser.

Most people assume if you want help, you would request it. So don't wait for someone to offer to help you.

Recognize when you are experiencing resentment or anger about your situation. What do you resent about being a caregiver? Why do you feel angry?

> I lift my eyes to the hills–where does my help
> come from? My help comes from the Lord, the
> Maker of heaven and earth (Ps. 121:1–2).

Take care of yourself. A healthy body is better able to tolerate stress. It is important to teach yourself how to relax. Try relaxation techniques. There are many books and online information to find relaxation techniques.

Take the time for affirmations such as journaling your inner thoughts, reading, meditation, and/or prayer.

Come to me, all you who are weary and burdened, and I will give you rest. Take my yoke upon you and learn from me, for I am gentle and humble in heart, and you will find rest for your souls. For my yoke is easy and my burden is light (Matt. 11:28–30).

Cast all your anxiety on him because he cares for you (1 Peter 5:7).

AFFIRMATIONS FOR POSITIVE THINKING:

Write down your inner thoughts by journaling. Journaling is a great place for venting.

Blog or e-mail people from within your support system. This is NOT an appropriate place for venting!

Send an uplifting card or letter to a friend who needs positive reinforcement as much as you do.

Read something inspirational or light and fun.

Diet and exercise is an important factor. As a caregiver, we are insisting on good healthy choices. You are likely providing great diet advice to the person you are caring for, but remember to take your own advice. Make sure to eat a well-balanced diet, exercise regularly, and get enough rest. Some people like to take those twenty-minute power naps. Do it if you can.

Take time off work. When you have vacation time, use it!

Keep a regular sleep schedule.

Get those annual physicals and dental appointments taken care of!

If you feel stress is too difficult to cope with, meet with a trusted person to pray and counsel with you. If you are still feeling hopeless, talk with your doctor about the stress in your life and make sure to follow doctor's orders. If you are supposed to be taking medications or supplements, make sure you are taking them.

He gives strength to the weary and increases the power of the weak. Even youths grow tired and weary, and young men stumble and fall; but those who hope in the Lord will renew their strength. They will soar on wings like eagles; they will run and not grow weary, they will walk and not be faint (Isa. 40:29–31).

Just say NO. Sometimes we take on too much. We want to help everybody do everything. We put way too much on our plates and then find ourselves frustrated and frazzled. Don't feel obligated to push yourself beyond your limits.

Prioritize. Set realistic goals and priorities. Instead of thinking of all the things you should be doing, just focus on one thing at a time. Make a checklist so you can enjoy a sense of accomplishment and regain a sense of control.

Don't expect perfection. Ease up on yourself and everyone around you, we all have our shortcomings.

REACTING TO BEHAVIORS:

Everyone has different behaviors and triggers. *How you react* to behaviors can make a difference on your stress levels. It is important to have a positive, acceptant attitude.

Self-differentiate. You were normal before you became committed to becoming a caregiver. *You still are.* The issues are theirs, not yours. Remind yourself of this often.

Disengage. Caregivers may run into emotional meltdowns. It is very easy to get sucked into an argument or a meltdown.

Count to ten, give yourself a time out. If it is safe, walk away for a few minutes. Don't try to have a rational argument with a child or someone who is emotionally, developmentally, or organically challenged. They don't get it! Let it go so you don't become very frustrated.

Pick your battles wisely and don't take it personal!

How's your love life? If you thought—what love life?—you have some work to do here! All people *need* loving, positive relationships. I want to emphasize *positive.*

Your spouse is not the person to vent with . . . I will explain that later in the book.

There is nothing better than being in love. So what are you doing about it? Use time to engage with your spouse. Shut off the TV, games, and/or computer off. Play cards or board games together. Take a walk together or go on a long drive. Use down time to create your own little haven together.

Your spouse needs to know when you are having a tough day, but don't take it out on them! Are they walking into the house and finding the atmosphere thick and heavy? Remember the first few seconds upon arrival will set the stage for the rest of the evening. You can make your home a sanctuary or a chaotic train wreck! Use those first few seconds wisely!

Sexual intimacy is a stress reliever and builds marital satisfaction! Schedule dates and mini vacations and make room for romance!

BUILD A RELIABLE SUPPORT SYSTEM.

Invite a trusted and experienced adult to spend time with you on a regular basis—especially during the tougher times. Having an experienced person around can give perspective. Someone to bounce off ideas, share the ups and downs, and talk thru situations that arise. They can give you someone to laugh with and help you to take things less seriously.

Talk to people with similar situations. Another family member that can relate to your situation. Make sure this person is not guilt ridden that they are not the caregiver. My *adult* daughter was an experienced caregiver and the perfect person to bounce things off with.

Talk at least once a day either online, by phone, or in person with someone else who gets it. Always remember your BFF!

Make sure you have spiritual supports in place. You may find a support group through a local church and Christian online supports. *Always* remember the HIPPA privacy laws—especially as a caregiver. Be sensitive to other's situations so not to offend them.

Anything online travels fast! Commit to sincere and tasteful discussions.

Again, ASK FOR HELP! Get as much information as you can. Study, learn, research. Surf the internet. Join online support groups. Read books and attend seminars. The more knowledge you have about the person you care for, the more you will be able to advocate for them and help them. List their diagnosis and medications. Know them inside/out. You will feel secure in making informed decisions with such preparation.

IF YOU ARE THE SUPPORT SYSTEM FOR SOMEONE:

Keep in touch. Send cards, pray for them, and let them know you are praying for them. If you offer to help someone, follow through with your promises. Be on time. If a person is relying on you to help them get somewhere, follow through.

MAKING DECISIONS AND PROBLEM SOLVING

Do not procrastinate. It will eat at you until your decision is made. Choose to get started. Ask for input from those who are knowledgeable about the person you care for (staff, social worker and/or family) to provide options and guidance toward your decision-making. Don't overwhelm yourself.

Evaluate each opinion and choose those that are win-win. Get expert advice and create new options when others won't do: Have a Plan A and a Plan B!

Research or investigate new and existing policies, every treatment and medication, and new findings about the diagnosis given.

Evaluate what makes the problem better or what makes the problem worse.

Discuss decisions with others and listen to their advice. Discern who you speak with. Are they respected and knowledgeable in the field?

Evaluate your own feelings before you act. Think twice about who you are advocating for! How will your decision affect other people?

Find joy in each day. Look for a moment of joy and hold on to the moment. Memorize it. Write it down. Sometimes, *one* moment of joy that is recognized is enough to get through to the next day. Try to find humor in everything—almost everything.

The right perspective can be funny. Seeing it as such can make all the difference.

Happiness is a choice.

BIBLICAL PRINCIPLES OF CAREGIVING:

Whatever you may be going through, whatever what your heart is feeling, whatever you are hoping for, the Bible has something for you to find wisdom, peace and a renewed perspective.

Be shepherds of God's flock that is under your care, serving as overseers—not because you must, but because you are willing, as God wants you to be; not greedy for money, but eager to serve; not lording it over those entrusted to you, but being examples to the flock. And when the Chief Shepherd appears, you will receive the crown of glory that will never fade away (1 Pet. 5:2–4).

Speak up for those who cannot speak for themselves, for the rights of all who are destitute, speak up and judge fairly; defend the rights of the poor and needy (Prov. 31:8–9).

May the Lord answer you when you are in distress, protect you, and remember your sacrifices (Psalm 20:1-3).

Be strong and courageous, and do the work. Do not be afraid or discouraged, for the Lord God, my God, is with you. He will not fail you or forsake you until all the work for the service of the temple of the Lord is finished (1 Chron. 28:20).

For God did not appoint us to suffer wrath but to receive salvation through our Lord Jesus Christ. He died for us so that, whether we are awake or asleep, we may live together with him.

Therefore encourage one another and build each other up, just as in fact you are doing (1 Thess. 5:9–11).

The Lord is good to those whose hope is in Him, to the one who seeks him; it is good to wait quietly for the salvation of the Lord (Lam. 3:25–26)

But the fruit of the Spirit is love, joy, peace, patience, kindness, goodness, faithfulness, gentleness and self-control (Gal. 5:22).

READING RESOURCES:

A Caregiver's Survival Guide: How to Stay Healthy When Your Loved One is Sick
By Kay Marshall Strom

Ambushed by Grace: Help and Hope on the Caregiving Journey
By Shelly Beach

The Art of Caregiving: How to Lend Support and Encouragement to Those with Cancer
By Michael S. Barry

Being a Caregiver in a Home Setting
By Elana Zucker

Chosen . . . to Never Walk Alone! An Inspiring Story of a Disabled Christian Woman's Life
By Susan J. Shanks, Ph.D.

Companioning the Dying: A Soulful Guide for Caregivers
By Greg Yoder

Compassionate Caregiving: Practical Help and Spiritual Encouragement
By Lois D. Knutson

Hope for the Caregiver: Encouraging Words to Strengthen Your Spirit
By Peter Rosenberger

Not Alone: Encouragement for Caregivers
By Nell Noonan

The Pastoral Caregiver's Casebook: Ministry in Crises
By John J. Gleason

QUESTIONS TO PONDER:

1. Do you have a disability?
   How has it affected your life?
   Do you resent the changes your disability has caused?
   Do you feel judged by others?
   Do you allow self-pity to get in your way?
   What is the best way for YOU to overcome negative issues?
   Do you work to keep a positive, healthy attitude?

2. Do you know someone with a disability?
   Are you at times suspicious of someone's actual disability?
   What would they gain from exaggerating their disability?

3. Are you comfortable being around people with disabilities?
   Do you feel impatient and/or annoyed by their disability?

4. What is the best way for a person to overcome their mind-set about disabilities?

5. Have you ever been or are you a caregiver of someone you love?
   Is your caregiver role your "choice?"
   What were you circumstances?
   What is your caregiver role?
   What is the best rewards from being a caregiver?
   What are the downfalls of being a caregiver?
   What are some of the things you need to do to prevent caregiver burnout?
   Do you have an alternate plan for when you need time off or just a break?

6 What makes you angry?
   How do you know when you are angry?

7. What are the five basic areas to you need to consider when you are caring for someone? Can you recognize the symptoms of grieving or loss?

8. What is the difference between empathy and sympathy? Why is it important to know the difference?

9. Why is it important to understand the diagnosis and the medications of the person you are caring for?
    Where can you obtain this information?

10. Would you be able to recognize the symptoms of caregiver burnout?
    Are you identifying any of them in yourself?

11. Do you have a reliable support system?
    Who do you know that is experienced that you can talk to?
    How often should you talk to someone who *gets it?*
    Who are your spiritual supports?
    Do HIPPA laws pertain to you?

12. Was any part of this chapter eye-opening for you?
    Does it motivate you to change anything?
    What verse or verses are important to you?

CHAPTER FOUR

MILITARY

WITH GRATITUDE

I feel it is important to have a chapter dedicated to our military families and veterans. As a military mom, it is with my humblest gratitude to acknowledge their hard work and bravery as a soldier, a military spouse and family.

    More than 7.3 Americans have served in the U.S. military. That's more than 1.3 million people. At least 10% of all veterans are women. Not only soldiers are affected, but the families of soldiers.

This chapter is dedicated to members of the military families and during their service

Most of our veterans suffer with some sort of damage caused during the service; from divorce and infidelity to physical and/or emotional trauma. Studies reveal that 30% of active duty and reserve military personnel deployed in Iraq and Afghanistan have a mental health condition requiring treatment—approximately 730,000 men and women, with many experiencing post- traumatic stress disorder (PTSD) and major depression. According to Anxiety and Depression Association of America (ADAA), 7.7 million Americans age eighteen and older have PTSD.

Less than 50% of returning Veterans in need receive any mental health treatment. The Veterans Administration reports that approximately twenty-two veterans die by suicide every day.

For physical disabilities, refer to Disabilities and Chronic Illness chapter.

POST-TRAUMATIC STRESS DISORDER (PTSD):

Defined: PTSD is a mental health condition triggered by experiencing or seeing a terrifying event. Extreme anxiety and trauma-related fear are characteristics of PTSD.

According to the Mayo Clinic, there are more than three million cases in the U.S. each year. Chronic PTSD can last for years—often a lifetime.

PTSD can be a debilitating condition. Those exposed to combat are likely to experience acute stress and symptoms of PTSD. Most people will recover from traumatic experiences, but people with acute PTSD continue to be severely depressed and anxious. According to ADAA, women are twice as likely to develop PTSD as men because there is the increased risk of exposure to sexual harassment, sexual assault, and rape. Children are not excluded from developing PTSD.

People exposed to mass violence have been shown to develop PTSD—a higher rate than those exposed to natural disasters or other kinds of traumatic events. Depression, substance abuse, and other anxiety disorders are found with people who suffer with PTSD.

WHAT DOES PTSD LOOK LIKE?

PTSD has a wide variety of symptoms. The most common symptoms are:

- Upset by things that remind you of the incident that occurred.
- Nightmares, vivid memories or flashbacks of the event that make you feel like the incident is happening all over again.
- Feeling emotionally cut off from others
- Feel numb or lose interest in things you normally care about
- Feel on guard at all times
- Irritable, angry outbursts
- Insomnia
- Unable to concentrate
- Jumpy or easily startled

REACTIONS THAT CAN DISRUPT
THE QUALITY OF LIFE:

- Avoid places or things that remind you of what happened
- Alcohol and drug use
- Harm yourself or others
- Thoughts of suicide
- Overworking to occupy your mind
- Isolation from friends and family

THERE ARE TWO EFFECTIVE TYPES OF TREATMENT FOR PTSD.

- Professional therapy or counseling is useful to understand their thoughts and reactions as well as to learn coping skills.
- Medications such as serotonin reuptake inhibitors are commonly prescribed for PTSD.

HOW CAN I HELP SOMEONE WITH PTSD?

Support from family and friends is important to the recovery process. Understand that getting better takes hard work. And it takes patience from those who care. With appropriate treatment from a mental health professional, a person can learn to manage or overcome PTSD.

Create a warm, comfortable environment, and be loving and caring. Be yourself around them. Help them to find joy, hope, and optimism. There is an adjustment of lifestyle to relieve PTSD symptoms.

Veterans experiencing PTSD, report exercise reduces their tension. Make sure family and friends are aware of the places or things that can cause a PTSD reaction. For example, a veteran may not handle living in an apartment complex because unforeseen loud noises can put a person with PTSD into a rage. A veteran I know cannot be touched when awaken. PTSD puts the veteran in war mode. When awaken by touch or a loud noise, the veteran may be startled thinking it is the enemy and react accordingly. The fourth of July fireworks can be tormenting to a veteran.

Keep in mind that with hidden and/or invisible wounds, nobody gets sympathy. But with physical wounds, people are more sympathetic. If you are a veteran, remember that recovery is contagious. Share your story of recovery. Your story could make a difference to someone's life.

As explained by VA.gov, evidence reveals that trauma can produce both positive and negative effects on peoples' spiritual experiences and perceptions. For some who have experienced trauma, depression and loneliness enforces their feelings of abandonment and loss of faith in God. And for some people, their experience increased an appreciation of life, they feel closer to God, they feel an increased sense of purpose in life and their spiritual well-being improves.

Research also reveals that having a healthy spiritual belief system can reduce the symptoms and clinical problems in people who have experienced trauma. Behaviors that include anger, rage, and revenge is decreased with forgiveness, spiritual beliefs, or spiritual practices.

For those whose core values are spiritually grounded, traumatic events may cause them to question the concept of their relationship with God. Survivors may question their belief in how a loving, all-powerful God can allow a person to be subjected to trauma or victimization. In this way, the experiences of their trauma may become the many ways in which trauma survivors define what it is to have faith.

Spirituality is used as a way to cope with traumatic death and loss. Research reveals there is a positive association between spirituality and grief recovery. For many, spirituality provides a way for which survivors can make sense of the loss. Survivors often benefit from supportive relationships provided by spiritual communities.

The spirituality of those with PTSD could affect important mental health issues (VA.gov) such as:

- Isolation and Social Withdrawal. Defining spirituality as a connection to the sacred, and encouraging trauma survivors to seek supportive, healthy communities can directly address these symptoms.
- Guilt and Shame. Though not part of the diagnostic criteria for PTSD, guilt and shame are recognized as important clinical issues. Spirituality may lead to self-forgiveness and an emphasis on compassion toward self.
- Anger and Irritability. Beliefs and practices related to forgiveness can address anger and chronic hostile attitudes

that lead to social isolation and poor relationships with others.

- Hypervigilance, Anxiety, and Physiological arousal. Inwardly-directed spiritual practices such as mindfulness, meditation, and prayer may help reduce hyperarousal.
- Foreshortened Future and Loss of Interest in Activities. Rediscovery of meaning and purpose in one's life may potentially have enormous impact on these symptoms.

MILITARY AND SUICIDE

According to Glenda Wrenn, MD, military women are six times more likely to commit suicide than men: one in four females to the one in one hundred males. Thoughts of suicide comes from their experiences during and after military service. Trauma can affect veterans many years later because they suppress their experiences and memories.

WHAT ARE THE SIGNS?

Veterans in crisis may show behaviors that indicate risk of harming themselves. Veterans who are considering suicide generally show signs of depression, anxiety, low self-esteem, and/or hopelessness. They may appear sad or depressed most of the time. With clinical depression, there is a deep sadness, loss of interest, trouble sleeping, and eating. They may exhibit anxiousness agitation, frequent and extreme mood changes.

Veterans often experience feelings of excessive guilt or shame. They may believe they are failures or that life is not worth living. They have no sense of purpose in their life. They show feeling of desperation because they believe there is no way out of a situation or solution to their problems.

Other signs include withdrawal from their family and friends. They may become recluse, neglect themselves and their personal welfare. They may neglect their jobs or education and/or lose interest in their hobbies or other things they used to care about.

Their behavior may dramatically differ from their normal behavior, or they may appear to be actively contemplating or preparing for a suicidal act through behaviors that include:

- Poor performance at work or school.
- Engaging in reckless or risky activities that could lead to death.
- Display aggressive behavior such as punching holes in walls and getting into fights, bouts of rage or uncontrolled anger or seeking revenge.
- Giving away prized possessions, putting affairs in order, tying up loose ends, and/or making out a will.
- Interest in obtaining firearms, pills, or other means of harming oneself.

National Suicide Support Number
1-888-784-2433 (1-888-SUICIDE)

HOMELESSNESS

I recall the first time I drove through Manitou Springs Colorado with my daughter—she and her husband were stationed at Fort Carson in Colorado Springs. While there on vacation, my daughter took my husband and I for the grand tour of Red Rocks and to walk the beautiful streets of Manitou Springs just below Pikes Peak.

We drove by gorgeous mansions—many of them being used as a bed & breakfast. We shopped at several of the little variety stores, enjoyed visiting stores filled with pottery, handmade jewelry, and artistry. Many of the buildings in town had the Aztec look of red clay walls. And there was a stream from the melting snow of Pikes Peak running, paving a luscious path of beauty in the midst of it all. We took in the mountain air, the warm sun and spring flowers everywhere. We dined at a quaint little vegetarian restaurant with hand carved tables and benches and bright colored walls. Manitou Springs is a pet-friendly town where you would find bowls of fresh water sitting at many store fronts. The sidewalks were decorated with boldly painted benches and huge red clay pots that held large colorful plants bursting out of each one of them.

There were also a number of long-haired, bearded, unkempt veterans with their army bag full of their only possessions. That was when the reality of veteran homelessness became real to me!

There wasn't just a few here or there. There were *many* of them.

I asked my daughter, an Iraqi Freedom Veteran, why are these military men homeless? I assumed if they were military, they should be cared for! How could they be homeless? She explained that many families reject their loved ones because they despise the war. By voluntarily enlisting in the military, it was condoning the war.

She further explained that excitement of the homecomings also came with fear. The homecoming troops wondered which soldiers would be greeted at the airport with family and loved ones, and which soldiers would be greeted by a stranger as they are served with divorce papers?

Another factor my daughter pointed out is that veterans are changed mentally and emotionally and often physically by the war. There is no longer a rigid schedule with a deluge of new responsibilities and expectations. And then there is the stigma—which is explained in this chapter.

The U.S. Department of Veterans Affairs estimates that 131,000 veterans are homeless on any given night. And approximately twice that many experience homelessness over the course of a year. Conservatively, one out of every three homeless men who is sleeping in a doorway, alley or box in our cities and rural communities has put on a uniform and served this country.

The Department of Veterans' Affairs (VA) funds temporary housing for homeless veterans, but these programs do not meet existing need.

The National Coalition for Homeless Veterans estimates that the VA serves about 25% of veterans in need—a figure that would leave approximately 300,000 veterans each year to seek assistance from local government agencies and voluntary organizations.

All homeless people carry a higher risk of contracting hepatitis C, HIV, and tuberculosis (TB) infections, and homeless veterans are at an even higher risk for hepatitis C and TB.

National Coalition for Homeless Veterans
1-800-838-4357 (1-800-VET-HELP)

MILITARY AND MARRIAGE

When a civilian is considering marrying a soldier, they need to remember that in a military marriage, duty is first; and everything else second.

There are beliefs that military marriages are unsuccessful due to infidelity.

A common issue for military couples is that it is difficult to plan things in advance. You can request a leave day, but you cannot make a plan until it has actually been approved.

Unfortunately, they can withdraw your leave without notice. This can be hard on couples, but also difficult for children who are disappointed that their parent was unable to attend something important to them.

The incredible amounts of time a family moves while in the military can be trying. There is usually little notice of the move and often the spouse takes on a majority of the move by themselves.

Homecomings can be difficult. While the reunion is thought to be exciting, there is a process of reintegrating back into the family can be the hardest for a military couple. Deployments are stressful for everyone in the family—service members, partners, children, and parents. It's probably a relief to know that your service member will soon be home. But it's important to know that life after deployment isn't going to be the same as it was before. It is a reality each family member has to deal with.

Generally, successful marriages occur with respect for their partner's service. They are resilient and have realistic expectations. They find coping skills to endure the separation and anxiety.

A wise military man I know said, "You either learn to work together or break apart trying."

FAMILIES OF MILITARY

Military families often deal with stresses such as frequent moves or the absence of a parent. With every move, they will need to make new friends and leave the friends they have already made.

Deployment creates additional issues for a family to handle. Families face a number of challenges before, during, and after deployment.

With sudden news of deployment, there may be short periods of strong emotions such as fear and anger. As their departure grows closer, a period of detachment and withdrawal may occur.

During deployment, family members may feel concern, worry, panic, loneliness, and sadness. They hold fear for their loved one's safety. Some will fear infidelity. Lengths of deployments are associated with more emotional difficulties among military children and more mental health problems among military spouses.

There are added family duties and responsibilities and being forced to learn new skills. They have to deal with problems on their own. They have a home to maintain, lawn mowing, and car maintenance. They have financial decisions and difficulties to make on their own.

There will be occasions of feeling overwhelmed—especially when there are children in the mix. Then add the responsibility of looking for schools with good academic reputations, find housing that coincides with the chosen school district, and reliable, safe sitters every time there is a move. It can be extremely frustrating.

Upon return from deployment, there will be the need to understand what your loved ones have been through. Often, the stay-at-home parent feels anger for having to take on everything while they were gone—while the person that was deployed feels they have missed family changes and milestones with their children, and the stay-at-home parent has become independent, that they are not needed anymore. Reintegration and adjusting to family roles takes time. Coming home from a deployment becomes the new normal for everyone.

MILITARY CHILDREN

Children with parents that have been deployed show elevations in anxiety and depression. They pay many of the same costs as their parents. Their reaction to deployment tends to depend on their age, maturity, and any other behavioral or mental health problems the child might have.

Military children feel the pain of missed birthdays, holidays, and important events, they worry about their parents. It can be difficult for a child to adjust when the absent parent comes home.

The child may not bond to the parent because of their absence. For children whose parent has been deployed a number of times, they are adjusting to a person that is in and out of their lives. The parent may be different—suffering with PTSD or physically disabled.

Military children often have adjustment disorders. They fear abandonment, feel anxiety over starting at new schools, worry about making new friends while grieving the separation of old friends.

However, some military children believe they are more resilient, worldlier, and adapt easily. They are excited about having experiences and friends from all over the world.

If parents successfully handle the stressors of military life and deployment, their children are less likely to have mental health or behavior problems. The #1 factor to a child being successful is the presence of a caring, mature adult in their life.

As a parent of a deployed soldier, I had to find coping strategies of my own. I refrained from news stations to avoid hearing about U.S. soldiers being attacked, bombed, and killed at war. I didn't want my imagination to get the best of me. I lived by the rule "No news is good news!" and I appreciated when others would respect that choice. I did *not* want to hear what was going on over there. My daughter was an Army musician—but she was a soldier first. Her primary time being deployed was to stand guard at the gates. She experienced things that would cause anyone to have nightmares. She is a strong woman!

HOW CAN I HELP?

It is very difficult when a family moves so often. First of all, they most likely don't know the area. Offer them information about the area—where the government center is located, the library, primary stores, and shopping centers, churches, and local attractions.

Holidays can be very lonely. To be invited to celebrate the holiday with someone can make a difference!

Invite military families to your church. They are usually away from family and don't know anybody in the area. Introduce them to people. Many churches offer childcare during their services and many churches offer support groups and services for military families and veterans.

Often when the spouse is deployed, there is a stay-at-home parent with young children and babies to care for. Make yourself available. Offer to mow the lawn or to babysit for them. They just may need adult interaction.

My daughter had three very young children at home—all under the age of five. She called me one day upset that the city had sent her a notice that her lawn must be mowed. Her husband was in Iraq and she couldn't leave the babies alone. We lived several states away so there wasn't anything we could do to help her. The one Army mom she knew moved away and she was desperate for help. She eventually got someone to mow it, but not easily. Oh how she would have been so grateful to have someone just simply offer to mow it for her.

Please, don't judge a person until you know the whole story.

WHAT DOES THE BIBLE SAY ABOUT WAR?

There is a time to love,
a time to hate,
a time for war,
and a time for peace.
(Ecclesiastes 3:8).

Some people are adamant that war is the presence of evil.

Pastors Bud and Betty Miller of BibleResources.org wrote a great article about war in the Bible which is referenced throughout this section. You will find war throughout the New and Old Testament. Archeologists have discovered many artifacts that verifies biblical records. Because of sin in the beginning of time (read the sin chapter), mankind has had the freedom to choose to do good or evil. We live in a world where evil men and good men are at war. Of course, God hates war. However, war is necessary to maintain order.

The first war that was recorded was the war in heaven where Satan and his evil angels fought against God and His angels. The war was won by the blood of Jesus (Rev. 12:7–11).

Then war broke out in heaven. Michael and his angels fought against the dragon, and the dragon and his angels fought back. But he was not strong enough, and they lost their place in heaven.

The great dragon was hurled down—that ancient serpent called the devil, or Satan, who leads the whole world astray. He was hurled to the earth and his angels with him.

Then I heard a loud voice in heaven say, "Now have come the salvation and the power and the kingdom of our God, and the authority of his Messiah. For the accuser of our brothers and sisters who accuses them before our God day and night has been hurled down.

They triumphed over him by the blood of the Lamb and by the word of their testimony; they did not love their lives so much as to shrink from death.

The world affairs has been threatening war and continues to threaten as countries build bigger and stronger weapons of destruction. The Bible warns us that it will increase over time as we are closer to the second coming of Christ (Matt. 24:6–8). You will hear of wars and rumors of wars, but see to it that you are not alarmed. Such things must happen, but the end is still to come. Nation will rise against nation, and kingdom against kingdom. There will be famines and earthquakes in various places. All these are the beginning of sorrows.

Christians often struggle with the actions of our government because we are taught as Christians to love our enemies. How do we reconcile this as a Christian?

The Bible defines the role of government as direction to protect their people from threats of invasions and to maintain law and order within its borders by use of military force. It is God's will to bless those who obey and live in harmony, not for those who are evil and destroy all that is good. War is a way God uses civil authorities to maintain order on earth. Even Jesus surrendered to governing authorities! Although war is a harsh form of punishment to evil-doers, the alternative would be worse.

In John 19:11, Jesus answered, "You would have no power over me if it were not given to you from above. Therefore the one who handed me over to you is guilty of a greater sin."

Romans 13:1–5: Submission to Governing Authorities

Let everyone be subject to the governing authorities, for there is no authority except that which God has established. The authorities that exist have been established by God. Consequently, whoever rebels against the authority is rebelling against what God has instituted, and those who do so will bring judgment on themselves. For rulers hold no terror for those who do right, but for those who do wrong.

Do you want to be free from fear of the one in authority? Then do what is right and you will be commended. For the one in authority is God's servant for your good. But if you do wrong, be afraid, for rulers do not bear the sword for no reason. They are God's servants, agents of wrath to bring punishment on the wrongdoer. Therefore, it is necessary to submit to the authorities, not only because of possible punishment but also as a matter of conscience.

No Christian soldier desires to kill another, however, the Lord did not chastise a soldier. The Lord commended this man for his understanding of authority and his great faith when he called upon the Lord to heal his servant. Our military need our prayers and the protection of the Lord anytime they go to battle. This should be the work of the church. Praying for our soldier's protection and prayer for our president. Our negative words will not change things, but prayer will. We must pray that we can return to peace. We need to especially pray for our enemies, that they might be saved. And pray that good will come out of what satan's evil intentions.

Matthew 8:5–10: The Faith of the Centurion

When Jesus had entered Capernaum, a centurion came to him, asking for help. "Lord," he said, "my servant lies at home paralyzed, suffering terribly." Jesus said to him, "Shall I come and heal him?" The centurion replied, "Lord, I do not deserve to have you come under my roof. But just say the word, and my servant will be healed. For I myself am a man under authority, with soldiers under me. I tell this one, 'Go,' and he goes; and that one, 'Come,' and he comes. I say to my servant, 'Do this,' and he does it." When Jesus heard this, he was amazed and said to those following him, "Truly I tell you, I have not found anyone in Israel with such great faith.

In 1 Timothy 2:1–6, God gives us instructions on worship; I urge, then, first of all, that petitions, prayers, intercession and thanksgiving be made for all people—for kings and all those in authority that we may live peaceful and quiet lives in all godliness and holiness. This is good, and pleases God our Savior, who wants all people to be saved and to come to a knowledge of the truth. For there is one

God and one mediator between God and mankind, the man Christ Jesus, who gave himself as a ransom for all people. This has now been witnessed to at the proper time.

IS KILLING IN A WAR CONSIDERED MURDER?

God knew when He created men with free will and that not all would follow and obey Him. He also knew that many would want to love and serve Him. In giving us free will, He also had to establish laws for us to live by.

The Ten Commandments listed in Exodus 20:1–17 reveals laws that were given for the good of mankind. In Exodus 20:13, God commands "Thou shalt not kill." Why would He decree governments to send men to war to kill other men?

The reason is that the Hebrew meaning of the word translated as "kill" actually means "murder" or "to slay someone in a violent manner unjustly." So in the Ten Commandments, God is saying, "Thou shalt not murder." Killing someone with the wrong motives of hatred, vengeance, greed, and jealousy is murder. Killing in self-defense to protect yourself is not considered murder.

Our nation's founders were known to carry a Bible in one hand and a musket in the other in order to defend the freedom they sought here. The freedom to worship God was one of those freedoms they fought for and died for.

WHAT DOES THE BIBLE SAY ABOUT MILITARY CODE AND CONDUCT?

In the Old Testament, there were guidelines about military conduct that would be beneficial to our armed forces. Many of the regulations used in the U.S. armed forces came directly from the pages of the Bible. Listed below are some of the rules given to them regarding military conduct and instruction:

AGE AND QUALIFICATIONS:

First, they were to take a census of the families indicating that there would be some discernment used in the selection of the males as they were numbered. The enlisted was spread across all of the states. The soldiers were drafted so that all would share in the burden of war. They had to be males at least twenty years of age and up and all must be physically fit. Those who were not up to their standards were not to be enlisted. They selected men of valor as they wanted their soldiers to be examples to the others and they wanted all to have a sense of national patriotism.

"Take a census of the whole Israelite community by their clans and families, listing every man by name, one by one. You and Aaron are to count according to their divisions all the men in Israel who are twenty years old or more and able to serve in the army. One man from each tribe, each of them the head of his family, is to help you" (Num. 1:2–4 NIV).

Then the officers shall add, "Is anyone afraid or fainthearted? Let him go home so that his fellow soldiers will not become disheartened too" (Deut. 20:8 NIV).

TRAINING AND PAY:

In 2 Chronicles 25:5–6, Amaziah called the people of Judah together and assigned them according to their families to commanders of thousands and commanders of hundreds for all Judah and Benjamin. He then mustered those twenty years old or more and found that there were three hundred thousand men fit for military service, able to handle the spear and shield. He also hired a hundred thousand fighting men from Israel for a hundred talents (approximately 3.4 metric tons of silver).

When the officers have finished speaking to the army, they shall appoint commanders over it. (Deuteronomy 20:9)

CHAPLAINS IN COMBAT:

Priests or chaplains were not used to fight in war. They were to be available as ministers to stand and pray before the Lord for the soldiers and the battle.

But the Levites after the tribe of their fathers were not numbered among them (Num. 1:47).

WOMEN IN MILITARY:

The decision to allow women in combat was a critical decision. There are reports of numerous problems in the armed forces. One recent incident has brought shame on our military with news reports of inappropriate actions of men and women involved with male prisoners in the war in Iraq. The sexual problems that arise when men and women are mixed in stressful conditions add to the problems of military life. Sexual temptations should not be added to the list of things that men must contend with while on the battlefield. Recent charges of rape and fornication have also been reported due to the close quarters of men and women in training and combat situations.

The women's liberation movement made an effort to liberate women in certain areas that were needed, and went to the point of pushing women to be equal with men in areas that the Bible does not condone. The Bible does not want women exposed to the rigors of war, but rather they are to be protected from it.

By nature, women are more emotional than men. In general, women are more suitable to serve in supportive roles in the military such as nurses, office personnel, technicians, managers, and overseers. Combat should be reserved for males only.

According to the scriptures, the only mention of a woman serving in the military was Deborah in the Old Testament and she served in leadership not in combat duty. She was a judge and leader directing the plan of war as described in Judges, chapter 4.

The Bible teaches men to honor and protect women as the weaker sex in 1 Peter 3:7: Husbands, in the same way be considerate as you live with your wives, and treat them with respect as the weaker partner and as heirs with you of the gracious gift of life, so that nothing will hinder your prayers. God made men stronger physically for the purpose of combat.

Another reason people believe women should not be in combat is to raise their children and to ensure the children are not left as orphans. Small children are more dependent on their mothers.

In Samuel 30:3, and 18-19, David was at war with the Amalekites and his wife and children were taken captive by them. It was David and his men that rescued the women and children. The women were not soldiers.

Greater love has no one than this, that he lay down his life for his friends (John 15:13). When you lay siege to a city for a long time, fighting against it to capture it, do not destroy its trees by putting an axe to them, because you can eat their fruit. Do not cut them down. (Deuteronomy 20:19)

EXEMPTIONS TO MILITARY DUTY:

The Old Testament listed reasons males should be excused from military duty:

- Those who have just moved into a new home and haven't had time to live in yet. Dedicate in the following scripture means "the first use of anything." Deuteronomy 20:5; The officers shall say to the army: "Has anyone built a new house and not yet begun to live in it? Let him go home, or he may die in battle and someone else may begin to live in it."
- Those that have just started a new business and have not yet had time to receive a return on it. Deuteronomy 20:6: "Has anyone planted a vineyard and not begun to enjoy it? Let him go home, or he may die in battle and someone else enjoy it."
- Those that are engaged to be married were not to go to battle. Deuteronomy 20:7: "Has anyone become pledged

to a woman and not married her? Let him go home, or he may die in battle and someone else marry her."

- If a man has just gotten married when war breaks out, he is not to go to war for a year. Deuteronomy 24:5: "If a man has recently married, he must not be sent to war or have any other duty laid on him. For one year he is to be free to stay at home and bring happiness to the wife he has married."

In the Bible, there are instructions about treating prisoners humanely, not violating women and children, caring for civilians, caring for the wounded soldiers, and not destroying the land. Godly morals were to be considered during battle.

BATTLE INSTRUCTIONS

When you lay siege to a city for a long time, fighting against it to capture it, do not destroy its trees by putting an ax to them because you can eat their fruit. Do not cut them down. Are the trees people, that you should besiege them? (Do not cut them down to use in the siege, for the fruit trees are for the benefit of people) (Deut. 20:19).

In Deuteronomy 23:12–13, the Bible provides instruction how to relieve yourself on the battle field: Designate a place outside the camp where you can go to relieve yourself. As part of your equipment have something to dig with, and when you relieve yourself, dig a hole and cover up your excrement.

This is also another reason women should not be on the battlefield, men do not get "caught with their pants down" as often as women when they must relieve themselves.

RULES OF ENGAGEMENT

The first thing before attacking a city, the Israelites were commanded to make peace with the enemy. If the enemy refused the conditions of peace, then they were to attack.

When you march up to attack a city, make its people an offer of peace. If they accept and open their gates, all the people in it shall be subject to forced labor and shall work for you. If they refuse to make peace and they engage you in battle, lay siege to that city (Deut. 20:10–12).

As to the extermination of foes, Israel had to remember that punitive war was in the interests of religion and morality and therefore her soldiers were to act, not as murderers, but as God-appointed executioners of divine judgment upon gross idolatry and iniquity (Deut. 7).

War was viewed as a divine method to exterminate evil wickedness that would defile the rest of the world. God still uses nations today to execute wrath on evil according to Romans 13.

Romans 13:1–7: Submission to Governing Authorities

Let everyone be subject to the governing authorities for there is no authority except that which God has established. The authorities that exist have been established by God. Consequently, whoever rebels against the authority is rebelling against what God has instituted, and those who do so will bring judgment on themselves. For rulers hold no terror for those who do right, but for those who do wrong. Do you want to be free from fear of the one in authority? Then do what is right and you will be commended. For the one in authority is God's servant for your good. But if you do wrong, be afraid, for rulers do not bear the sword for no reason. They are God's servants, agents of wrath to bring punishment on the wrongdoer. Therefore, it is necessary to submit to the authorities not only because of possible punishment but also as a matter of conscience.

This is also why you pay taxes for the authorities are God's servants, who give their full time to governing. Give to everyone what you owe them: If you owe taxes, pay taxes; if revenue, then revenue; if respect, then respect; if honor, then honor.

READING RESOURCES:

There are some fabulous books and articles available for military families. Take advantage of them!

Beyond Trauma: Hope and Healing for Warriors: A Guide for Pastoral Caregivers on PTSD
By Dean Bonura

Children's Books for Young Children in Military Families
http://articles.extension.org/pages/64821/childrens-books-for-young-children-in-military- families

While My Soldier Serves:
Prayers for Those with Loved Ones in the Military
By Edie Melson
While My Child is Away:
My Prayers for When We Are Apart
By Edie Melson

Tour of Duty: Preparing our Hearts for Deployment
A Bible Study for Military Wives
By Sara Horn

Military Families Learning Network
https://blogs.extension.org/militaryfamilies/child-care/

PTSD Relationship Book and More for Couples Coping with PTSD
www.ptsdrelationship.com/

HOTLINES:
National Coalition for Homeless Veterans
1-800-838-4357 (1-800-VET-HELP)

National Suicide Support Number
1-888-784-2433 (1-888-SUICIDE)

QUESTIONS TO PONDER:

1. Were you or anyone in your family enlisted in the military? How has the military changed you or your loved one?

2. Were you aware of the homelessness and mental health issues of our soldiers? Was any of this surprising to you?

3. Were you aware of the suicide rates of military troops and veterans? Were you aware of the issues brought on by PTSD?

4. Did you know there were military standards in the Bible? Did any of them surprise you?

5. We have many females in the military. Do you feel a female should be allowed in combat? Why?

6. Do you feel chaplains should be allowed in combat? Why?

7. What can we do as a church to help military families? What can YOU do to help military families?

8. Was any part of this chapter eye-opening for you? Does it motivate you to change anything?

9. What verse or verses are important to you?

CHAPTER FIVE

ABORTION

First, I want to remind you there are extreme risks with an abortion that people should be made aware of when considering abortion. There are legal, emotional, and physical implications that comes with abortion.

According to a number of articles I researched, Planned Parenthood has been accused of not providing potential patients with enough counseling to be fully informed before performing an abortion. Researchers used undercover agents revealing abortion clinics use consistent persuasion to set abortion appointments before being connected to a counselor. The standard procedure is to overbook to ensure there are no open slots when a patient does not show up. This practice decreases good care and personalization at a critical decision in the patient's life. Understand that these clinics are not looking at your best interest! The famous actor, Chuck Norris said, "Instead of baby, we say fetus; instead of killing, we say aborting, instead of dissect, we say research; instead of extermination chambers, we say abortion clinics."

STATISTICS:

National Abortion Federation reports that one in three American women will have an abortion by the age of forty-five.

With back alley abortions, women died or suffered serious medical complications due to untrained and unsanitary conditions. In 1973, when abortions were legalized, there was a dramatic decline in pregnancy related injuries and death.

AbortionNO.org reports that there are forty-two million abortions per year worldwide.

115,000 per day worldwide. 3,315 per day in the U.S.

This website also reveals abortion imagery and graphic details.

Guttmacher Institute released a Fact Sheet in February 2014 with these statistics: 21% or 4 in 10 pregnancies are terminated, half of them have had at least one prior abortion.

Reasons Given for Abortion:

75% are concerned for taking on the responsibility of other individuals.

75% cannot afford to have a child.

75% feel it would interfere with their careers, school and/or caring for other dependents.

50% do not want to be a single parent or have problem with their spouse or partner.

1% rape or incest

6% health problems

51% used a contraceptive method.

90% of women tested positive for Down syndrome abort their children. According to Rayna Rapp, there is an adoption waiting list for Down syndrome children.

Guttmacher Institute reports that the average abortion costs $451, whereas a vaginal birth with no complications costs more than $9,000.

World Expert Consortium for Abortion Research and Education, Wecare found that there are high rates of physical, sexual, and emotional violence among women seeking abortion. It was stated that intimate partner violence (including history of rape, sexual assault, contraception sabotage, and coerced decision-making) was associated with abortion. They also found that women in violent relationships were less likely to reveal their abortion from partners compared to women who were not victims of violence.

Wecare found when an abortion took place while living in a violent relationship, there is a high probability that they will suffer psychological consequences as a result that further compound a life marked by significant suffering. Numerous studies have documented the fact that women, who feel pressured by partners, abortion counselors, other people in their lives, and/or by life circumstances, are more likely to experience post-abortion mental health problems.

According to the Guttmacher Policy Review, Vol. 16, #2, they reviewed women with post- abortion psychological experiences. It states abortion does not increase women's risk of mental health problems. However, I read many articles substantiating mental health concerns coincide with the feeling of stigma, need for secrecy, lack of support, and interpersonal concerns. There were negative mental health concerns with exposure to antiabortion picketers. The concerns also coincide with hormonal changes similarly to postpartum depression.

It is ludicrous to believe that having an abortion does not cause negative psychological experiences. We have statistics that prove extremely high numbers of people experiencing mental health problems in the general population (See Mental Health Statistics). That was one good reason for writing this book. We know that stressors (including difficult decision making and guilt) will increase the risk of having mental health issues.

Human Life Alliance reports that some men suffer emotional pain and regret when their partners have an abortion.

CAN YOU LIVE WITH YOUR DECISION?

It is imperative to speak with a trusted Christian. Go to someone you know will guide you without judgment. If you are a minor, speak with a trusted adult. Do not try to handle this decision alone. It is a decision you will live with the rest of your life. As you mature, you will feel differently about life.

It is argued that we would be full of children with bigger problems because people who have abortions don't want the babies. They would become another welfare recipient, a burden to society. If abortion isn't legalized, it would be done as termed back alley, which is medically unsupervised, unsterile conditions.

As a young adult and a baby Christian, I was absolutely pro-abortion. I believe now that my opinion was based on the many times I had been molested as a young child. I didn't want anyone to tell me what I can and cannot do with my body. As a Christian woman full of life's lessons and biblical teaching, I have become much more reserved. There are alternative options. Over the years, I have met a number of people that had to go through other countries to find a baby to adopt.

I enjoyed reading the article, "Two Amazing Singers Who Were Almost Victims of Abortion," written by Sarah Terzo of LifeNews. com, dated 05/26/14. Terzo writes about Andrea Bocelli and Celine Dion, both being internationally renowned singers, both explaining their mother's circumstances and reasons for refusing abortion. Dion's mother was devastated when she was pregnant with child number fourteen. Her Catholic priest denied her permission for an abortion. Andrea's mother was hospitalized while pregnant and was advised by the doctor to get an abortion because her child will be disabled. Andrea's mother refused. Andrea was in fact born blind. Both almost aborted, both extremely talented and famous. In this e-article, there was a clip of the two of them singing "The Prayer" together.

WHAT DOES THE BIBLE SAY ABOUT ABORTION?

There are no specific words in the Bible about abortion because that is modern terminology.

Historically, ancient Greeks and Romans performed abortions. For hundreds of generations, abortions were practice by way of drinking herbal and root concoctions to force menstruation among some brutal methods in other areas of the world. In Ecclesiastes 1:9, Solomon writes that history repeats itself. As we know, it most certainly does!

IS ABORTION CONSIDERED MURDER?

This is such a controversial topic! This is an awful question for those who have had abortions or performed abortions. Exodus 20:13 from the Ten Commandments says "Thou shalt not kill." The problem is that for centuries, people have shared different opinions as to whether or not an unborn baby is considered a living being from the time of being conceived. If someone hits a woman (even accidentally) and she gives birth prematurely, they will be judged accordingly.

"The punishment will match the injury. A life for a life, an eye for an eye" (Exod. 21:22–25).

"Do not kill the innocent and righteous for I will not acquit the wicked" (Exod. 23:7). "Anyone who murders a fellow human must die. If anyone takes a human life, that person's life will also be taken by human hands. For God made human beings in his own image" (Gen. 9:5–6). But there is hope. Keep reading!

GRIEVING

Grieving is very painful. For most, there is an extraordinary amount of guilt and regret that comes with abortion. If you are grieving, understand that you may experience lengthy bouts of emotional turmoil. People need to understand that everyone handles grief in their own way and their own time. You cannot change the situation. You cannot turn time back.

Do *not* use alcohol, drugs or food to relieve your pain. Make sure you have a support group that you can call on. There is strength in others. Pray and/or meditate.

If your abortion happened several years ago and you are suffering with shame and guilt as a new Christian, remember your sins are forgiven. The sin of abortion is as forgivable as any other sin. Whether you are the woman that had the abortion, a person that encouraged an abortion, or the person that performed the abortion, Christ will forgive you through faith. John 3:16, Romans 8:1, and Colossians 1:14, all reminds us that through faith in Christ, all sins can be forgiven.

What the Bible teaches about the unborn child:

Psalm 139:13–16: "You made all the delicate, inner parts of my body, and knit them together in my mother's womb." Thank you for making me so wonderfully complex! It is amazing to think about. Your workmanship is marvelous—and how well I know it. You were there while I was being formed in utter seclusion! You saw before me I was born and scheduled each day of my life before I began to breathe. Every day was recorded in your book.

Psalm 127:3: "Behold, children are a heritage from the Lord, the fruit of the womb a reward."

Genesis 1:26–27: "And God said, Let us make man in our image, after our likeness: and let them have dominion over the fish of the sea, and over the fowl of the air, and over the cattle, and over all the earth, and over every creeping thing that creeps upon the earth. So God created man in his own image, in the image of God created by Him."

Exodus 1:15–21" "Pharaoh, the king of Egypt instructed Hebrew midwives to kill all Hebrew boys as they were born and to save the girls. But the midwives feared God and did not obey the King allowing the boys to live. And God blessed the midwives for being God-fearing women, and gave them children of their own."

Jeremiah 1:4–5: "The Lord said, "I knew you before you were formed within your mother's womb; before you were born I sanctified and appointed you to speak to the world." (This verse supports life in the womb.)

Job 12:7–10: "In His hand is the life of every creature and the breath of all mankind."

In the first chapter of Matthew, it tells the story about Joseph and Mary, and the birth of baby Jesus. Joseph did not want to wed Mary because she was pregnant (obviously this baby was not his child) and that was when being a virgin upon marriage was vital. It was assumed that women like Mary who was pregnant were considered harlots. Who would believe she was a pregnant virgin? An angel of God told Joseph to take her home to be his wife anyway. Hallelujah!

WILL I MEET MY BABY IN HEAVEN?

You *will* meet your baby in heaven! See chapter 8. In 2 Samuel 12, we learn about David's affair with a woman named Bathsheba. Bathsheba became pregnant from this affair. Nathan (a prophet) warned David that their child would die because he betrayed God. So David fasted and prayed to the Lord that He would not carry out His judgment. When the child died, 2 Samuel 12:19, David stopped praying and fasting. When asked why he stopped fasting and praying, David replied, "I shall go to him and he will not return to me" (2 Samuel 12:23). This clearly indicates that he will be with his child one day in heaven.

Though they were not yet born and had done nothing either good or bad (Rom. 9:11).

Another important point is found in Romans 6:23; the wages of sin is death. An unborn or aborted baby has never sinned.

Jesus invited children to come to Him (Luke 18:16).

READING RESOURCES:

A Scarlet Cord of Hope
By Sheryl Griffin

Surrendering the Secret: Healing the Heartbreak of Abortion
By Patricia Layton

You're Not Alone: Healing through God's Grace after Abortion
By Jennifer O'Neill

Healing after Abortion: God's Mercy is for You
By David Powlison

QUESTIONS TO PONDER:

1. Did you or anyone close to you have an abortion?
    How has it changed you or the person you refer to?

2. Were you aware of the mental health implications of an abortion?
    Was any of this surprising to you?

3. What would you say to someone that confides they are considering an abortion?
    What if that person is a minor?
    What can we do as a church to help someone that suffers guilt and regret from having an abortion?
    What can YOU do to help someone through the aftermath of an abortion?

4. Was any part of this chapter eye-opening for you?
    Does it motivate you to change anything?
    What verse or verses are important to you?

CHAPTER SIX

ADDICTION

People are slaves to whatever has mastered them
(2 Pet. 2:19).

ALCOHOL AND DRUG ABUSE

What we have learned over the years about alcohol and drug abuse is that it is one or all of the combined components; pre-disposed genetics, a product of their environment, or self-treatment for mental illness.

According to (NCADD) National Council on Alcoholism and Drug Dependence (NCADD) estimates 17 million Americans currently have an alcohol use disorder and only a fraction of people with alcohol problems seek professional help.

At this time, prescription drugs are popular. It is not just a Hollywood problem. According to HHS.gov (Health and Human Services), opioid abuse is considered an epidemic. One in five teens have tried prescription drugs recreationally. They feel invincible. People assume that because these drugs are a prescribed medication, they are safe to use when actually they can be more powerful than street drugs—especially when they are mixed with alcohol.

Kids will not tell on other kids. Often parents are in denial or simply won't do anything about it because they are afraid of ruining their picture perfect family persona.

The addict will do a number of things to get their drugs. They will go from urgent care to urgent care because they know if they whine and fuss enough, they will get what they want. They may go doctor shopping until they find a dirty doctor or steal and/or print prescription pads. There have been cases where they will get doctor information so they can order them from pharmacies. They steal for drugs to purchase on the street or order them through mail order facilities.

Addiction affects every aspect of their life—from relationships with their family and friends to their financial situation.

"Remember that nobody intends to destroy their life.
It's a slow, steady compromise that leads to destruction."
Unknown Author

First of all, understand that the Bible does not state that drinking alcohol is a sin. The Bible reveals problems when you are no longer in power of the alcohol. 1 Timothy 5:23 reveals alcohol in moderation is acceptable.

How many times has the addicted person heard, "All you have to do is pray harder!" Or "You must not be taking your spiritual life seriously."

Addiction is a substance or behavior that interferes with life, love and relationships. It creates a dependency on itself. The tolerance level builds needing more and more to feel "normal." In Ephesians 4, Paul writes that when we turn from God, we separate ourselves from the life of God. We are left with an insatiable need for more. Research reveals that when the satiation cycle ends, the addicted person becomes irritable and anxious. As a Christian, *choose* mercy and compassion. Nobody wants to be an addict (Prov. 20:5). Though good advice lies deep within the heart, a person with understanding will draw it out.

Allow me to explain how alcohol/drugs can be used for different substitutions. Remember that this example can look like a highly educated business person or a stay-at-home parent—both striving for perfection. It can be a student, teacher, doctor, lawyer, deacon, or pastor. It can be any one of us.

The addict may totally isolate themselves not allowing anyone in. His/her addiction substitutes the wall they built. Some addicts are people pleasers and always walking on eggshells. Their addiction is used to substitute their burnout. And there is the addict that is a harsh and merciless judge. Or they are a perfectionist. This type of addict uses their addiction to substitute self-loathing.

Addiction afflicts *all* walks of life for different reasons with very destructive results. You most likely know at least one person that fits one of these categories.

OTHER COMMON DRUGS:

OPIODS – THE NATION'S BIGGEST DRUG RELATED THREAT

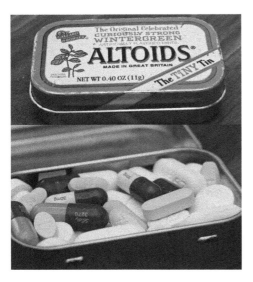

Hospitals, treatment centers and law enforcement are inundated with the results of opioid addiction. Opioid deaths have nearly doubled. People start using prescribed opioids post-surgery and become addicted to the medication. With the crack-down on prescribing opioids people are resorting to street drugs including heroin. Heroin is favored because it is cheaper and easier to access than pain medications. Unfortunately, street drugs are laced with deadly drugs such as Fentanyl to increase its strength causing overdose and death. Heroin use is found in all age and economic levels.

- Opioids are prescribed medications used for pain after surgery and chronic pain. They are highly addictive. They include Oxycontin, Vicodin, Norco, Suboxine, Codeine, Oxymorphone, Fentanyl, Demerol, Dilaudid, Methodone and Morphine.
- Street Drug Opioids include opium, heroin and hashish. These drugs are referred to as Black Stuff and Smack.

SEDATIVES AND TRANQUILIZERS:

- Prescribed Sedatives are medications used for anxiety, seizures, and to induce sleep. They include Xanax, Lortab, Valium, Ativan and Ambien.
- Street Drug Sedatives and Tranquilizers include Barbiturates, benzodiazepines, methylenedioxymet (MDMA).

STIMULANTS:

- Stimulants are prescribed medications used for treating ADHD, narcolepsy, asthma, obesity and depression. Medications include Adderall, Concerta and Ritalin.
- Street Drug Stimulants are often used by students for performance enhancement, increased focus and weight loss. These drugs include amphetamines including Biphetamine and Dexadrine. They are referred to as Bennies, Crosses, Speed and Uppers.
- Catha edulis, or Khat is a plant used to treat obesity and prevent hunger in areas of meager food supplies. It is referred to as Khat, Chat, African Salad and Abyssinian Tea.
- Cocaine is a powder form also known as Coke, Toot, Snow, Bump and Blow.
- Methamphetamine increases energy, sleeplessness, paranoia and aggressive behavior. It is known as Meth, Crystal, Ice, Tweak and Crank.

DISSOCIATIVE DRUGS:

Dissociative drugs causes feelings of separation from the body and hallucinations.

- Phencyclidine (PCP) aka Angel Dust. When PCP is mixed with marijuana, it is known as Zombie Weed.

- Salvia divinorum is a psychoactive plant known as Magic Mint. It causes dissociation and confusion.
- Ketamin is a veterinary tranquilizer used as an anesthesia. It is known as Kit Kat, Special K, Cat Valium, Super Acid, K-Hole and K.
- Dextromethorphan is found in cough and cold medications. It is known as Dex, Skittles, Robo, and Robo-tripping. Higher doses causes hallucinations and paranoia.

HALLUCINOGENS:

- Dimethyltryptamine is known for its short and intense highs. It is known as a Businessman's Trip.
- Psilocybin Mushrooms has several species of psychoactive fungus known as Magic Mushrooms, Cubes, Shrooms and Gold Caps (depending on species)
- Methylenedioxy or Methamphetamine (MDMA) increases energy and is a hallucinogenic. It is known as Ecstasy, Lover's Speed, X, Molly and Eve. Lysergic Acid Diethylamide (LSD) causes drug-induced psychosis. It has a variety of names depending on color and form including Acid, Microdot, Yellow Sunshine, Cubes and Dots.
- Mescaline causes perceptual disturbance. It is found in cactus. It is known on the street as Peyote, Cactus, and Buttons.

CLUB DRUGS:

- Gamma-Hydroxybutyric Acid (GHB) is a date rape drug called G and Liquid X.
- Flunitrazepam (Rohypnol) is considered date rape drug called forget-me-pill, Mexican Valium and roofies.
- Gamma-Hydroxybutyric Acid (GHB) is a date rape drug called G and Liquid X.

OTHER:

- Synthetic Cathinones are Bath Salts also known as Flakka, Gravel and Zombie Drug. It causes erratic behavior, paranoia and psychosis.
- Synthetic Cannabinoids is a potent synthetic marijuana has a medical benefits. Used on the streets, Synthetic Cannabinoids are called Spice and Fake Weed.
- Steroids are drugs used to treat medical conditions but often abused to boost performance and increase muscle mass also known as Doping, Gym Candy and Roids. Steroids can cause a number of medical and psychiatric disorders including drug dependence, aggressive behaviors and depression.

Inhalants: fumes and vapors of solvents, glue and gases inhaled (called huffing) to induce a psychoactive or mind altering effect. It too can cause a number of medical conditions as it starves the body and brain of oxygen causing heart disruption and nosebleeds. Long term use includes organ damage, brain damage, and losing senses of hearing and smell.

MARIJUANA USE

I want to address marijuana because I know so many people that believe it is a safe drug primarily because it is organic. However, most people do not understand that through the processes of street drugs, often marijuana is dipped and/or mixed in chemicals. For years, it was common to dip marijuana cigarettes into chemicals such as embalming fluid or PCP (Pentachlorophenol) to increase their potency. Another consideration is that over the years the THC (tetrahydrocannabinol) in marijuana has become stronger making it more difficult to know how strong the marijuana is.

A lot of people believe that you cannot get addicted to marijuana, but that has been proven a myth. Research suggests that more than 10% of all marijuana users become addicted. And this number increases among those who start using as teens.

Marijuana use is linked to less academic and career success. They are more likely to drop out of school, higher absences, accidents, and injuries. There is significant proof that long-term effects of marijuana causes a reduced resistance to common illnesses, suppressed immune system, growth disorders, increased abnormally structured cells in the body, reduction of male sex hormones, rapid destruction of lung fibers and lesions to the brain, reduced sexual capacity, study difficulties due to reduced ability to learn and retain information, apathy, drowsiness, lack of motivation, personality and mood changes, and the inability to understand things clearly.

Marijuana has both short-term and long-term effects on the brain. Short-term problems includes disorientation, lack of physical coordination, and slowed reaction time increasing your risk of being involved in a car accident. Next to alcohol, marijuana is the second most frequently found substance in the bodies of drivers involved in fatal accidents.

It is imperative that young adults understand that it affects brain development. For long-term users of marijuana, people may lose their memory and learning functions. Studies prove loss of IQ points with ongoing cannabis use. And the lost mental abilities may not fully return after they quit using.

Marijuana use can cause breathing problems, decreased blood pressure, and increased heart rate, increase risk of bleeding, liver disease, and diabetes. It can cause problems with fetal development during pregnancy. It can cause mental health problems such as depression, anxiety and suicidal thoughts especially among teens. Long-term marijuana use is linked to mental illness including hallucinations, paranoia, psychosis, and schizophrenia.

According to Dr. Peter H. Grossman, plastic surgeon, warns about a drug trend sending significant numbers of people to the hospital due to the dangers of "Dabbing." DABS or BHO (Butane Hash Oil) is known as Honey Oil, Wax, Shatter and Budder. It is highly concentrated doses of cannabis made by extracting the THC using solvents like butane or carbon dioxide making a sticky substance generally vaped rather than smoked. The substance can be dried to paper thin honey colored sheets that are very fragile (thus the name shatter). The production of DABS is as dangerous as a meth lab. It causes explosions, fires, burns and serious injuries.

DABS or BHO can be up to five times more potent than high grade buds. The THC is up to nine times higher levels of THC.

Overdosing is a risk to even experienced users as these concentrated levels are so high. As with any drug, overdosing is potentially deadly.

If you are using marijuana or any type of THC substance, you are at risk of addiction and sin.

CAN PEOPLE GET TREATMENT FOR MARIJUANA ADDICTION?

The answer is yes. Withdrawal symptoms will include mood swings, irritability, sleeplessness, decreased appetite, anxiety, physical tension, and craving the drug. Behavior support for treating marijuana addiction includes therapy and motivational incentives.

OTHER NATURAL DRUGS:

As I mentioned in the marijuana section even if the drug is all natural, it can be addictive. A lot of those natural herbs and plants are not regulated. People who use Kava and Kratom have no idea of the exponential damage they are causing their bodies because they believe the natural substance is safe. According to the Food & Drug Administration, FDA, Kratom is as addictive as morphine and other opiates. It is extremely toxic to the organs including the respiratory and nervous system. It is reported to cause psychosis, convulsions, hallucinations, stomach sickness, sweating, dizziness, chest pain, and confusion. Like any mood altering drug, it carries the potential for addiction. Although The Botanical Legal Defense will argue with these findings as it is their mission "to fight over-reaching government criminalization of nature's most significant gifts."

People find no harm in using Ayahuasca, which is an entheogenic or psychotropic brew because it is natural. This Ayahuasca vine is associated with shamanism. It is used as a spiritual medicine or as a sacrament. Ayahuasca has been used to clear the body of worms and parasites which means it causes the body to purge. It has cardiovascular effects that can increase your heart rate and blood pressure.

Some people have reported extreme psychological stress such as panic attacks, anxiety and fear.

These natural herbs and plants can cause ruin in your life; physically and financially. If you are an addict of any kind, it is not safe to transfer one drug for another.

I am addicted to smoking cigarettes. Although I have not smoked for more than twenty years, I still crave a smoke when I go fishing. The cravings are tied in with relaxation. When at work, it is difficult to take a break because I really crave that cigarette! I know a number of ex-smokers that quit smoking but still puff on e-cigarettes. They need that e-cig just like they did when they were getting the nicotine. So for many, the addiction is a relaxation behavior.

RELAPSE

According to Camp Recovery Center, be aware of common triggers for relapse. This includes avoiding social situations where drugs and alcohol may be accessible. Do not use drugs, alcohol, or any mood-altering substance. Don't be overconfident thinking you can use once and you will fine. Avoid reminiscing about partying and drug use. Complacency can get you into trouble.

Beware!

Don't allow yourself too much social isolation. Isolating yourself causes bouts of depression. Try to prevent stress, boredom and self-pity. Often that is not only a trigger but an excuse to use.

Mental illness can cause relapse. If you are taking medications for a mental health disorder, you must continue taking them per doctor's order—even when you are feeling great and think you don't need them anymore. Remember, you are probably feeling great because of your medications.

Physical illness and pain can cause relapse when given medications that are mood altering. You may become bored and isolated due to illness and pain. And commonly feel an increase in sadness and depression.

WHAT DOES THE BIBLE SAY ABOUT ALCOHOL AND DRUG USE?

Again, let me reiterate that the Bible does not state that drinking alcohol is a sin. The Bible reveals problems when you are no longer in power of the alcohol. Therefore, I urge you to realize that this is in representation of any mind-altering drug; alcohol, chemical, or plant.

Proverbs 201:1 reveals alcohol leads to brawls.

Proverbs 23:19–20 reveals alcohol's deceptive power: Solomon tells his son whose life was spinning out of control to stay focused, warning him that alcohol and gluttony would end in poverty.

Proverbs 23:29–30 reveals alcohol's destructive power: People that are addicted to drugs or alcohol will experience woe and sorrow in an assortment of problems including financial ruin, injury, and conflicts. Proverbs 20:1 whoever staggers (because of wine and beer) is not wise.

Proverbs 23:31–35 reveals alcohol's addictive power: People may start using drugs and alcohol for recreation or relaxation. Over time, the need grows, increasing in use or dosage until it becomes a toxic poison. Solomon describes the typical cycle of a drunkard in Proverbs 23:33–35.

Proverbs 31:4–5 reveals alcohol's power to distract: Lamuel's mother warned Lamuel to stay away from alcohol if he wants to be an effective ruler or King.

Proverbs 31:6–7: Alcohol used as a sedative: Lamuel's mother tells Lamuel those who drink strong alcoholic drinks have lost hope in their life. It is then a sedative to help the poor and oppressed forget.

GAMBLING ADDICTION:

Gambling addiction is known as compulsive or pathological gambling. It is an uncontrollable urge to gamble despite the negative effects it might have in their lives. It devastates not only the addict but also the addict's family. Two out of three gambling addicts will engage in illegal activity to pay off their gambling debts. Gambler's Anonymous found through a study that forty-eight percent of their members had considered suicide and thirteen percent had attempted suicide.

Gambling addiction (like any addiction) is associated with other problems including mood disorder, anti-social personality disorder and depression.

Gambling addition is more prevalent with thanks to the internet. Technology can allow you to play with instant access to your banking account and charge accounts. Online gambling is one of the fastest growing and profitable businesses in existence today. There is a trend of gamblers on college campuses using their student loan funds to support their gambling. Also, elderly adults on a fixed income with too much time on their hands. It is believed that one in five online gamblers are addicted, and four percent of gambling addicts are teenagers.

Recent statistics reveal more than eighty percent of U.S. adults have engaged in gambling at least one time. At least 2.9 percent of the adult population are addicted spending more than $500 billion annually on wages. Problem drinkers have an increased risk of developing an addition to gambling.

GAMBLING ADDICTION SIGNS AND SYMPTOMS:

1. Preoccupation with gambling: reliving gambling experiences, planning the next gambling session, and how to find the money to continue gambling.
2. Needing to spend more money to gain the desired level of excitement.
3. Unsuccessful attempts to reduce or stop gambling.
4. Irritable or restless when attempting to reduce or stop gambling.
5. Using gambling to procrastinate things that need to be done, avoid a problem or improve a mood.
6. Trying to gamble back lost money.
7. Lying to family, friends, therapists to cover up lost money due to gambling.
8. Involvement in illegal activities which include robbery, forgery, and fraud to recover from gambling debts and/or to continue gambling habits.
9. Difficulties with relationships, job, or education as a result of gambling.
10. Relying on others for money to get out of desperate financial situations caused by gambling.

YOUR ACTIONS HURT AND AFFECT OTHERS

If you gamble or use drugs, you are hurting and affecting others.

Some people think because they have a job and pay the rent, they are supporting the family financially. Often that is not the case. I thank God my dad sobered up during my junior high school years (now called middle school). I was able to graduate with a class I knew for more than a few months, we became active with a small baptist church and we shared real family time together. I truly cherish those years!

Drugs, alcohol and gambling effects your loved ones physically; sleep deprivation, eating too much or too little, stomach ulcers, chronic illnesses, etc.

It causes emotional turmoil. Children are traumatized by watching their parents fight. There is a propensity to move frequently. My Dad's alcoholism caused me to attend 21 different schools. Emotional turmoil causes depression and anxiety. My family moved so often, I became less social. With a sudden move to California, I had a heavy Midwestern accent. I was horribly bullied and began to stutter.

Here is another example: Suppose you get arrested for stealing at the local Walmart–or walk into the Walmart drunk and loud. Perhaps your child has a friend or a friend's parent that works there. Or a teacher's aide from school, or someone from the Sunday school class your child attends. Your child(ren) will suffer mockery and ridicule as a consequence of *your* behavior.

When you have a family, you need to think about how your actions may affect others.

FOOD ADDICTION:

As we all know, there is an epidemic of obesity in the United States. You've all heard the numbers! As a young child, I recall being impressed to hear when older people lived into their eighties. But with great medical strides, more and more people are living into a full century.

Unfortunately, as our generations change with our need to do it all in this fast-paced lifestyle, we have resorted to a society of computers and fast food. This lifestyle has slowed our metabolisms immensely. High stress jobs and obesity are proving to lower life expectancy. Last time I had my BMI and other factors checked, my life expectancy was seventy-two years of age. And I don't smoke!

IS OVEREATING A SIN?

Yes, overeating is a sin.

It affects your body image, your self-image, your health, and the acceptance from others. There is a stigma with being obese. Many people feel obesity is caused from a lack of self-control and tend to be lazy. Obesity can affect the types of jobs you can do and your stamina.

SO HOW IS THAT A SIN?

Because God does not want us to indulge ourselves in anything; this includes food and wine:

- He who is a companion of gluttons humiliates his father (Prov. 28:7).
- Do not associate with heavy drinkers or gluttons (Prov. 23:20).
- Eat only what you need (Prov. 25:16).
- So whether you eat or drink, or whatever you do, do it all for the glory of God (1 Cor. 10:31).
- It is not good to eat too much honey (Prov. 25:27).
- A sated man loathes honey, but to a famished man any bitter thing is sweet (Prov. 27:7).

Like all bad habits, overeating can be broken with determination and discipline. Like trying to quit any addiction, you keep trying until you find the right method to get your life back.

OVERWORKING AND MONEY:

There is no dispute that money causes conflict when it gets in the way of marriage, family and friends. For the love of money is the root of all kinds of evil. (1 Timothy 6:10)

- Avoid desires for luxuries and riches (Prov. 23:3).
- Avoid working just to gain wealth (Prov. 23:4).
- Avoid dishonesty in business agreements (Prov. 23:10).
- I will not be controlled by anything (1 Cor. 6:12).

INTERNET ADDICTION:

The Internet is a primary tool for communication, socialization, education, business, and entertainment. When used responsibly and in moderation, it can provide us with an infinite amount of information and can contribute to the quality of our lives.

CAN PEOPLE REALLY BECOME ADDICTED TO THE INTERNET?

A common belief is that Internet addiction happens because people use the internet to avoid the real world and responsibility to ignore emotions including loneliness, reduce stress, depression, or anxiety. Using the internet in moderation to manage emotions or simply to relax is fine as long as it doesn't take away from dealing with the real world. When it becomes obsessive or problematic, then it may be considered addictive behavior like gambling.

Generally, we think of addictions that pertain to nicotine, drugs, and alcohol that eventually increases with tolerance. You become dependent and suffer withdrawal when discontinued. Any behavior or activity that produces a reward can become addictive in that it becomes an obsession which may include a preoccupation of food, sex, exercise, and even stock trading. Research has proven that psychological addiction is real and is associated with neurochemical and biological changes in the brain.

When does normal use cross the line into excessive use or addiction? When the virtual world is used in excess and becomes more important than the physical world—this can be a serious problem. If a person uses the internet to escape real world responsibilities or difficulties creating more problems in their life suggests addiction to the internet.

Would this include cell phone use?

Yes. Almost all cell phones are connected to the internet. Without the internet, you are connected to a social media by way of texting. We all know someone that cannot live without the ability to text constantly. I know too many people that just cannot separate themselves from their phones. Not even to eat a meal or watch a movie.

SIGNS OF INTERNET ADDICTION

Similar to the symptoms of video game addiction, the signs of Internet Addiction can be broken down into four distinct categories—psychological, physical, behavioral, and relational.

PSYCHOLOGICAL

- Feeling guilt after spending too much time online
- Difficult to refrain from the Internet for more than a few days in a row
- Lose track of time when online
- Frustrated or tense when unable to go online
- Justifying extreme use
- Minimizing the negative effects of excessive Internet use ("I could be doing worse things than this.")
- No longer involved with hobbies or activities you used to enjoy
- Only happy or content when online
- Obsessing about what is going on in your virtual world while at school, work, or out with friends.

PHYSICAL

- Carpal tunnel syndrome
- Headaches, neck aches, back problems
- Tired, dry, and/or red eyes
- Irregular, unhealthy eating habits causing significant weight gain or weight loss.

BEHAVIORAL

- Marathon internet use
- Eating meals while on the computer or not eating at all.
- Regularly using the Internet until very late at night despite having to get up early the next morning
- Several attempts to decrease Internet use with little or no success
- Going online with every small opportunity
- Often going online while neglecting other important responsibilities

Education: Students decrease time spent studying causing poorer academic performance

Work: Getting to work late and/or tired because you stayed up late to be online. Sneak opportunities to go online when you should be executing work objectives.

Family: Preoccupied parents = Unsupervised children. Enough said!

Household tasks (yes, this is gender generalizing—and no, this is not how it always works at my house):

Men: outside of the obvious like the grass getting mowed, there are vehicles to keep maintained, a window and tub that need caulking, a faucet that needs to be replaced. When's the last time you organized your garage? The list goes on . . .

Women: there is seasonal clothing and repairs to tend to. A good vacuuming is overdue as well as shining up those wood floors. When is the last time you cleaned those blinds and dusted the ceiling fans? The list goes on . . .

RELATIONSHIPS

- Displaying anger or resentment toward anyone that may comment or question how much time is spent online
- Relationship problems and frequent arguments stemmed from spending too much time online
- Blaming loved ones for the amount of time spent on the internet: "If you were more_____, I wouldn't be online so much."
- Losing real friends because you spend too much time with virtual friends
- Others are concerned about your Internet use. You are angered by mere comments regarding your internet use.
- Decreased socializing with family and friends.

- Deceiving people about the amount of time you spent on the Internet.

Internet Addiction Disorder (IAD) is often associated with mental disorders including impulse control problems, attention deficit/hyperactivity disorder (ADHD), and depression.

IAD is divided into six categories: gaming, social networking, cyber-sex/pornography, shopping, gambling, and general surfing.

One out of eight people have Problematic Internet Use (PIU). This has become a bigger issue since most everyone carries a cell phone with internet access. Some people are so addicted to their online life that they will risk texting while driving. A study reveals more than 91% of drivers with cell phones admits to texting while driving.

According to the U.S. Department of Commerce, the internet is being misused in the workplace. The study reveals thirty to forty percent of internet use in non-business related, sixty percent of all online purchases are made during regular work hours, and there is a forty percent loss of productivity due to personal internet use. The study reveals that seventy percent of all pornography is during normal work hours.

AM I ADDICTED TO THE INTERNET?

- Am I preoccupied to go online when the computer or internet is not available?
- Am I missing out real life because of my Internet use?
- Am I self-sufficient and proud of who I am today?
- Am I forfeiting the ability to achieve life goals?

INTERNET ADDICTION TREATMENT

Because Internet Addiction is a fairly new psychological problem, specialized treatment options are limited. Although some psychologists and counselors are taking an interest in working with online obsessions, finding a specialist can be difficult.

Change is never easy, but it is required for personal growth and development. As difficult as changing your Internet habits may be, it is not nearly as difficult as living with the regret of lost relationships, missed opportunities, and unrealized potential. People who are online often believe there is a sense of anonymity, when in actuality, they can be found (as the Subway spokesperson Jared Fogle found out when he used his fame to become a sexual predator).

Our virtual friends cannot take place of real friends. Chatting cannot replace spending time with others in person. And video game accomplishments cannot be substituted for achieving personal goals in the real world.

With proper treatment, support from others, and a genuine commitment to change, it is definitely possible to overcome Internet Addiction and live a happier and more fulfilling life.

There are a number of free parental control systems that can assist you in limiting computer or internet time. Most of them are easy to install and use with high security.

THERAPY FOR INTERNET ADDICTION

Most therapy for Internet Addiction follows a cognitive-behavioral model. This form of treatment is used for a wide variety of issues to include recognizing unhealthy behaviors, developing coping skills, and then changing the actual behaviors. The most effective treatments will not only target the unhealthy behaviors, but also any possible underlying contributors to Internet Addiction such as depression, social anxiety, or relationship problems.

If a therapist who specializes in treating internet addiction is not available, potential clients may wish to choose someone who works with other addictions such as Pathological Gambling Disorder. Depending on the nature of the online obsession, it may also make sense to choose a therapist who has experience treating pornography addiction. If excessive internet use is caused by another issue such as depression, anxiety, or a lack of self-confidence, it would obviously be wise to select someone who specializes in these issues.

COMPUTER GAMING ADDICTION:

Gaming is addictive in the same way gambling is addictive. A gamer addict will isolate themselves ignoring relationships and responsibilities. The high is the hunt to obtain a higher score, higher status, or ranking. Gaming addiction leads to psychosocial problems and withdrawal symptoms such as irritability, anxiety, and sadness (as in gambling and substance abuse) when internet access is denied. Recent studies reveal a correlation in elementary grade children between problematic internet use (PIU) and Attention Deficit Hyperactivity Disorder (ADHD). There is interest in exploring possible links between video games and psychiatric disorders that include bipolar disorder, depression, and social anxiety.

SIGNS AND SYMPTOMS OF COMPUTER GAME ADDICTION:

- It interferes with education, work, or relationships
- Avoid or do not follow-through with commitments in order to keep playing games
- Prefer gaming over social invitations
- Using most or all of one's free time for gaming
- Regularly playing late into the night and which results in poor sleep habits
- Lose interest in other favored activities
- Regular gaming "binges" of eight hours or more nonstop

PORN AND SEXUAL ADDICTION:

A person who is addicted to sex and pornography often engage in risky sex and tend to have many sexual partners. They also have other risky behaviors that includes drug and alcohol use to numb their control of inhibition.

This addiction is rapidly growing and a common problem. It is reported that 90% of all teens have looked at pornography. Clinical psychologist Karen Stewart reports nine out of ten college-age males and over one third of college-age females look at pornography on a regular basis.

According to Gert Martin Hald, PhD, and colleagues in The APA Handbook of Sexuality and Psychology (Vol. 2), International studies reveal pornography consumption rates at fifty percent to ninety-nine percent among men, and thirty percent to eighty-six percent among women.

Is this really an addiction or is it an impulse control disorder? Experts refer to sexual behaviors such as these as a compulsive sexual behavior. Studies only revealed sexual compulsivity exists, but there are differences in how it presents itself. There are differences in effective therapy; suggesting SSRI anti-depressants and/or cognitive behavior therapy to deal with trigger situations.

Porn and sexual addiction can ruin marriages, increase unhealthy behaviors and encourage sexual aggression. It changes the way you think about human beings. It kills the intimacy of sex. "People become objects and body parts" reports Terry Crews, former NFL player on Today.com.

The internet has made pornography practically ubiquitous. While many porn viewers don't seem to suffer ill effects, porn can become problematic for others. The Kinsey Institute survey found nine percent of porn viewers said they were unable to stop. Understanding what drives the behavior is necessary to control the behavior.

Participants of pornography claim erotica enhances their sex lives. However, studies reveal that women who perceive their partner's porn use to be problematic experienced lower self-esteem feeling unattractive, undesirable, and unable to measure up to the porn stars. With that, there is less intimacy, and increase of porn use which will inadvertently create more relational problems. It is typical with men in heterosexual couples that use porn on a regular basis has a tendency to withdraw from their spouse emotionally. They also reported the increased secrecy caused them to feel less intimacy and more depressed.

In married couples interviewed, it was found that the cycle is a combination of the male whom turns to pornography because he feels sexually unsatisfied, and the woman pulls away from her husband because he is choosing to spend his attention on porn.

Addiction to porn not only gets in the way of their real-life relationships, but can cause problems in other areas of life. People lose jobs from visiting porn sites at their place of employment.

Valerie Voon, MD, PhD, a neuropsychiatrist at the University of Cambridge tested compulsive pornography by scanning brain activity of porn users while viewing erotic images and compared them to the brain scans of alcoholics and drug users viewing drinking and drug paraphernalia.

The brain activity patterns were similar. A 2013 study by researchers at the University of Leicester in the United Kingdom suggests that a penchant for porn may be more compulsion than addiction. Researchers found that certain traits including neuroticism, agreeableness, conscientiousness, and obsessional checking behaviors were correlated with high pornography use (Journal of Sex & Marital Therapy, 2013)

BREAK THE ADDICTION:

I will not be controlled by anything!
(1 Cor. 6:12)

How do you escape addiction? Break the habit? Whatever you are addicted to or has become habitual can be stopped. Here are some self-help tips:

You need to understand why you do whatever it is you are doing. What is the purpose you are doing these things to the point you have to ask yourself these questions?

- Are you avoiding something, escaping an emotion, anxiety or stress?
- Is it creating a problem for you? Do you argue with your spouse over it?

- Are you not getting enough rest because of it? Are you missing class or work?
- Are you ashamed of it?

Are you being honest with yourself? For example; if you are an alcoholic, you are not drinking because you are thirsty or you like the taste. You are medicating yourself.

> If you don't learn to transform the pain, You'll just transfer it.
> –Pete Wilson

Whatever your addiction is, it is somehow affecting your life in a negative way, or you wouldn't be concerned about it.

According to psychologists, you don't break bad habits, you have to replace them with good habits. If you are drinking or using drugs to numb emotional pain without replacing it with something, you will most likely go back drinking or using drugs again. People often find relief with breathing exercises or relaxation techniques.

Know what your triggers are. Are there certain activities you need to avoid? Is there a certain time of day that are your triggers? Pay attention to what those triggers are and make an effort to fill that time or activity with a positive enforcement. Make sure you are not setting yourself up to fail. Clear your addictive choice from your home, office, car, or wherever you are getting your addiction satisfied. Make sure you do not have access to your addiction. Sometimes it helps to ask a trusted person to be your prayer partner and support system. It has to be someone you know will not be afraid to be confrontational with you if you are wavering. Make sure people know you are working on breaking this habit so they will not inadvertently tempt you. You may have to change your break times at work so you are not around other smokers. You may need to leave from work at a different time so you are not tempted to go to the bar with your usual crowd.

Get involved in support groups through a local church. Request a mentor to keep in touch with you. Hospital and county social workers are able to refer you to appropriate support groups.

Beating an addiction can be extremely difficult. Sometimes, you need to reward yourself through the process to continue your success. Invite your support person to lunch or coffee and dessert to celebrate your success with you. It is a reward your support person would appreciate as well.

BIBLICAL VERSES TO WORK THROUGH ADDICTION:

Repentance is the first step to redemption after committing a sin. It says in 1 John 1:19, "If we confess our sins, He is faithful and just to forgive us our sins and cleans us from all unrighteousness."

Behave properly as a follower of Christ (Rom. 13:13).

The Lord knows my ways. Psalms 139:1–3: Oh Lord, you have examined my heart and know everything about me. You know when I sit down or stand up, you know my thoughts even when I am far away. You see me when I travel and when I rest at home. You know everything I do.

Resist sin by dependence on God. Hebrews 2:18: Since He himself has gone through suffering and testing, He is able to help us when we are being tested.

Look for the way to bear it. 1 Corinthians 10:13: The temptations in your life are no different from what others experience. And God is faithful. He will not allow the temptation to be more than you can stand. When you are tempted, He will show you a way out so that you can endure.

In this passage, Paul wants the Corinthians to understand that temptation happens to everyone. Others have resisted temptation, so you can too. God will help you, but you must pray for God's help. You must resist people and situations that may get you into trouble. You should run from anything you know is wrong. Seek other Christians that will off help when you are tempted.

My grace is sufficient for thee, for my strength is made perfect in weakness (2 Cor. 12:9).

The Lord will deliver me from evil (2 Timothy 4:18). The Lord will deliver me through every evil attack and will bring me safely into his heavenly Kingdom.

The battle is not yours, it is God's (2 Chronicles 20:15, 20 15). Listen! This is what the Lord says: Do not be afraid. Don't be discouraged by his mighty army, for the battle is not yours, but God's. Verse 20; Believe in the Lord your God, and you will be able to stand firm.

In those scriptures, we are reminded that we may not be fighting an army, but we fight the temptation and pressure of everyday life. We have to know what our limitations and weaknesses are so that we can fight the battle against the enemy with God's help.

Be thankful at the end of the battle (1 Corinthians 15:57). Thank God because He gives us victory over sin and death

It is never too late to be what you might have been.
–George Elliot

ENABLING

Most of us have heard of enabling. Sadly, it is common in every kind of addiction. It doesn't all happen in a day. It sneaks up on you over time. In the meantime, the people in your life find ways to make it through day to day living without realizing they are making up for the addicted persons' deficiencies.

People who try to help addicts often feel helpless. They become caregivers. Caregivers want to give advice because they want to feel better about feeling hopeless. They want to rescue or fix the addict by helping them get out of jail, lending them money, or helping them to find another job. The enabler tells a little white lie here and there to protect the addicted person from sabotaging themselves (because the failures inadvertently affects the enabler). The longer the enabler rescues the addict, the longer it takes for them to *hit bottom*.

To rescue an addict is to *walk on eggshells* to prevent the addict from getting upset. Really the enabler is projecting their own pain and failure.

ARE YOU AN ENABLER?

Ask yourself these questions . . .

1. Do you avoid confrontation or potential problems to prevent conflict?
2. Do you mask your feelings to prevent confrontation?
3. Are you in denial?
   Do you minimize the situation?
   Have you been told to "get real?"
4. Do you treat him/her like a child by lecturing, blaming or criticizing them?
5. Do you cover for him/her, lie for him/her?
   Do you pick up their slack or bail them out of trouble?
6. Do you financially support him/her?
7. Do you keep finding excuses for him/her, giving him/her another chance to stop the addictive behavior? Do you hope it's a phase and assume it will get better?
8. Do you join in with the addicted person? I have heard many people say, "If I drink (or use) with them, I will be able to keep them safe." "If I go to the casino with him, I might be able to control his spending."

If you answered yes to any of these questions, you are probably an enabler.

When you enable an alcoholic or drug addict, you are risking their lives and you could possibly be risking your own life.

Celebrate Recovery offers this advice:

1. Allow the addict to feel the consequences of their actions.
2. Refrain from judgment.
3. Be honest. Let them know you have difficulty trusting them and that you fear them when they are under the influence. Do not offer comments about their self-destruction as that will come off as judgmental.

4.   Allow the addict shame and grace. They have a great problem, but you are still their friend.
5.   For more information about enabling your alcohol or drug dependent person, look into advice and supports with people who are informed and experienced. Al-Anon or Nar-Anon offer discreet, anonymous support and resources. It is a worldwide fellowship for those affected by someone else's addiction.

> As iron sharpens iron,
> So a friend sharpens a friend
> (Prov. 27:17).

When you are dealing with adolescents (we are talking beyond peer pressure), a diagnostician should be considered to check for biological, brain chemistry, and other risk factors.

As a teacher or leader, offer grace and truth. Be warm but be strict. Make sure you engage with family, and try to get permission to work with their therapist. Have resources available and easily accessible.

RECOVERY RESOURCES:

The most common recovery resources are Alcoholics Anonymous (AA) and Narcotics Anonymous (NA). There is Ala-Non and Ala-Teens for family supports as well. It is a twelve-step recovery process with regular attendance of meetings for continued supports. You can find support groups of this kind in a variety of addictions: Gamblers Anonymous, Overeaters Anonymous, etc.

Celebrate Recovery has a holistic approach to treat emotions, brain chemistry, metabolism, hormones, and relationships. It is a biblical and balanced program that helps us overcome our hurts, hang-ups, and habits. It is based on the actual words of Jesus rather than psychological theory. It was designed as a program to help those struggling with hurts, habits, and hang-ups by showing them the loving power of Jesus Christ through a recovery process.

Teen Challenge USA is a non-denominational Christian resource for intervention and support. There are more than two hundred residential centers located across the US.

"To provide youth, adults, and families with an effective and comprehensive Christian faith-based solution to life-controlling drug and alcohol problems in order to become productive members of society. By applying biblical principles, Teen challenge endeavors to help people become mentally-sound, emotionally-balanced, socially-adjusted, physically-well, and spiritually-alive."

IN ADDITION:

When looking online at Christian-based/faith-based treatment facilities, I found many, many selections. You should always check their satisfaction surveys before you even start checking their policies and other admission details.

Drug-Free America 1-800- 662-4357

READING RESOURCES:

The Addiction Recovery Skills Workbook: Changing Addictive Behaviors
By Suzette Glasner-Edwards, PhD

The Daniel Plan
By Rick Warren, Dr. Daniel Amen and Dr. Mark Hyman

The Enabler: When Helping Hurts the Ones You Love
By Angelyn Miller

Healing the Addicted Brain
By Dr. Harold C. Urschel

Mind-Body Workbook for Addiction: Effective Tools for Substance-Abuse Recovery and Relapse Prevention
By Stanley H. Block, MD, Carolyn Bryant Block and Guy du Plessis, MA

Picking up the Pieces Handbook: Creating a Dynamic Soul Care Ministry in Your Church
By Chuck Hannaford

The Power of Right Believing: 7 Keys to Freedom from Fear, Guilt, and Addiction
By Joseph Prince

Reclaiming Stolen Intimacy: When Your Marriage is Invaded by Pornography
By Clay and Renee Crossnoe

Resources for Christian Counseling: Counseling Those with Eating Disorders
By Raymond Vath

The Secret Seductress: Breaking the Destructive Cycle of Pornography
By Mark Laaser

Steps: Gospel-Centered Recovery
By Matt Chandler and Michael Snetzer

Truth and Lies: The Unlikely Role of Temptation
By Tim Chaddick

Your First Step to Celebrate Recovery: How God Can Heal Your Life
By John Baker

QUESTIONS TO PONDER:

1.   Were you surprised by the addictions brought up in this chapter?

2.   Do any of the addiction descriptions describe you or someone you know?

3.   What can we do as a church to help someone dealing with addiction?

4.   How can we as a church help a family through addiction? Does your church have information and resources available to help a person or family member afflicted by addiction? Do YOU have information and resources available to help a person or family afflicted by addiction?

5.   What would you say or do if someone confided about themselves or a family member with an addiction? What would you do if this person was a minor?

6.   Was any part of this chapter eye-opening for you? Does it motivate you to change anything?

7.   What verse or verses are important to you?

CHAPTER SEVEN

I FEEL LIKE A FAILURE

We all feel like a failure at one time or another. Unfortunately, we replay that internal junk in our mind. Don't worry about failure in itself, worry about a pattern of failure. If you failed and you recognize it, learn from it. If you are showing a pattern of failure, that is your sign to change!

There is no wonder we feel like failures! When we are prone to selfish, fleshly desires including riches and fame, we are bound to find failure in our lives. We see obscene TV programs that over time can cause poor self-image and body image. Here are some statistics to realize;

According to PolitiFact.com, it was estimated in 2012 that the probability of divorce is 40% to 50%.

According to the U.S. Small Business Administration, over 50% of small businesses fail in the first five years.

According to Alcoholrehab.com, drug and alcohol rehab statistics show that the percentage of people who will relapse after recovery ranges from 50% to 90%.

And according to researcher, Richard Wiseman, 50% of all Americans set a New Year's resolution. And approximately 88% of all those set resolutions fail. That's approximately 156 million people every year that failed their resolutions and disappoint themselves.

Some people sabotage themselves by setting outrageous or unrealistic goals. According to Psychology Today, one innate issue with goal setting relates to how the brain works.

Neuroscience research shows the brain works to be protective, being resistant to change. With goals that require a major behavioral change or thought-pattern, the brain will be resistant. We are wired to not only seek rewards, but to avoid physical and emotional pain or discomfort including fear. When fear of failure occupies the mind of the person setting goals, they lose motivation desiring comfortable behavior and thought patterns.

Some people sabotage themselves through media. TV and other media has made illicit behavior, overt sexuality and immorality the new normal. Over time, this consistent feeding of negative information poses poor self-image and body image.

I will attempt to identify the emotions behind failure and share scripture that coincides with it. It is my prayer to help you understand how to help yourself through this.

After hearing ugly words like "failure, loser, ugly, fat," it often becomes that internal dialogue. People are changed by abuse. They lose their power. Or they are feeling defeated when they are laid off and cannot find another job. Many, many older people have been laid off. They may be educated and desire a career they worked hard for! Now this unemployed person may be a couple decades older, most likely several pounds heavier, probably have medical issues and most likely carrying debt.

That could make a strong, secure person feel like a failure. It is an emotionally painful feat. What is your internal language? What do you keep telling yourself?

First of all, let go of what other people think! How many of us worry about what somebody is thinking or what they may be saying behind your back? Are you going to be able to change their perception of you? Is it really you? Or is it them? Think about how you perceive what people are thinking. What do you do with that perception? You can't control what others say and do. But you can control what you do. It is *your* decision to allow someone's opinion or malcontented attitude to control you.

About a hundred years ago—or what seems that long ago, there was a saying about Stinkin' thinkin'. Think about what you are telling yourself, push the negative thoughts away. Be around people who build you up, edify you, make you feel good about who you are and willing to help you through tough times.

We cannot be perfect. Ever. We can blame the fall of Adam and Eve for that! We all have faults, downfalls and weaknesses. Do not be overly-critical of yourself and others.

FEAR

Fear is an emotion that can dictate your whole being. If you fear relationships, you will avoid them. If you fear storms, you will overreact when one is about to arrive. If you fear others are judging you, you will fear being around people. Fear can totally control your life and paralyze you from normalcy. A commonality of experiencing extreme fear is having an anxiety disorder. I know of an elderly female that is so afraid of the affairs overseas, she has nightmares about it. Even though this lady professes to be a Christian, she is terrified that these people will come after American Christians and torture, shoot, and/or behead them as they have been doing overseas. My point in telling you about this is that people are judged when they are Christians. People will ask, "Why do you fear anything if you are a Christian?" What is not understood is that this lady is suffering with mental health issues. She cannot control those emotions any more than she can control the weather. She can alleviate some of the suffering with self-calming remedies, dependent on the severity of her obsessing. But for her, medication and counseling is her saving grace. And understanding from those around her.

The Bible has plenty to say about fear!

In Proverbs 18:21, it says that life and death are in the power of the tongue. Your tongue possesses a power of the spoken word. Your words have the power to create or destroy you. If you allow doubt and fear into your spirit, you will begin to speak failure, destruction, and even death. And by the power of your own tongue, what you speak you will produce.

We all have a need for security or certainty. I believe this is a reflection of experiences. Due to alcoholism and gambling, I lived with a lot of broken promises, witnessed domestic violence and moved several times. As I have mentioned, I attended nineteen different grade schools until my father sobered up, which then I attended one junior high and one high school for a total of twenty-one schools. I grew up believing that nothing is certain. Ever. When good things were going on, I feared what was about to happen because bad things were inevitably going to happen.

My husband and I suffered with my insecurities the first few years we were married.

Throughout my entire childhood, I witnessed sexual addiction, promiscuous adults, and infidelity, both males and females, and experienced a three-year relationship that proved to be no different. It made for a couple of good country songs I wrote, but it was difficult for my husband to convince me that he is an innocent man. He paid the price in that I constantly checked up on him, wanted to know who he was with, why he was home later than he should be, etc. It was a hardship on our marriage.

Insecurity comes with living above your means. Many feel like failures with comparison of others to measure their own success. If you are one that compares your failures by other people's successes, you will always struggle with self-worth. If you struggle with comparison, stay off of Facebook and the like. Remember that people generally don't discuss their bills that go with the stuff they are bragging about. And often, they exaggerate their experiences and good fortune.

If you experience mental and physical exhaustion to keep up with your lifestyle, you are probably using your *status* as a measure of self-worth. Some people actually thrive on stress. If you choose to live a stressful lifestyle, you are missing internal peace.

SELF-DOUBT OR "SUPPOSED TO"

When we think of those words, is it because you know you should be doing something other than what you are doing? That is the Holy Spirit working on you to keep a clear conscience.

WHAT DOES THE BIBLE SAY ABOUT HAVING FEELINGS OF INADEQUACY?

There is no condemnation awaiting for those who belong to Jesus Christ (Rom. 8:1).

The Holy Spirit testifies together with our spirit that we are God's children, and heirs of God, and coheirs with Christ—seeing that we suffer with Him so that we may be glorified with Him (Rom. 8:16–17).

The Lord will fulfill His purpose for me.
(Psalms 138:8)

You were bought at a price, therefore use every part of your body to give glory back to God, because He owns it (1 Cor. 6:20).

To the praise of His glorious grace that He favored us with in the beloved (Eph. 1:6).

4 But God who is rich in mercy because of His great love that He had made for us. 6 Together with Christ Jesus, He also raised us up and seated us in the heavens (Eph. 2:4&6).

Even before He made the world, God chose us to be His very own; making us holy in His eyes, without a single fault—we who stand before him is covered with his love (Eph. 1:4).

I am sure that God who began the good work within you will keep right on helping you grow in His grace until His task within you is finally finished on that day when Jesus Christ returns (Phil. 1:6).

You are chosen for His possession so that you may proclaim the praises of the One who called you out of darkness into His marvelous light (1 Pet. 2:9).

For the Lord is watching his children and listening to their prayers (1 Pet. 3:12).

READING RESOURCES

Brave Enough: Getting Over Our Fears, Flaws and Failures, to Live Bold and Free
By Nicole Unice

Failing Foreword: Turning Mistakes into Stepping Stones for Success
By John C. Maxwell

Failure: The Back Door to Success
By Irwin W. Lutzer

I Tried Until I Almost Died: From Anxiety and Frustration to Rest and Relaxation
By Sandra McCollom

(Un)Qualified: How God Uses Broken People to Do Big Things
By Steven Furtick

QUESTIONS TO PONDER:

1. What things have made you feel like a failure?
    How did you react to it?

2. Do you or someone you know have "Stinkin' Thinkin'?"
    When you catch yourself in that mode, what do you do to
    change it?

3. When someone calls you or approaches you in that mode,
    what do you say or do?

4. What can we do as a church to help someone with low
    self-esteem?
    What can YOU do to help build someone's self-esteem?

5. Was any part of this chapter eye-opening for you?
    Does it motivate you to do anything?

6. What verse or verses are important to you?

CHAPTER EIGHT

FAIR FIGHTING
MARRIAGE AND RELATIONSHIPS

"How you make others feel about themselves
Says a lot about you."
–Unknown Author

LOVE AND MARRIAGE

One of the greatest blessings in my life is my husband. We have been married for over thirty years. We have a wonderful marriage, but it hasn't always been a bed of roses! We both came into this marriage with our own baggage, trust issues, fears, behaviors, and habits that were unpleasant to each other. We had to willingly grow up together and to grow together. Our success is from having similar core values. The rest is all built from fulfilling dreams and experiences with each other.

I'd like to think we can all live in a rosy world with the perfect mate and live happily ever after. But it doesn't always work out that way. With years of working in family court and in the mental health field, I am not naive to think all marriages can be preserved. When a family is in an immediate dangerous situation, you have to do everything you can to protect yourself and your children. A person should be pro-active with intervention when living in *any* potentially dangerous situation.

Some people experience difficulty with relationships because they have built unrealistic expectations about people in their lives. They have a mindset of what their special someone is all about. With the expectations of this kind of person, they have the propensity to think they will fix their special someone. Often, depression will become an obstacle in their relationship as they get to know their special person, as they realize their special someone is not the person they invested in.

Another issue I see in relationships is comparing previous relationships. As I mentioned in a previous chapter, I was horribly distrusting of my husband because I witnessed infidelity throughout my childhood. Then I had a long relationship that only proved that theory was right.

It took me a long time to realize that people love differently.

WHAT DOES THE BIBLE SAY ABOUT LOVE AND MARRIAGE?

In John 13:34–35, Jesus says that we are to love as He has loved you. Your love for one another will prove to the world that you are His disciple. And in 1 Corinthians 13:13, we are reminded that there are three things that will last forever; faith, hope and love—and love is the greatest of these.

In Corinthians 13:4–7, we are reminded that God's love is unselfish. Love is patient and kind. Not rude, boastful, proud, or rude. Love is not irritable, demanding, and keeps track of being wronged. Love never gives up, is always hopeful and endures through every circumstance.

LOVE Galatians 5:22–23

I will show love to my spouse every day.

I will invite the joy of the Lord to rise in me continually. I will walk in peace, not stress.

I will be patient with my spouse and not lose my temper. I will show kindness to my spouse no matter what.

I will do good for my spouse in every way. I will be faithful to my spouse in all I do.

I will be gentle and not harsh with my spouse. I will not allow myself to get out of control.

WHAT DOES THE BIBLE SAY ABOUT MARRIAGE?

First of all, we have to remember that marriage was God's plan (Genesis 2:18–24). He wants us to commit to our marriage because commitment is essential for a successful marriage (Genesis 24:58–60 and Malachi 2:14–15). Marriage was designed to raise children. (Malachi 2:15)

A boyfriend does *not* have the same privileges as a husband.

Give honor to marriage, and remain faithful to one another in marriage. God will surely judge those who are immoral and those who commit adultery (Heb. 13:4). Unfaithfulness breaks the bond of trust (Matt. 5:32).

We are to submit to one another (Eph. 5:21–33).

We need to romance each other (Song of Songs 4:1–19; 1 Cor. 7:2–5).

Marriage holds times of great joy (Jer. 7:34).

Husbands: 1 Peter 3:7, if a man does not honor his wife, his prayers will not be heard.

Women: You need to dress modestly, wear decent and appropriate clothing. Do not draw attention to yourself with showy hairstyles and expensive clothes and jewelry. Women who are devoted to God should make themselves attractive by the good things they do (1 Tim. 2:9–10).

Your beauty should not come from outward adornment, such as elaborate hairstyles and the wearing of gold jewelry or fine clothes. Rather, it should be that of your inner self, the unfading beauty of a gentle and quiet spirit, which is of great worth in God's sight (1 Peter 3:3–4).

Better to live in a desert than with a quarrelsome and nagging wife (Prov. 21:19).

Better to live on a corner of the roof than share a house with a quarrelsome wife (Prov. 25:24).

A quarrelsome wife is like the dripping of a leaky roof in a rainstorm (Prov. 27:15).

FAIR FIGHTING:

WHAT FEELINGS CAN BE DESCRIBED WITH CONFLICT?

Generally speaking, a person in conflict feels hurt, angry, and mis-understood. With these feelings, the goals you have in mind are to prove how right you are and how wrong the other person is. There is no better measure of a person's integrity than the behavior they display when they are wrong!

In every conflict, you need to ask yourself what part of this issue should you own and what part of this issue should you apologize for? There are two sides, no right or wrong (Prov. 15:1). All people come with baggage that exaggerates the issue adding an emotional response to the conflict. Pride brings a person low, but the lowly in spirit gain honor (Prov. 29:23).

Control your reaction. Remember that conflict is short-term. But if you have to regret your reaction, the memory of the conflict

JUDITH ISAACS-HERRIG, M.ED, QIDP

becomes engrained in your memory. Always ask yourself "If I knew the conversation was being recorded and shared, how would this change my behavior? Let your gentleness be evident to all. The Lord is near (Phil. 4:5).

A good man brings good things out of the good stored up in his heart, and an evil man brings evil things out of evil stores up in his heart. For the mouth speaks what the heart is full of (Luke 6:45).

ARE YOU ASSERTIVE OR AGGRESSIVE?

According to Oxford Dictionary, assertive is defined as having or showing a confident and forceful personality. To be self-confident, firm, or forthright. The definition for aggressive is ready or likely to attack or confront; characterized by or resulting from aggression. To be hostile, belligerent, or antagonistic.

All people have their own way to respond when in conflict. My husband is likely to do nothing at all. He stands in front of me like a deer with headlights in the eyes. I am not sure if his mind is somewhere else and he is even listening to me. I would get angrier when he would not respond. What I discovered at a workshop we attended together is that he does nothing because he fears he will say the wrong thing. I have had to learn a different approach with him (no, I have not perfected this technique).

The best time to talk to him is in the car because we are generally alone and there is no other distractions. However that would not be appropriate if we had our children in the car. When our children were living at home, the easiest place to talk to him was in bed. Talking to him while the TV is on is like talking to the wall. So it is important to find a time to talk where there are no people to hear the conversation, and there are no distractions such as the TV and electronic devices.

A common problem I have heard from women is that their husbands don't want to help with the housework. Do you accuse him of being lazy? Here's a thought—maybe his priorities are different than yours! Does he work full-time? Do you both work? Where can you compromise?

My husband is an admitted procrastinator—always has been. There are things that need to be done around the house that I physically cannot do. To prevent argument, we found discussing what needs to be done in advance of his day off is the best approach for him. Now, if he doesn't get going in *my* time, I will assert myself by letting him know that I am going to start preparing what needs to get done, rather than aggressively nag him.

It is important to watch your tone and how you say things. Check in on your own attitude before you talk. Stop whatever busy things you are doing and make the effort to not only talk, but to listen. Honestly listen to what he is saying, without interruption, and without judgment or reaction.

"Do not let any unwholesome talk come out of your mouths,
But only what is helpful for building others
up according to their needs,
That it may benefit those who will listen."
(Ephesians 4:29)

There are many books available that refer to differences in male and female thinking. There *is* a difference and it is up to you to learn how to communicate. How does your spouse differ from your perspective? Are you willing to put yourself in their shoes, to try to understand what your spouse is thinking?

Gary Chapman of the Five Love Languages has excellent books and resources about marriage and communication. He provides the following statistics:

- 50% of wives report to have husbands that do not communicate.
- 86% of divorced couples report deficient communication.

Communication is an act of will, it is a choice. Gary Chapman reminds us that we all hear differently, and we also listen differently.

Are you allowing distractions to interfere with communication? Do you tell your spouse you are going to quick check your emails and two hours later you are still on the computer? Are you a gamer and spend too much time gaming on your computer? Or out with your buddies? Are you too busy or you overbook yourself? It is difficult sometimes, but important to set boundaries for your marriage and your family. These are just a couple of examples that will allow you to drift apart from each other.

Communication in marriage is important because it offers a deeper sense of intimacy. With communication, you are sharing your life with your spouse. Only you know you. For what man knows the things of a man except the spirit of the man which is in him? (1 Cor. 2:11)

You should not only share the day to day events, but how you feel about the events. And as you communicate decision making, communicate your feelings about the decision you are making.

When conflict arises, do you disagree strongly or is it just a difference of opinion?

Communicate what you are feeling so it is understood by your spouse. Ask your spouse to clarify so you know you are both on the same page. Practice listening when your spouse is talking. Try to understand what your spouse is thinking and feeling by putting yourself in their shoes.

If the communication is getting distorted by anger, you need to call a temporary time-out. Don't sin by allowing anger control you, and don't go to bed at night while you are still angry. Get rid of all types of angry behavior (Eph. 4:26, 31). Solomon describes effects of anger or foolish actions such as having a temper or to manipulate others will become hated (Prov. 14:17). Fools vent their anger and the wise hold it back (Prov. 29:11).

Instead, be kind to each other and forgive one another (Eph. 4:32). God blesses those who work for peace (Matt. 5:9).

Examine your anger. Rid yourself of all malice, deceit, and envy (1 Peter 2:1). Is this something you can work out together? What can you do to help solve this problem? Are you willing to agree to disagree? Is there room for compromise? Is it your way or the highway?

ARE YOU A BUTTON PUSHER?

You know—when you are in a heated argument and you know exactly what to say or do to set the person off? The little things that are *sooooo* personal, exploiting the person's insecurity or irritability that an outsider may not even notice. As an adult, we are generally better at disguising the motives.

To define button pushing, it is a matter of knowing what topics that make a person most vulnerable. In marriages and close relationships, it is important to know that you may break the emotional trust of your loved one by exposing their unguarded vulnerability. Bottom line is that it brings up insecurity because they are feeling a sense of humiliation and rejection.

A person that pushes buttons is a person looking to get the upper hand in an argument, or to feel superior. It is incredibly cruel to take advantage of those buttons.

Often it is easier to blame others for their reactions rather than taking responsibility for the way you react. Then communication will sound like, "I feel bad when you . . ." or "you made me . . ." or "You always . . ." Do you have the *I* factor or the *You* factor?

It is abhorrent how some people speak to family members. Words can be hurtful and cutting into the hearts of your loved ones. Swearing and calling them names, or using demeaning comments at them is degrading and humiliating. It will never leave them, it will haunt them forever. Even if they forgive you, they will never forget how they felt around you. This kind of abuse affects people like PTSD. There will be things that brings those feelings to surface. It is never forgotten. Always regard people respectfully. If you love a person, why would you hurt them? Comfort and edify each other (1 Thess. 5:11).

Kind words are like honey. Sweet to the soul and healthy for the body (Prov. 16:24).

Recognize the power of your words.
(Proverbs 18:9-21)

A gentle answer turns away wrath, But a harsh word stirs up anger (Prov. 15:1).

Never bring up the past. Think before you speak. The one who has knowledge uses words with restraint, and whoever has understanding is even-tempered. Even fools are thought wise if they keep silent, and discerning if they hold their tongues (Prov. 17:27–28).

Those who guard their mouths and their tongues keep themselves from calamity (Prov. 21:23).

Never be rude or disrespectful. Woe to the world because of the things that cause people to stumble! Such things must come, but woe to the person through whom they come! (Matt. 18:7). Be an example. Whoever loves a quarrel loves sin; whoever builds a high gate invites destruction (Prov. 17:19).

How do you speak to each other in front of others? Gracious words are a honeycomb, sweet to the soul and healing to the bones (Prov. 16:24).

How do you speak to others in front of your children? Would you want the communication you have with your spouse to be replicated by your children?

Get rid of all bitterness, rage and anger, brawling and slander, along with every form of malice. Be kind and compassionate to one another, forgive one another as Christ forgave you (Eph. 4:31–32).

Pick your battles! Often, a man will complain about the woman taking his tools and not returning them in the proper place. My case is different. My husband doesn't put his tools away, so neither one of us can ever find them. Instead of arguing or being frustrated about it, we purchased a tool set of my very own. It is even PINK!

Don't overbook yourself. Do you feel as though you are consistently letting the people closest to you down? Do you disappoint your husband, children, family and closest friends because you are always late, interrupted during conversations by your phone, or vacant because your mind is elsewhere? I proudly wore my busy badge of honor. Busyness made me feel productive and needed, and I overlooked the havoc it created in my life. God made us with limitations. We need to pay attention to them.

According to Audrey Barrick of the Christian Post, The Obstacles to Growth Survey found that on average more than four in ten Christians say they often or always rush from task to task.

> The LORD will fight for you; you need
> only to be still" (Exod. 14:14).

The American Psychological Association released a study stating, "In general, Americans seem to understand the importance of healthy behaviors like managing their stress levels, eating right, getting enough sleep and exercise, but they report experiencing challenges practicing these healthy behaviors. They report being too busy."

Christians are simply becoming too busy for God.

When I am busy or in a hurry it is impossible for me to maintain quality relationships with people or God. Think about it! If the Devil can't make you sin, he can make you too busy.

Prayer is the most powerful weapon against trials. The most effective medicine against sickness and the most valuable gift to someone you love.

Above all, love each other deeply because love covers over a multitude of sins (1 Peter 4:8).

Whenever you are having issues with your spouse, you should go to him/her directly. Not on Facebook or with family and friends. It is disturbing to see the derogatory comments people make about others publicly. That is despicable behavior.

We know from Bible studies that Peter was a loudmouth. Jesus spoke to Peter privately, then publicly. If your brother or sister sins, go and point out their fault, just between the two of you. If they listen to you, you have won them over (Matt. 18:15).

The Bible teaches us to guard against gossip. A gossip betrays a confidence, but a trustworthy person keeps a secret (Prov. 11:13).

Whoever gives heed to instruction prospers, and blessed is the one who trusts in the LORD. The wise in heart are called discerning, and gracious words promote instruction (Prov. 26:20–21).

But if they will not listen, take one or two others along, so that every matter may be established by the testimony of two or three witnesses (Matt. 18:16). Where two or three are gathered together in my name, I am there in the midst of them (Matt. 18:20).

Some of those things that irritate you now are often what actually attracted you. Define the problem. Can it be changed by you? Love can grow stronger by being tested (Hos 2:14–16).

Maturing in Christ means giving someone a piece of your heart when you really want to give them a piece of your mind (The Pretty Girl's Life).

ANGER

Anger is not a productive emotion. It is a battle of who is right and who is wrong. Are you a right fighter? What is your end goal?

A fool gives into his anger, but a wise man keeps himself under control (Prov. 29:11).

Just because you're mad at someone
doesn't mean you stop loving them.
–Unknown

Avoiding a fight is a mark of honor; only fools insist on quarreling (Prov. 20:3).

Anger is considered an evil behavior as written in Galatians 5:20. Galatians 5:21 reminds us that anyone living that sort of life will not inherit the Kingdom of God.

VIOLENCE IN THE HOME

Domestic violence should never be tolerated. Remember that it can start out small and can become increasingly dangerous not only to the spouse but their children and extended family members. There are studies that show abuse is a gradual process that generally starts with verbal and emotional abuse leading up to breaking things, slapping and hitting to even murder. We hear it over and over again—but tend to think, "It won't happen to me!"

If your relationship has come to the point of abuse, make sure you are away from the children. Do not engage in the argument if the person is angry and/or irrational. That includes texts and messaging. If you are unable to communicate in a civil manner, seek a Domestic Abuse Advocate. If you have children, request a Guardian ad Litem to advocate for your children.

When you have called the police a number of times, and you have filed an Order for Protection (OFP), you may need to leave your home to be safe.

Important: If you are being abused, your children are being abused too. Children who are living in a home where there is violence are victims of child abuse even if they aren't physically being hurt. Studies show psychological damage to children when they witness violence in the home. Children who have continued exposure to violence often display delinquent behavior by the time they reach adolescence. They also tend to continue the cycle of violence into their own relationships.

You have both a moral and legal responsibility to protect your children. Child protection services may deem you an unfit parent if you fail to protect your child by removing yourself and the children from the abuser.

Do not tolerate abusive behavior from your spouse. Call 9-1-1 if you are in immediate danger.

Another source of help is the National Domestic Violence Hotline at 800-799-SAFE (7233) or 800-787-3224 (TTY). Help is available 24 hours a day, 365 days a year. Keep this number with you at all times.

SAFETY MEASURES TO TAKE:

- File an Order for Protection (OFP) and keep it with you at all times.
- Always consider the use of a shelter to keep yourself and your children safe.
- Make sure to lock your home doors and windows—even when you are home. It is best to have another adult with you.
- Lock your car doors when you are driving. Make sure if your windows are open that they cannot reach a hand through it.
- If at all possible, try to change your patterns. Some people tend to have lights to come on with a timer. Changing timers to different lamps and times offer a change in patterns as well.
- Secure your finances so you have the ability to pay bills and buy groceries.
- Stay off social networks.
- Make sure to document everything! Save all texts, recorded messages, and e-mails.
- Have a safety plan for your children at school and at home.
- Always be ready to leave again. Keep life simple so you can pull roots quickly if needed.

FINANCIAL

We know the number one subject couples fight over is money. Because we are all raised by different parents, we all have different traits and attitudes about money.

My husband is one that panics over bills and would pay them regardless of the consequences. I would have a tendency to load up on major groceries for the month to make sure I could feed the family. The bills would freak him out and the lack of gas and groceries freaked me out. One way we were able to compromise with that issue was to have two separate checking accounts.

He had a salary so he paid the primary bills. My checks were irregular, so I would pay what was left over with my checks. Then I felt more control over groceries, the kids' extra-curricular activities and occasional trips up north (that's about all we could afford). We really had less arguments when we had separate accounts.

There are a couple of financial principles I am going to bring attention to:

LOVE OF MONEY

A work filled life is an empty life. Everything can be so meaningless like chasing the wind (Eccles. 2:1–17). The love of money is the root of all evil (1 Tim. 3:3, 6:10). Don't wear yourself out trying to get rich (Prov. 23:4).

Don't love money. Be satisfied with what you have (Heb. 13:5). Avoid desires for luxuries and riches. Proverbs 23:3 We are reminded that we can say in confidence; "The Lord is my helper so I will have no fear." (Heb. 5:6)

The greedy bring ruin to their households, but the one who hates bribes will live (Prov. 15:27).

When Christ, who is your life, appears, then you also will appear with him in glory. Put to death, therefore, whatever belongs to your earthly nature: sexual immorality, impurity, lust, evil desires and greed, which is idolatry (Colossians 3:4–5). Avoid envying sinners (Proverbs 23:17).

In 2 Timothy 3:1–5, Paul informs Timothy that in the last days, people will love themselves and their money. They will be unloving and unforgiving and slandering others. They will lack self- control. They will be puffed up with pride and act religious.

Avoid working just to gain wealth (Prov. 23:4).

ARE YOU A PRISONER OF WANT?

Some people are prisoners of want—they are unable to find contentment. They are allowing their wants to get in the way of the important things in life. Americans are obsessed with the rich and famous. They work too much trying to keep up with the Kardashians. We are reminded not to wear ourselves out trying to get rich because our wealth can disappear in the blink of any eye (Prov. 23:4–5). We all know that from the 9-1-1 terrorist attack that caused Americans the most detrimental economic crash in history!

The godly eat to their hearts content, but the belly of the wicked goes hungry (Prov. 13:25).

Paul explains that everything is worthless when compared with the infinite value of knowing Jesus Christ. He discarded everything so he could become one with Christ. He further explains that God's way of making himself right depends on his faith. He was looking to experience the mighty power of Christ. He did not claim perfection, but focused on releasing his past and looking forward to what is ahead of him. His goal was to press on to reach the end of the race and receive the heavenly prize for which God is calling us (Phil. 3:7–15).

There is nothing more disappointing than having someone close to you that cannot be happy for you when something exciting is going on in your life. They have jealousy rather than joy for you. Or those who get pleasure out of knowing you have been wronged, disappointed, or run into a hardship. Family members often compete and compare their successes, trials and failures with each other. Sibling rivalry doesn't stop at adolescence.

BEING BROKE

We sometimes have no control over our circumstances. Many suffered bankruptcy after the 9-1-1 crises. We can praise God that He rescues the poor from the cutting words of the strong, and rescues them from the clutches of the powerful. At last the poor have hope, and the snapping jaws of the wicked are shut (Job 5:15–16).

Do you have a spending problem? Studies reveal that spending (especially with finding great deals) releases dopamine in your brain like a drug. If you find yourself obsessed with shopping, and experience buyer's remorse because of compulsivity, you have a serious spending problem.

He who loves pleasure will become a poor man; He who loves wine and oils will not become rich (Prov. 21:17).

Do you use people for your own benefit?

- Do you use or exaggerate your circumstance to gain sympathy?

- Do you exaggerate your circumstance to gain unwarranted gifts from kind and generous people?
- Do you exaggerate you circumstance for financial assistance?

In 1 Thessalonians 4:6,11-12 it says; No one should wrong or take advantage of a brother or sister. The Lord will punish all those who commit such sins. In verses 11-12, it says to live a quiet life, to mind your own business and to work with your hands so you will be respected and not dependent on anybody.

Are you broke because you don't want to work?

Lazy hands make for poverty, but diligent hands bring wealth (Prov. 10:4).

As the head of the family, a man should provide, not just for himself, but for his whole household (1 Timothy 5:8).

Blessed is the man who trusts in the Lord, and whose hope is the Lord. For he shall be like a tree planted by the waters, which spreads out its roots by the river, and will not fear when heat comes; But its leaf will be green, and will not be anxious in the year of drought, or will cease from yielding fruit (Jeremiah 17:7–8).

Therefore do not worry about tomorrow, for tomorrow will worry about itself. Each day has enough trouble of its own (Matt. 6:34).

ADULTERY

An affair with a married person disrespects the union. No one commits adultery without first being able to justify their behavior to themselves.

With infidelity, the spouse will experience betrayal and anger. Most will experience bouts of anxiety and/or depression. The spouse will feel unworthy and undesirable.

Some spouses may get over the betrayal of adultery but only after much suffering. Adultery can cause severe psychological damage. Many relationships cannot be mended because the wounded person can no longer trust their spouse.

Adultery is extremely selfish. They don't think about those close to them that will be affected negatively by their actions. Family, their children—even friends who care about you as a couple will suffer the anguish caused from this unfaithful act.

Do not discuss jealousy and infidelity with your children. This kind of discussion is not appropriate with your child. Intimacy and marital issues are not your child's business. They are not your best friend. You need to be their rock so they can come to you.

WHAT DOES THE BIBLE SAY ABOUT INFIDELITY?

Can a man scoop a flame into his lap and not have his clothes catch on fire? Can he walk on hot coals and not blister his feet? So it is with the man who sleeps with another man's wife. He who embraces her will not go unpunished (Prov. 6:27–29).

In Proverbs 6:32–34, the man who commits adultery is an utter fool for he destroys himself. He will be wounded and disgraced. His shame will never be erased. For the woman's jealous husband will be furious and he will show no mercy when he takes revenge.

Let there be no sexual immorality, impurity, or greed among you. Such sins have no place among God's people (Eph. 5:3). In 1 Thessalonians 4:1-2 it says that we are instructed to live in order to please God, authority of Jesus Christ. Continued in that chapter are clear instructions to avoid sexual immorality, to control your own body in a way that is holy and honorable.

JEALOUSY

Simply put—jealousy is insecurity. It is a real feeling generally brought on by baggage from previous relationships.

In Proverbs 14:30, jealousy is compared to having bone cancer.

What we need to know about jealousy is that it is a behavioral choice in how you react to that emotion. Are you going to do the repetitive calling to check in on him/her? Are you going to be demanding with accusations and questioning? Are you isolating your spouse?

Do not allow past experiences cloud your vision of relationships. If this is an area you cannot move on with, connect with an experienced relationship counsellor to help you gain control of it.

DIVORCE

Most people who jump into divorce are not truly ready for Divorce. Considering divorce tends to be a knee-jerk reaction caused from anger and pain.

It is not wise to divorce if you are feeling emotional about it. You should never react when you are angry or distressed. You may regret the decision you made while you were in an emotional state.

When you think about divorce, are you thinking about how it will affect your children? Are you displaying animosity? Are your children in the crossfire? There will be a fracture in this family causing them to experience new feelings and instability.

Have you done everything you can to preserve your marriage? Are you BOTH "in it to win it?" Have you consulted with your pastor for spiritual guidance? Have you received marital counseling? Do you need mental health care? Have you read self-help books?

Divorce can cause a multitude of emotions. Generally a divorcee will go through stages similar to the stages of grieving death. All people react differently and in their own time. Support groups can be effective for many people. If you or someone you know is stuck in the grieving process where the grieving becomes a mental health issue, please seek a mental health professional immediately.

Suppose you are seriously considering divorce: What about years later? When you have children, what will you say when they are older and start asking questions like, "Why did you get a divorce?" What will they feel when you respond with "Because I was angry and hurt." If you are able to tell your children that you have done everything you could do to make your marriage work, it will help to understand that you didn't just walk out. It was carefully considered.

Never burden your children with adult issues because they cannot control those situations. Your children are not your friends, so do not expect them to provide you with companionship or support. Do not allow yourself to fall into the guilt trap and overindulge them or baby them.

Be careful not to use your children for pawns. Make sure you are not running your own agenda. Your children need love, stability, and assurance. Keep them safe at all times. Do not ever argue and fight near them.

Another important reminder is to make sure your children are free of guilt or feel responsible for the separation or divorce. When my parents would fight, I always wondered what I could do to make the fighting stop. I worried about the future of my family. Will the police be called? Will we (my brother and I) be taken away? Will we be kicked out of this rental and have to go to another school? How far will this fight go?

WHAT DOES THE BIBLE SAY ABOUT DIVORCE?

When do you choose divorce? You will find different opinions from different people. There are biblical answers to seriously consider:

Couples should enter marriage prepared for a lifetime commitment (Matt. 19:6 and Mark 10:9).

Paul writes in 1 Corinthians 7:10–11, those who are married, I have a command that comes not from me, but from the Lord. A wife must not leave her husband. But if she does leave him, let her remain single or else be reconciled to him. And the husband must not leave his wife.

"The man who hates and divorces his wife," says the LORD, the God of Israel, "does violence to the one he should protect," says the LORD Almighty (Mal. 2:16).

Husbands, in the same way be considerate as you live with your wives, and treat them with respect as the weaker partner and as heirs with you of the gracious gift of life, so that nothing will hinder your prayers (1 Peter 3:7).

In this same way, husbands ought to love their wives as their own bodies. He who loves his wife loves himself (Eph. 5:28).

With the grace of God, only death should dissolve a marriage (Rom. 7:2–3).

Husband and wife are bound as long as they both live. One may remarry only when his spouse has died (Rom. 7:2–3).

MISCARRIAGE

Miscarriage is a very difficult, painful time for a couple to experience. Especially when they have gone through a long wait or were medically altered to achieve their pregnancy.

Because miscarriage is such a traumatic event, it can change a person emotionally. It may be detrimental to their marriage.

For many women, there is an extraordinary amount of guilt as they think about the things they should have or could have done. "Did I drink too much coffee? Did I let work get too stressful for me? Is God punishing me for something I did earlier in my life?"

Some husbands blame themselves for a miscarriage as he regrets that his wife had to work while she was pregnant. He loathes his inability to raise a family on his income alone.

Some people suffer the loss of their perceived future with that child.

Their grieving is very painful. It does not only affect the parents. We need to remember the children of the family who was awaiting their new sibling as well as the grandparents and extended family members.

If you are grieving, understand that you may experience lengthy bouts of emotional turmoil. People need to understand that everyone handles grief in their own way and their own time. Do *not* use alcohol, drugs or food to relieve your pain.

Make sure you have a support group that you can call on. There is strength in others. Pray and/or meditate.

WHAT THE BIBLE TEACHES ABOUT THE UNBORN CHILD:

Psalm 139:13–16: You made all the delicate, inner parts of my body, and knit them together in my mother's womb. Thank you for making me so wonderfully complex! It is amazing to think about. Your workmanship is marvelous—and how well I know it. You were there while I was being formed in utter seclusion! You saw before me I was born and scheduled each day of my life before I began to breathe. Every day was recorded in your book.

Psalm 127:3: Behold, children are a heritage from the Lord, the fruit of the womb a reward.

Genesis 1:26–27: And God said, Let us make man in our image, after our likeness: and let them have dominion over the fish of the sea, and over the fowl of the air, and over the cattle, and over all the earth, and over every creeping thing that creeps upon the earth. So God created man in his own image, in the image of God created by Him.

Exodus 1:15–21: Pharaoh, the king of Egypt instructed Hebrew midwives to kill all Hebrew boys as they were born and to save the girls. But the midwives feared God and did not obey the King allowing the boys to live. And God blessed the midwives for being God-fearing women, and gave them children of their own.

Jeremiah 1:4–5: The Lord said "I knew you before you were formed within your mother's womb; before you were born I sanctified and appointed you to speak to the world. (This verse supports life in the womb)

Job 12:7–10: In His hand is the life of every creature and the breath of all mankind.

In the first chapter of Matthew, it tells the story about Joseph and Mary, and the birth of baby Jesus. Joseph did not want to wed Mary because she was pregnant (obviously not his). That was a time when being a virgin upon marriage was vital. It was assumed that women like Mary who was pregnant were considered harlots. Who would believe she was a pregnant virgin? An angel of God told Joseph to take her home to be his wife anyway. Hallelujah!

WILL I MEET MY BABY IN HEAVEN?

You *will* meet your baby in heaven. In 2 Samuel 12, we learn about David's affair with a married woman named Bathsheba. Bathsheba became pregnant from this affair. In 2 Samuel 12:14, Nathan (a prophet) warned David that their child would die because he betrayed God. So David fasted and prayed to the Lord that He would not carry out His judgment. When the child died (II Samuel 12:19), David stopped praying and fasting. When asked why he stopped fasting and praying, David replied "I shall go to him and he will not return to me." 2 Sam. 12:23. This clearly indicates that he will be with his child one day in heaven.

Though they were not yet born and had done nothing either good or bad (Rom. 9:11).

Another important point is found in Romans 6:23; the wages of sin is death. An unborn or aborted baby has never sinned.

Jesus invited children to come to Him (Luke 18:16).

FAMILY

When you have come home from a long day of work, what is your attitude? Even though you are tired and really want to be left alone, remember that the first four minutes from the time you walk in the door sets the tone/mood in the house. Make a conscious effort to think about that as you are walking into your home. A few minutes of time with your children will allow them to go play because they got that out of their system. Think about this—a few minutes of time up front or an evening of negative attention. You *are* making a choice!

As mentioned in your marriage, are you allowing distractions to interfere with family life? *Do* you make yourself emotionally available? Do you spend too much time on the computer? Are you working so much you are never home for meals or to see your children's activities? Do you participate in making decisions with them? How are you participating in their life?

According to 1 Peter 3:8–12, All of you should be of one mind. Sympathize with each other. Love each other as brothers and sisters. Be tenderhearted, and keep a humble attitude. Don't repay evil for evil. Don't retaliate with insults when people insult you. Instead, pay them back with a blessing. That is what God has called you to do, and he will grant you his blessing. For the Scriptures say, "If you want to enjoy life and see many happy days, keep your tongue from speaking evil and your lips from telling lies. Turn away from evil and do good. Search for peace, and work to maintain it. The eyes of the LORD watch over those who do right, and his ears are open to their prayers. But the LORD turns his face against those who do evil."

> "Two things to remember in life:
> Take care of your thoughts when you are alone
> And take care of your words when you are with people."
> –Unknown

GOD, HUSBAND, WIFE THEN CHILDREN

There is a role for each of us as a family unit. As we become more and more versed with the Bible, we will understand those roles (Eph. 5:21–33).

God commands that our primary relationship is with him. You must love the Lord your God with all your heart, all your soul, and all your mind. This is the first and greatest commandment (Matt. 22:37–38). Love the Lord your God with all your heart and with all your soul and with all your strength (Deut. 6:5).

If you are married, your spouse comes next. A married man is to love his wife as Christ loved the church (Eph. 5:25). Husbands should follow God first, then his wife. In the same way, wives are to submit to their husbands "as to the Lord." A woman's husband is second only to God (Ephesians 5:22).

Intimacy is an important part of marriage. A husband and wife can help each other by meeting the other's needs through physical and emotional intimacy (1 Corinthians 7:2–5).

In 1 Corinthians 11:3, scripture says, "But I want you to realize that the head of every man is Christ, and the head of the woman is man, and the head of Christ is God."

God made Adam and Eve husband and wife before he made them parents. He established marriage as the primary relationship between man and woman (Gen. 1:24).

If husbands and wives are second only to God in our priorities, it stands to reason that the result of the marriage relationship is having children, which therefore, should be the next priority.

Children who will be the next generation should be raised to love the Lord with all their hearts (Prov. 22:6 and Eph. 6:4).

> I'd rather have others consider me weak
> because I am submissive to my husband
> than to be considered weak to the Lord
> because I submit to the view of others.
> –Unknown

HUSBANDS

A husband has his responsibility in a marriage.

He is called to be a leader. But I want you to understand that Christ is the head of every man, and the man is head of a woman, and God is the head of Christ (1 Corinthians 11:3)

A husband is to love his wife as he loves himself; to feed and care for her (Eph. 5:22–30).

He is to love his wife unconditionally (Ephesians 5:25). Husbands, love your wives and do not be harsh with them (Colossians 3:19).

The husband should let her know she is loved. In Proverbs 31:28, the scripture says "Her children rise up and call her blessed; her husband also, and he praises her."

He needs to provide for his wife and family (1 Timothy 5:8).

WIVES (1 PETER 3:1–5)

Being a married woman, I have attended a number of Christian women's seminars to learn the biblical principles of love, marriage, and being a woman of faith. I might have to write another book to share more with you.

A changed life is the most effective way to influence a family member. Peter instructs wives to develop their inner beauty so their husbands will be won over by their love. We are to remember our roles.

Wives, you must accept the authority of your husbands. Authority does not mean allowing for abuse or behaving as a slave master. Then, even if some refuse to obey the word of God, your godly lives will speak to them without any words. They will be won over by observing your pure and reverent lives.

Don't be concerned about the outward beauty of trendy hairstyles, expensive jewelry, and name brand clothes. That is matters of the worldly. You should commit to exuding inner beauty, the unfading beauty of a gentle, quiet spirit which is so precious to God. Wise women put their trust in God and accept the authority of their husbands.

A WIFE OF NOBLE CHARACTER

PROVERBS 31:10–31, NLT

[10] Who can find a virtuous and capable wife? She is more precious than rubies.

[11] Her husband can trust her, and she will greatly enrich his life.

[12] She brings him good, not harm, all the days of her life. She is ethical and professional.

[13] She finds wool and flax and busily spins it.

[14] She is like a merchant's ship, bringing her food from afar.

[15] She gets up before dawn to prepare breakfast for her household and plan the day's work for her servant girls.

[16] She goes to inspect a field and buys it; with her earnings she plants a vineyard.

[17] She is energetic and strong, a hard worker.

[18] She makes sure her dealings are profitable; her lamp burns late into the night.

[19] Her hands are busy spinning thread, her fingers twisting fiber. She is compassionate.

[20] She extends a helping hand to the poor and opens her arms to the needy.

[21] She has no fear of winter for her household, for everyone has warm clothes. She is practical and intelligent.

[22] She makes her own bedspreads. She dresses in fine linen and purple gowns.

[23] Her husband is well known at the city gates, where he sits with the other civic leaders.

[24] She makes belted linen garments and sashes to sell to the merchants.

[25] She is clothed with strength and dignity, and she laughs without fear of the future.

[26] When she speaks, her words are wise, and she gives instructions with kindness. She is dedicated to family.

[27] She carefully watches everything in her household and suffers nothing from laziness.

[28] Her children stand and bless her. Her husband praises her:

[29] "There are many virtuous and capable women in the world, but you surpass them all!"

[30] Charm is deceptive, and beauty does not last; She is devoted to the Lord. but a woman who fears the LORD will be greatly praised.

[31] Reward her for all she has done. Let her deeds publicly declare her praise.

READING RESOURCES:

The 5 Love Languages: The Secret to Love that Lasts
By Gary Chapman

Ever After: Life Lessons Learned in My Castle of Chaos
By Vicki Courtney

Getting the Love You Want; A Guide for Couples
By Harville Hendrix, Ph.D.

Healing Your Marriage When Trust is Broken: Finding Forgiveness
and Restoration
By Cindy Beall, Forward by Craig Groeschel

Honor Begins at Home: The Courageous Bible Study
By Michael Catt, Stephen Kendrick and Alex Kendrick

Love for a Lifetime Bible Study
Dr. James Dobson

Recovering From Divorce: Overcoming the Death of a Dream
By Ramon Presson

Unfaithful: Hope and Healing After Infidelity
By Gary and Mona Shriver

Violence Among Us: Ministry to Family in Crisis
By Brenda Branson and Paula J. Silva

QUESTIONS TO PONDER:

1. Were you aware of the male and female roles in marriage are found in the Bible?

2. What is your perception of submitting to your spouse?

3. When in a heated argument, do you tend to be passive, assertive or aggressive?

4. After reading this chapter, do you feel you fight fair?
   What pushes your buttons?
   Are you a button pusher?

5. Do your arguments ever become physical? If so, what are you willing to do about it?

6. What is your attitude when you come home from work?
   What can you do to improve the tone when you come home from work?

7. Has your relationship been stained by infidelity?
   Are you holding on to the pain?
   Are you allowing jealousy to cloud your healing?

8. Everyone knows someone that has been divorced. How do you feel about divorce?

9. Was any part of this chapter eye opening for you?
   Does it motivate you to change anything?

10. What verse or verses are important to you?

CHAPTER NINE

CHILDREN; WHY DID WE GO THERE?

Whether you are raising your biological children, stepchildren, grandchildren, or foster children, you have probably asked yourself this question a number of times! Modern times are causing more and more of us to be rearing other people's children, namely our own grandchildren.

Raising children is not an easy feat. People are born with genetic encoding meaning all children are going to differ from each other. That makes it difficult to compare one parents' battle to another.

Children are not born with instructions, and there are no set patterns, regimens, or rules.

When you are caring for other people's children—especially due to a crisis, they will likely come to you with a bundle of emotional baggage. They may come with little to no clothing. When my husband and I were doing foster care, often we would have children come to us with nothing more than the clothes on their back. The children most likely will display anger and show signs of anxiety and/or depression. They have been removed from their own surroundings, their own things, family members, pets, school, and friends. In general, you will be dealing with major behavior problems. Their chronological age may differ from their mental age, social age, and emotional age. Their emotional level will be depend on their emotional age. And their social and learning skills will be dependent on their upbringing. Sadly, children will look for love and attention in some very unlovable ways.

CHILDREN LEARN WHAT THEY LIVE.

The loudest lesson to a child is to learn by example. Children learn what they live. The sweetest gift to give to your child is to be a Godly husband and wife (Prov. 6:23).

A mirror will reflect your face, but the kind of friends you choose reflects the kind of person you are (Prov. 27:19). We are to live by example, as we are to parent by example. Remember that the Lord is the maker of us all (Prov. 22:2).

We are not criticize others. Treat others the way you want to be treated (Matt. 7:1, 2, 12).

It is written that if you teach a child the right path, that when he becomes an adult, he will stay with it (Prov. 22:2 and 6). If you listen to fools, you will start acting like them (1 Corinthians 15:33).

CHILDREN LEARN WHAT THEY LIVE

By Dorothy Law Nolte

If children live with criticism,
They learn to condemn.

If children live with hostility
They learn to fight,

If children live with fear,
They learn to be apprehensive,

If children live with pity,
They learn to feel sorry for themselves.

If children live with jealousy,
They learn to feel envy.

If children live with ridicule,
They learn to be shy.

If children live with shame,
They learn to feel guilty.

If children live with tolerance,
They learn to be patient.

If children live with encouragement,
They learn to be confident.

If children live with praise,
They learn to appreciate.

If children live with acceptance,
They learn to love.

If children live with fairness,
They learn justice.

If children live with security,
They learn to have faith.

If children live with sharing,
They learn generosity.

If children live with kindness and consideration,
They learn respect.

If children live with approval,
They learn to like themselves.

If children live with acceptance and friendship,
They learn to find love in their world.

BIBLICAL EXAMPLE FOR PARENTS

A wise child accepts a parent's discipline. A mocker refuses to listen to correction (Prov. 13:1). Listen when your father corrects you and listen to your mother's correction. If sinners entice you, turn your back on them (Prov. 1:8–9, and 15). Turn your back on them, stay far away from their paths (Prov. 1:15).

If you listen to your parents, you will have a long and happy life. Learn to be wise and develop good judgment and common sense, (Proverbs 4:4). Wisdom and common sense will bring you honor and respect (Prov. 3:22).

As a parent, be as involved as possible. Remember that times are a lot different than they were when you were their age. You need to connect with them by keeping up with what is going on in their lives. Practice communicating with them by talking about the little things.

Remember that you are not your children's friends. You are their *parent*. The difficult part of becoming friends is that the boundaries become confused.

Children need their parents for security.

As a parent, you need to keep your fears in check. Children need to feel safe. My mother is irrationally terrified of storms and fires. To this day, she calls us to tell us we have weather watches and warnings. She watches the sky like she is going to change it by keeping an eye on it. She irrationally worries about leaving something on (coffeemaker, fan, etc.) in fear of it catching on fire. This irrational worry caused me to fear some of the same things—to the point of being irrational as well. It was a struggle not to freak out about the same things in front of my own children, but I didn't want them to become obsessed by these irrational fears.

As a parent, keep your own insecurities in check. Whether the fear is fires, storms, jealousy, or self-loathing. Your children depend on you to keep them safe. Because they are not able to discern what is an irrational fear, your child/children will likely emulate your reaction or behavior.

DISCIPLINE AND CONSEQUENCES

As a parent, we need to allow mistakes and natural consequences to happen. There are consequences to sin (Prov. 1:18–19). By trying to cover your child's mistakes and fix things for him, he will not learn natural consequences.

When you are enforcing or making rules, you should always explain to your children why it is important to you. By doing this, it will help your child to understand your logic.

The character of even a child can be known by the way he acts (Prov. 20:11). A youngster's heart is filled with rebellion, but punishment will drive it out of him (Prov. 22:15).

Do not fail to correct your children (Prov. 23:12–13). Punishment that hurts chases evil from the heart (Prov. 20:30).

CONSIDERATIONS WITH DISCIPLINE AND CONSEQUENCES

- With discipline, make sure that the discipline is not out of anger of frustration.
- What is a consequence that is age appropriate and worthy to your child?
- Be committed to your values. Don't just throw a consequence at a child without explaining why they are getting the consequence and how that goes against your values. It is important they understand the correlation.
- Be realistic. This doesn't mean to bend "with the times." Give your child a consequence that you can live with and/or you are able to follow through.
- Be consistent. Don't give in one time and expect the child to understand the next time. By being inconsistent, your child will receive mixed messages. Don't give in when your child starts fussing and getting loud because you will have taught your child that if he has a big tantrum, he will get out of the consequence. That will not work in school, work or in

prison. Teach the discipline and respect of rules while they are young. Discipline your son in his early years while there is hope. If you don't, you will ruin his life (Prov. 19:18).

As a parent, if we love our child, we are to discipline him (Prov. 13:24). Train up a child in the way he should go: and when he is old, he will not depart from it (Prov. 22:6).

When I was a teen, on my way out the door to hang out with my friends, my father's famous statement he whispered privately in my ear was "Don't disappoint your daddy." That sweet statement stuck with me. It resonated in my ear. Offer sincere encouragement (Prov. 21:13).

All people including children, need to feel they have a purpose in their lives. Make sure to find ways to give them a sense of control somewhere in their life. They are surrounded by rules at home, at school, at church, even at playgrounds. Make sure they are aware of what they can and cannot control. For example, homework is a non-negotiable. But curfew can be negotiated under the right circumstances.

How often have you heard, "But my friends are going!" We have to teach our children this verse as well as why it is important. Do not be deceived; Bad company ruins good morals (1 Cor. 15:33).

Remember that your children need to hear the good things. Catch your child doing something right—Tell them that you believe in them and are proud of them.

DO YOU USE SHAME FOR CORRECTION?

There is nothing more disturbing to a person's self-identity than shaming. In the context of normal development, shame is the source of low self-esteem, diminished self-image, poor self-concept, and deficient body-image.

Shame itself produces self-doubt creating a lack of security and confidence. It can become an impediment to the experience of belonging and to shared intimacy.

In pathological development, shame causes alienation, loneliness, inferiority, and perfectionism. It can also play a role in many psychological disorders as well including depression, paranoia, addiction, narcissism, and borderline conditions. Sexual disorders and many eating disorders are largely disorders of shame.

Both physical abuse and sexual abuse also significantly involve shame. Shame has been found to be a very strong predictor of Posttraumatic Stress Disorder.

REPORTING VS. TATTLING

You want your children to know it is safe to tell you anything. But sometimes reporting becomes tattling. It is important to know the difference and to teach your child the difference.

Tattling can be used as a form of bullying. Know what the motivation is for tattling. Never underestimate a child's ability to manipulate an adult.

Reporting:	Tattling:
Purpose is to keep someone safe.	To get someone in trouble.
Need help from an adult.	Could have solved problem themselves.
Important	Unimportant
Harmful/Dangerous	Harmless
Behavior is on purpose	Behavior is an accident

SIBLING RIVALRY VS. SIBLING ABUSE

Sibling Rivalry is defined as: competition between siblings especially for the attention, affection, and approval of their parents

Sibling Abuse is defined as: the physical, emotional, and/or sexual abuse of one sibling by another. Though several studies indicate that sibling abuse is far more common than other forms of family abuse, chronic maltreatment by siblings has only relatively recently become the subject of serious clinical study and concern.

Most households tend to have both parents working, and there are a lot more single parents trying to make ends meet leaving children to fend for themselves.

Sibling abuse is a serious problem! Studies reveal more than 50% report sibling abuse. As explained throughout this book, abuse of any kind leaves a lifelong impact on people. It changes them forever.

HOW DO I KNOW IF MY CHILD IS BEING ABUSED BY THEIR SIBLING?

Do you have one child that tends to be aggressive? Does this child tend to get rougher and more aggressive with siblings and peers?

Does your child avoid a sibling? When we had foster care in our home, a younger child cried when I tried to get the child to go outside and play with the other children. I found out that this child was being abused outside.

Does your child have bruises, scrapes, and/or cuts? How much teasing is considered bullying? My brother would hold me down and drool on my face. He would incessantly tease and provoke me. And I did my share of return fire.

When does the parent draw a line in the sand? Parents should make sure their children clearly understand that teasing and making fun of others is unacceptable behavior.

Unfortunately I always told my daughters "If you aren't bleeding, I don't want to hear about it." That kind of thinking allows your child to be bullied. Don't tell children to fight their own battles. Ask more questions to discern when you should step in to protect them.

Is your child having difficulty sleeping and/or having nightmares?

Does your child not want to eat a meal at the table with family members? We had an elderly foster person living with us for a short period of time. Neither one of my daughters wanted to eat meals at the table because this woman was extremely rude and aversive to be around.

Does the "victim" child act out the abuse in play? I worked with a child that displayed sexual abuse through playing with her Barbie dolls. I heard her talking in her room. What was going on in there was definitely sexual. When I peeked around the corner, I realized she was verbalizing what she was doing with her Barbie dolls.

If your child is showing any of these signs, talk with your child's pediatrician immediately. If you are already seeing a family counselor or psychologist, it is appropriate to address this information with them. To protect your child's integrity, you should not share this information with outsiders. It is important to seek counseling for your child(ren). If your child exhibits signs of sexual abuse, you will need to supervise your child to prevent acting out sexually with other people (including their siblings and playmates).

BULLYING

What is bullying?

Bullying happens when one or more children repeatedly hurts another child verbally or physically. It involves repeated physical, verbal, or psychological attacks or intimidation directed against a child who cannot properly defend themselves because of their size or strength, or because the child is outnumbered or less psychologically resilient.

Bullying includes assault, tripping, intimidation, rumor-spreading and isolation, demands for money, destruction of property, theft of valued possessions, destruction of another's work, and name-calling.

Some researchers believe females value social relationships more than males do, so female bullies tend to disrupt social relationships with gossip, isolation, silent treatment, and exclusion. Females tend to bully females while males bully both genders.

OTHER FORMS OF BULLYING;

- Bullying of teachers by students.
- Hazing; painful embarrassing initiation rituals used to join gangs or fraternities.
- Bullying to recruit and retaining youth gang members, compelling them to commit crimes.
- Sexual harassment including propositioning, unwanted physical contact, exhibitionism, and voyeurism.
- Harass people based on perceived sexual orientation.

All children deserve a school environment where they feel safe and can learn to the best of their abilities. The levels of violence among young people in our communities and schools have increased immensely. Studies show that sixty percent of children identified as bullies in middle school go on to have arrest records. It is important to address bullying at an early age before they are involved in even more serious behavior problems. As a result of bullying, the victims of bullies may experience anxiety and depression and low self-esteem. They have poor school attendance to avoid the abuse.

Bullying affects students' sense of security. Bullying is widespread and perhaps the most underreported safety problem on American school campuses.

WHY ARE PEOPLE RELUCTANT TO REPORT BEING BULLIED?

Surveys reveal that most students do not report bullying to adults. Surveys confirm that many victims and witnesses fail to tell teachers or even parents. As a result, teachers and school officials underestimate the extent of bullying in their school.

If victims are so miserable, why don't they report it so they receive help? Surveys suggest that children believe most teachers do not intervene when told about bullying, the adult responses have been disappointing.

REASONS FOR NOT REPORT-
ING BEING BULLIED;

- fear of retaliation,
- ashamed that they are unable to stand up for themselves,
- they won't be believed,
- they don't want to worry their parents or teachers,
- they lack confidence that anything will change if they report it,
- their parent's or teacher's reaction could make the problem even worse,
- the teacher or school official might reveal the name of the person that reported the bullying
- to be thought of as a snitch.

The same is true of student-witnesses. They may agree that it is wrong but most likely won't report it.

EFFECTS OF BULLYING

Victims of bullying suffer consequences beyond embarrassment. Some victims experience psychological and/or physical distress, are frequently absent and cannot concentrate on schoolwork.

Research reveals victims generally have low self-esteem that can lead to anxiety and depression, years after the victimization. Those who were bullied frequently experienced poorer physical and mental health. Some bullied students stay at home to avoid being bullied, while some have reported to have considered suicide as the only possible solution.

SCHOOL POLICIES FOR BULLYING

Before you admit your child into a school, consider asking them questions to evaluate if your child will be safe at this school. Feel free to use, copy and share the *checklist* at the end of this chapter.

To address bullying, schools should ensure that all their teachers have effective classroom management training. Research suggests that classes containing students with behavioral, emotional, or learning problems have more bullies (and victims). Teachers in those classes may require additional tailored training in spotting and handling bullying.

School administrators should review the school bullying policy with all late-enrolling students. This removes any excuse new students have for bullying. It also stresses the importance the school places on countering it.

Get involved! I know everyone is busy, but you have to make your child a priority! What happens in their life now will affect them the rest of their lives. Get on school mailing lists, attend PTA meetings, and attend school events.

HOW CAN I TELL IF MY CHILD IS BEING BULLIED?

Your child may be the victim of bullying if he/she:

1. Comes home from school with torn or dirty clothing, or damaged books
2. Has cuts, bruises, or scratches
3. Has few, if any, friends
4. Hesitates going to school, or frequent complaints of headaches or stomach pains
5. Insomnia and bad dreams
6. Loses interest in schoolwork and school activities
7. Seems sad, depressed, anxious or moody
8. Negative attitude, poor self-esteem
9. Unusually quiet, overly-sensitive, or passive

If your child comes home upset because another child is verbally or physically abusive, *do not* tell them things like "Oh, (s)he must have a crush on you." Your child should never believe for one second that a person that likes them will abuse them. Don't ever assume they will understand the difference.

If you believe your child is being bullied, talk to your child. Ask them what is troubling them. Schedule a meeting with the school to see if they share the same concerns.

HOW CAN I TELL IF MY CHILD IS BULLYING OTHERS?

Your child may be bullying others if he or she:

- Teases, threatens, or kicks other children and animals
- Is hot-tempered or impulsive, or has a hard time following rules
- Is aggressive toward adults
- Is calloused, shows no sympathy for children who are bullied
- Has been involved in other antisocial behavior, such as vandalism or theft.

If your child shows these warning signs, it is possible that your child is bullying others. You need to address your child about his/her behavior, and schedule a conference to talk about the issue with school staff and social worker. Your child may need professional help beyond what you and the school can do.

CHILD TRAUMA

Most people have accepted that terrorist attacks are the new normal. Tornadoes, hurricanes, and natural disasters occur around the world daily. But we struggle with the effects of trauma. Especially with children. They will react differently depending on their personality, maturity level and their circumstances.

Parents and teachers are generally the people children rely on for support after experiencing a traumatic event. Parents need to discern how much information they should divulge with their child.

ADAA member Aureen Wagner, PhD, Director of The Anxiety Wellness Center in Cary, North Carolina, offers this recommendation for parents: "Remain as calm as possible; watch and listen to your child to understand how upset he or she is. Explain a traumatic event as accurately as possible, but don't give graphic details. It's best not to give more information than your child asks for. Let your child know that it is normal to feel upset, scared or angry. If older children or teenagers want to watch television or read news online about a traumatic event, be available to them, especially to discuss what they are seeing and reading."

These tips are important for children and adolescents of all ages:

- Reassure them of their safety.
- Encourage them to talk openly and ask questions.
- Answer questions honestly.
- Discern what they don't need to know.
- Avoid discussing worst-case scenarios.
- Limit graphic replays of the traumatic event.
- Consistent routine.

SIGNS OF DISTRESS:

- Restless, difficulty sleeping
- Change in appetite
- Clingy or whiney
- Re-experiencing the event through nightmares, recollections, or play
- Avoidance or denial of the event
- Anxious, jumpy
- Persistent fears

If your child continues to show these signs, a mental health professional should be sought. There are many effective treatments available.

DEALING WITH NEGATIVE BEHAVIORS

*A rebellious son is a grief to his father
and a bitter blow to his mother (Prov. 17:25).*

Why is this bad behavior happening? As a parent, we need to recognize bad behavior as a loss of parental control.

Lack of respect and aggressive behavior is a power struggle between you and your child. How you react to it is going to make or break you. *Never* allow aggression in your home! Remember that you are the example. Your child will emulate you! So if you are angry and throwing things, slamming doors, yelling, or swearing, is that the example you want to set for your child? *Been there, done that!* The best way to handle a heightened situation is to think about how you would handle this situation if you were being recorded for all the world to see.

Pick your battles. Even when they are rolling their eyes, they can still hear you. Yes it is disrespectful, but is it worth nagging when there are things more urgent to address?

While dealing with your child, always stay calm. Do not react to the negative behavior. The negative attention they receive from you feeds the behavior. Listen to your child. Focus on their internal dialogue. What are they telling themselves? What are their beliefs? Why do they believe that?

Set consequences and stick to them. If you have a spouse, make sure you are *both* on the same page. Consequences only work with consistency. You may have to push the consequences until your child realizes the bad behavior doesn't work anymore.

Set up a reward system. If your child has everything, they have nothing to work for. So you may have to take their privileges away and make your children earn them back.

Wives: Women tend to take their children's behavior very personally. They see their children's behavior as failure of how their children have been raised. Don't be a martyr, be a mother.

Husbands: Remember that males are a powerful role model in a child's life. You are more to a child than a financial provider. So think about your role in your child's life. Are you giving them a nurturing environment?

Children look to their parents as a safe place. And that is all threatened through divorce and mixed families. This may very well be an underlying frustration in your child. This is an old saying, but it is *sooooo* important! Catch your child doing the right things *and* acknowledge the good behavior!

WE ARE ALWAYS FIGHTING OVER CHORES!

Make sure your children understand that as a family, we *all* need to do chores. The family needs to work as a team.

Use a chore chart type check list so each person can refer to it. Do you need picture guides? Do the supplies need to be arranged? Would it be helpful to label drawers and cabinets?

You can offer rewards for completed work. Allow them to have their privileges. Don't harp on them to get the chore done. You should only have to remind them once. Anything past that is a control issue. Then you let them experience natural consequences—take away their privileges. Always be consistent and *do not* give in. Don't let it pass this time and be angry that they aren't listening to you the next time. When you give in you are taking away your authority and they will never believe you when you give them a consequence. Consistency is the key!

We *all* need to do chores. You are to model positivity and responsibility of your chore. Do it correctly and make sure to have fun. If you are assigned a chore and don't do it, your children will notice. If you cannot possibly do a chore, make sure you talk to your family about trading a chore. This is a great way to teach your children camaraderie. Make sure it is all in writing so you cannot forget what you agreed to.

Oversee their work from a distance. Make sure you are dishing out deserved compliments and that they outnumber the corrections.

If you follow these suggestions, you may see some resistance—especially if they are not used to you keeping your word. As a parent, this will teach your children skills they will use in the real world. You are doing them no favors by doing the work for them or letting it go because you want to escape the confrontation. It may be tough the first few weeks, but in the long run, it will be worth it!

MY CHILD HAS LOW SELF-ESTEEM

You are not born with a self-image. It is learned through your environment, how you were raised, and how you choose to respond to it. We may have no control over our environment, but we do have control over how we respond to it. Nobody grows up in perfect circumstances. A lot of people think the grass is always greener on the other side of the fence. But those same people would be yearning to be on the other side of someone else's fence because they interpret that it is the circumstances that needs to change.

Our feelings are a chosen reaction.

Sadly, those with low self-esteem tend to be self-loathing. They tend to fight depression and anxiety, they suffer with anorexia or drug abuse. Receiving a simple compliment is difficult. You can change your self-concept with learning where this unhealthy behavior stems from. It is important to be aware of how you think of yourself because your self-image reveals how you look at life. It is a reflection of how you believe others see you. With that being said, can you believe God loves you? It is difficult to have a healthy view of God if you do not have a healthy view of yourself.

No one can make you feel inferior without your consent.
– Eleanor Roosevelt

If you have a positive self-image, you tend to be more optimistic. If you have a negative self- image, you tend to be more pessimistic. Paul refers to it as seeing through dark glass in 1 Corinthians 13:12.

Your self-image determines your happiness. You can destroy your damaged self-image with biblical truths! Paul teaches us that our body is the temple of the Holy Spirit, who lives in you and was given to you by God. You do not belong to yourself for God bought you for a high price. You must honor God with your body (1 Cor. 6:19–20).

In 2 Corinthians 3:17–8, Paul tells us we can be recreated to the image of our Heavenly Father. We have to realize that this transformation does not happen the instance you become a new Christian. You have to make a continuous effort in the process of changing your self-image. As he thinks within himself, so he is (Prov. 23:7).

Remember that God loves his children and wants us to love ourselves. It is stated in Proverbs 19:8 to acquire wisdom is to love oneself. This is not condoning self-centered behavior or to fulfill selfish interest. This is simply stating that if you love yourself, you will seek wisdom.

He wants us to know that you are valuable to God. In Mark 8:36, Jesus declares each human being to be worth more than the total wealth of the whole world. Wow! Now that is valuable!

If your self-loathing is caused from sin, refer to Chapter 11; Christians Sin?

A person's self-image reflects how the person thinks others see them. No child is born with a self-image. Once the self-image is formed, it tends to be resistant to change. Do not be the parent that reflects their insecurities on their children;

- "If you eat too much of that, you will be as fat as I am."
- "Your teeth are crooked, so don't smile big in the camera."
- "Don't bother with trying out for sports. Neither one of us (parents) were any good at sports. "You are as graceful as a bull in a China shop."
- "I gained a pound. I hate my hair. I never can do anything right."

SELF-LOATHING

Your view of life is generally a product of your self-image.

As hard as I tried, I know I have made these mistakes with my own daughters. I inherited large hips and thighs, among other unfavorable traits I dislike. I had huge spaces between my teeth and have a lazy eye that does not move with the other eye. I am very conscientious of how my face is turned when talking to people (so people know which eye to look at) or having a photo taken (which I avoid like the plague). I know God loves me as I am, yet I struggle with this fight every day.

Give your children a sense of achievement and self-esteem.

Acknowledge when they do something good. Have fun, be positive, and enthusiastic with them.

Pick your battles, know when to offer criticism and critiques.

Just a few months ago, I was going through some unpacked boxes from our move to Tennessee. I found two boxes that contained school papers and report cards for both of my daughters. I also found several notes that were written back and forth to my children's teachers and was struck right between the eyes with a truth about my parenting skills that I am not proud of. All I could think is "Good Lord, those girls were just children! What was I thinking?" I was very hard on them. My expectations were unrealistic!

> The words you speak become the house you live in.
> –Hafiz

At an American Association for Intellectual and Developmental Disabilities (AAIDD) seminar, I heard about a teacher that practiced humor around a sensitive issue. When she walked into her classroom, she found a number of swearwords on the board. As she erased them, she remarked, "At least the words were all spelled right." Because she didn't get her shorts in a bundle over it, it didn't give them the negative response they were expecting. This teacher also praises her students for bringing their supplies and class work in. She reports great attendance and cooperation in her classroom.

The human spirit can endure a sick body, but who can bear a crushed spirit (Prov. 18:14)?

Use words that help and heal (Prov. 25:11–12).

KEEP YOUR OWN HONESTY IN CHECK!

- Do you eat the grapes or cherries in your shopping cart while you are shopping? I have known people who have put new clothing and shoes on their children in a store and then have them walk out to the car without paying for them.

- Do you lie to people? How many times have you lied to someone in front of your child and they KNEW you were lying?
- Do you hide purchases so your spouse doesn't know you were out shopping again? Do you pull cash out of your account so your spouse doesn't know why or how you are really spending?
- Do you ask your children to keep secrets? I know parents that have had extramarital affairs that told their children to not tell their spouse they "visited" this person. They were awarded secrecy gifts and treats. They were also told that it was fair game because the other parent is doing the same thing. This behavior will teach a child that all adults are adulterous. They will have trust issues in their own marriage.
- "What they don't know won't hurt them." Do you think your child will say the same thing about you?

As I stated earlier in this chapter, your children are watching you! You are an influence!

A meager diet is as satisfying as a feast with love in the home (Prov. 15:17). We are expected as parents to teach our children and grandchildren about God and Jesus Christ. In Deuteronomy 4:9, Moses urges parents to teach their children about God's miracles. And in 2 Timothy 1:5, Timothy's mother and grandmother taught Timothy of their Christian faith. We are to plant seeds of the Good News. And in 2 Timothy 3:15, Timothy became a Christian through the teachings of the holy scriptures taught by his mother and grandmother. We are ambassadors for Christ, 2 Corinthians 5:20.

FRIENDS AND PEERS

Friendships impact our children's future. Friendships should be a firm non-negotiable standard with your children. Start making this a priority while they are younger, and remember that it is never, ever too late.

Birds of a feather flock together.
–Plato

Do not be deceived: "Evil company corrupts good habits" (1 Cor. 15:33 NKJV).

If sinners entice you, turn your back on them. Don't go along with them, stay far away from their paths (Prov. 1:9–15). Walk with the wise and become wise; associate with fools and get in trouble (Prov. 13:20). Don't befriend angry people or associate with hot-tempered people or you will learn to be like them and endanger your soul (Prov. 22:24–25).

"Show me your friends
and I will show you your future."
–Maurice Clarett
Proverbs 1:8–22

"Show me your friends and I will show you your future." It is vital that our children understand the wisdom of this sentence.

As iron sharpens iron, so a friend sharpens a friend (Prov. 27:17). As a Christian, it is important to be around like-minded people to stay strong in your walk with Christ; be very careful when making choices; sure they are consistent with your Christian walk. This does not mean a Christian cannot be a friend to a non-Christian. But if they affect your Christian walk negatively then protect your faithful heart and put distance in that relationship.

As a parent, we are faced with making choices for our children. First, pick your battles by leaning on what is negotiable and what is non-negotiable. Teach your child compromise by explaining clearly both points of views and how either of you can make that compromise. Make sure you are setting clear guidelines. Stand firm on what is important and compromise only what is negotiable.

Teach your child(ren) about loving your friends. What does that mean? Don't just pretend to love others. Really love them. Hate what is wrong, hold tightly to what is good. Love each other with genuine affection and take delight in honoring each other (Romans 12:9–10).

CHILD MOLESTATION

Most offenders are known to the child; they may be family members, relatives, family friends, teachers, coaches, youth leaders, babysitters, and other people in positions of authority. If you are thinking that it wouldn't happen to any of your children because they are good kids, think again.

Understand that children most susceptible to sexual abuse have obedient, compliant, and respectful personalities.

Offenders target children from unhappy or broken homes, physically and/or emotionally neglected because they may be eager for attention and affection. Children who are victims of sexual abuse may display behaviors that include withdrawal from family or friends, poor academics, experience depression, anxiety, or exhibit aggressive and self-destructive behavior. They may lure children with pets, balloons, candy, or toys. Often it may involve activities that would attract children and exclude adults. They give them lots of attention, affection, and gifts.

As a parent, you should always ask questions. Why are they being so nice or so attentive with your child? What are their motives? Make sure to monitor time spent together — even showing up unannounced.

Research reveals startling statistics every parent needs to know:

- Before the age of 18, 1 out of every 4 girls is sexually abused and 1 out of every 6 boys is sexually abused.
- The median age for reported child abuse is 9 years old.
- More than 90% of abusers are people children know, love and trust. Young victims may not recognize their victimization as sexual abuse. 30 to 40% of victims are abused by a family member. 50% are abused by someone outside of the family whom they know and trust.
- 85% of child abuse victims never report their abuse.
- The way a victim's family responds to the abuse plays an important role in how the incident affects the victim. Sexually abused children who keep their abuse a secret or who "tell" and are not believed are at greater risk than the general population for psychological, emotional, social and physical problems often lasting into adulthood.
- The average age of sex offenders is 27 years old. Nearly 70% of child sex offenders have between 1 and 9 victims and at least 20 % of child offenders have 10-40 victims.
- 1 in 5 children are solicited sexually while on the internet.

Victims of child sexual abuse are more likely to be sexually promiscuous. An estimated 60% of teen first pregnancies are proceeded by experiences of molestation, rape, or attempted rape.

I am going to explain my story in hopes that you will consider how you might handle this situation.

As a child I had been molested a number of times. At three or four—pre-kindergarten age—I thought I was special because the offenders chose me. By kindergarten, as the molestation continued, I felt guilty because by then I knew that those areas being touched were private and what was going on was a sin. I told my babysitter about the abuse and she reported it to my parents. I found out later that my father threatened to kill the offender (one offender was divorced and nowhere to be found) Although it was gallant on my father's part, it was an overreaction. My father was belligerent and compulsive due to drugs and alcohol abuse. I realized that was why these very important people in my life suddenly moved out of state. The reaction to revealing this secret had left me devastated!

Later, the molestation continued by another trusted adult. I was about eight or nine. This perpetrator's sexual abuse made me believe I was ingratiating and adultlike. He only stayed at our home a short duration. After he left, the guilt was progressively gnawing at my heart and soul. I decided I needed to go to my mother to confess what we did, clear my child-minded conscience. As I started the conversation with her, she turned toward me with the over- exaggerated eyes and tight lips and said, "Oh Judith Rae!" She then walked past me. End of discussion.

How did I feel by my mother's reaction? Rejected! In retrospect, I think back to my Dad's reaction last time I reported being molested. I am sure my mom feared similar results with this news.

My mom has always distrusted the motives of people—especially men. She would tell me that all men are pigs. I am sure her perception is equated to her disruptive, abusive childhood. She was given away to the foster care system as a child. As I reflect on her history, I can understand her lack of empathy.

HOW CAN I PROTECT MY CHILD FROM BEING MOLESTED?

Always remember that it can happen to your child. Remember that young children who have been molested will generally reflect in play with other children.

Talk to your child about molestation before it happens. They need to understand that a perpetrator can be someone they trust, love, and respect.

In early childhood, teach your children the name of their genitals just as you teach them the names of other body parts. This teaches that the genitals, while private, are not so private that your child can't talk about them with you. You should teach young children about the privacy of body parts, and that no one has the right to touch their bodies. They should also learn to respect the privacy of others.

Talk about bad touch and the importance of telling you if they have been touched inappropriately. If they are told to keep it a secret, they are to tell you anyway because bad touch is unacceptable and is never to be kept a secret. Someone that asks them to keep a secret are probably doing something they shouldn't do.

Make sure to give your child a plan so they know what to do before it happens.

If your child is in daycare or other educational programs, make sure they have an open door policy that allows you to drop in unannounced and allows you to observe or participate in activities.

Children should be taught to beware of adults who offer them special gifts or toys, or adults who want them to get in or near a vehicle. Pay attention to adults who make a big deal of your child, wanting to take him/her on a special outing or to special events.

You should always know where your child is, where they are going and what time you can expect them home. With the availability of cell phones, your child should be able to text you if he is going someplace other than you were expecting and text you when they are leaving so you can judge a reasonable amount of time for your child's arrival.

God gives us the Holy Spirit to talk to us. That is what we call our *gut instinct*. Listen to what your gut is telling you.

Be cautious with older siblings and playmates. Avoid closed doors. Children are often curious about the body parts of others and may attempt to explore them behind closed doors. Keep in mind that sleepovers are opportunities for those incidents to happen.

Always monitor what your children are doing online and what your children are watching on TV. There are controls to limit the degree of sex and violence your children have access to. Use them. If you don't know how, find someone that does. Remember that children may act out what they are exposed to. Know what your children's friends are allowed to watch too.

Ask questions—not just once but every time. Don't ever assume just because your child has been safe at a certain place that it is always good. Things can happen! Never ask questions in front of the possible perpetrator.

Never start out with questions like:

- Did you behave?
- Were you good?
- Did you listen?
- Did you do everything you were asked to do?

You won't get a real answer with these questions. You need to be your own detective with questions that force a conversation rather than yes/no answers.

- What all did you do while you were gone (or) while I was away?
- What was your favorite part?
- What was your least favorite part?
  o Did you feel uncomfortable?
  o Did you feel safe?
- Is there anything you might want to share?
  o Did anyone touch you somewhere private?
  o Did anyone ask you to keep a secret?

Always pray for the protection of your children.

Always keep an open door policy for your children. They should be comfortable in telling you things whether it is good or bad. As children become pre-teens, your children should be able to discuss sexual topics comfortably at home. Share news and reports of child sexual abuse to start discussions of safety, and reiterate that children should always tell a parent about anyone who is taking advantage of them sexually.

Visit Family Watchdog for information about sexual predators in your neighborhood.

WHAT IF MY CHILD TELLS ME HE OR SHE HAS BEEN MOLESTED?

If your child offers any information of sexual abuse, listen carefully, take it seriously. Too often, children are not believed, particularly if they implicate a family member as the perpetrator.

Don't overreact or freak-out! Calmly—contact your pediatrician, the local child protection service agency, or the police.

Please, please, please remember to keep this matter as private as possible. As a victim, I can assure you—I didn't want my aunts and uncles and family friends and the prayer chain to know my big, dirty secret. Remember that a lot of prayer chains are gossip chains!

If you don't intervene, the abuse will most likely continue. Your child may come to believe that home is not safe and/or that you are not available to help.

Make sure your child understands that (s)he is not responsible for the abuse.

Bring your child to a physician for a medical examination, to ensure that the child's physical health has not been affected by the abuse. It may be necessary to test your child for a sexually transmitted disease (STD). Your physician can discuss your concerns, examine your child, and make necessary referrals and reports.

Most children (and their families) will need professional counseling to help them through the mixed emotions and start a healing process.

TROUBLED TEENS

Pixabay / MGN

Do you ever wonder what makes some teens think they are so entitled? Do you have a teen that thinks they shouldn't have to put up with rules? They think they shouldn't have to deal with school? Do they hang with older friends that are sexually active, and have drugs and alcohol accessible? Have they been caught shoplifting, steal money from you, or maybe even steal your car? Are they carrying weapons? Do your teens have meltdowns when you attempt to enforce a rule? Do they break things? Are they physically and verbally threatening you? Do they hurt themselves or others?

What do you do about it? Do you dole out money? Do you hand them the keys just to shut them up? Do you make threats and not follow through with them?

A parent should not worry about making their child mad. Rules are a part of adulthood. It is not easy to parent! Teaching children that they don't have to follow rules is going to create a young adult in jail. Your child will not respect authority (police/laws, professors, bosses, etc.) if you don't teach them respect at an early age.

When my children made poor choices, I felt like a failure of a parent. My mind worked overtime to try to protect them from making mistakes that would affect them the rest of their lives.

We are often free to make choices
but powerless to choose our consequences
(Prov. 14:12, 13:24).

Make sure you have a reliable support system. Our saving grace was our Bible study leader. He was a great advisor and prayer warrior for my husband and I.

MY CHILD REFUSES TO ATTEND CHURCH

We have to remember that we have raised children with entitlement. We reward kids for doing things they should do! So it is my advice that you find a good Bible teaching church that does not use the fear of hell, fire and damnation—but of love and forgiveness. The church should have activities that your child(ren) will enjoy. Get involved by attending their programs and volunteer for some of their activities.

My husband and I had a rule that anyone living with us will attend church with us. Period. It was our job as a Christian parent to give our children a foundation to stand on. If you are on again, off again church goers, you are going to have a hard time gaining respect there. I know through experience that if you are fed the word, you will desire more of the word. The word IS the truth.

TEEN DATING

HOW DO I KNOW IF MY TEEN IS BEING ABUSED BY THEIR PARTNER?

Teen dating violence is defined by CDC.gov as the physical, sexual, psychological, or emotional violence within a dating relationship including stalking. It can occur in person or electronically and might occur between a current or former dating partner. Teen violence is often unreported because they are afraid it may result in serious consequences

Teens often think teasing and name calling are a normal part of a relationship. But sometimes, these behaviors can become abusive and develop into more serious forms of violence.

Teen violence can have short-term and long-term effects, people are changed with experiences in their relationships. Healthy relationships can have a positive effect on a teen's emotional development. Unhealthy, abusive, or violent relationships can have severe consequences and short- and long-term negative effects on a developing teen such as mental and physical health as well as on their school performance.

Teens experiencing dating violence are more likely to experience symptoms of depression and anxiety. They may display rebellious behaviors such as tobacco, alcohol, and drug use. They may become anti-social and/or show signs of depression including sui-cide. Unfortunately, teens who are victims of dating violence in high school are at higher risk for victimization during college.

Here are some shocking statistics:

- 1 in 3 teens know someone their age that has been abused by a date or partner
- 1 in 4 have been involved with a violent partner.
- 98% of abused people stay with the abuser.

Early intervention and public awareness is important if we want to stop violence in youth relationships before it begins and keep it from continuing into adult relationships. We need to teach teens how to communicate with their partner, to manage uncomfortable emotions like anger and jealousy, and to treat others with respect.

WHAT IF I SUSPECT MY CHILD IS USING DRUGS?

Do you have an open relationship with your child? Will they ask you to come pick them up from a party because they or the person driving had partied too much? You may want to attempt creating that relationship so your child is safe.

Don't ever assume you can trust your children. Trusting parents are easy to take advantage of. Kids with exemplary behavior and great grades to back it up are still kids. Kids make mistakes and bad choices. So if you are going out of town and leaving your trustworthy child at home, don't leave them the opportunity to temptation. Lock up the liquor cabinet and medications.

Don't assume your child is too young to experiment with drugs and alcohol. Alcohol was around me my entire childhood and could sneak it easily. And the first time I smoked marijuana, I was either eight or nine years old as it was accessible in my home.

Know who your child's friends are, where they live, and how to get ahold of a parent. You *must* have that information. If the child won't give you that information, you have a problem. That should be a non-negotiable rule!

Stay on top of their school attendance. Most schools have online attendance and grade records. As a parent, it is your responsibility to know if your child is staying in class and doing the work. Skipping school and poor grades may be a sign of too much partying.

Watch closely for physical signs of drug and alcohol use such as slurring words, unusually tired or opposite—extremely wired. Certain types of drugs will make people dizzy, shaky, aggressive, and cranky. Is your child using Visine (to get the red out), hiding their eyes with their hair or a hat, always popping mints or gum in their mouth, or simply avoiding you when they come home?

Does your child tend to have a lot of excuses for coming home late? Learn to be a detective. Make sure you know ways your child may be able to sneak in or out of the house. Know where your children are. If they tell you they are going somewhere, check to see that is where they really are. It may not be convenient, but bailing your child out of jail or putting them through treatment is even more inconvenient!

Check their bedrooms for hidden drugs, prescription bottles, alcohol, or drug paraphernalia. It is getting to be more and more difficult now that there are bath salts, smoking devices, and inhalants. If you are finding unusual numbers of spray cans, glue, markers, computer dust spray, there is a chance they are huffing. Is there leafy herbal pieces and seeds, burn marks on foil or in spoons, or white powder or pasty substances on top of flat surfaces such as a mirror, CD case or table top? Search under their mattress, attached behind the headboard or under and behind dressers and drawers. Check bags, trinket boxes, shoe boxes, and pencil cases. Check inside the shoes they don't wear and in clothes pockets.

Check your child's car in the same way! From under and in the crevices of the seats, in the ashtray, glove box, trunk, or any other storage area. Search bags, clothes, and containers.

Don't assume when your child asks you for money to buy clothes or eat out, that is actually what is being purchased. Handing over money may actually be supporting a drug habit.

Give random drug tests. It makes sense to request one following a late night out. There needs to be a consequence for a positive test or a refusal to take a test.

As a parent, we need to keep our child safe. But we must also teach them responsibility and trust. Make sure you are allowing your child privacy and trust—unless they give you reason to no longer trust them. And only then.

MY CHILD IS LGBT (LESBIAN, GAY, BISEXUAL OR TRANSGENDER).

There are so many different beliefs regarding homosexuality. Some people believe it is a form of rebellion. Or it is a learned behavior by way of sexual abuse or sexual curiosity. Many people experiment with the gay lifestyle. A gay person might experiment with a heterosexual relationship.

The LGBT population in general will tell you they never were comfortable with the gender they were born with. They may hide it because they feel ashamed of their sin and are concerned about church and family members. Others hide it because they are in denial and struggle between the two worlds.

MIXED REVIEWS OF
STUDIES REGARDING SEXUALITY;

Some scientist believe that homosexuality is not a learned behavior, that sexual orientation is inherited; meaning you are wired that way.

> Genes are hardware . . . the data of life's experiences are processed through the sexual software into the circuits of identity. I suspect the sexual software is a mixture of both genes and environment, in much the same way the software of a computer is a mixture of what's installed at the factory and what's added by the user.
>
> —P. Copeland and D. Hamer (1994)The Science of Desire (New York: Simon and Schuster).

> Various theories have proposed differing sources for sexual orientation . . . However, many scientists share the view that sexual orientation is shaped for most people at an early age through complex interactions of biological, psychological and social factors.
>
> —From the A.P.A.'s booklet, "Answers to Your Questions About Sexual Orientation and Homosexuality."

> (1) There is a genetic component to homosexuality, but 'component' is just a loose way of indicat-

ing genetic associations and linkages. 'Linkage' and 'association' do not mean 'causation.'

(2)There is no evidence that shows that homosexuality is genetic—and none of the research itself claims there is. Only the press and certain researchers do, when speaking in sound bites to the public."

—Jeffrey Satinover, M.D., The Journal of Human Sexuality, 1996, p.8.

Like all complex behavioral and mental states, homosexuality is . . . neither exclusively biological nor exclusively psychological, but results from an as-yet-difficult-to-quantitate mixture of genetic factors, intrauterine influences... postnatal environment (such as parent, sibling and cultural behavior), and a complex series of repeatedly reinforced choices occurring at critical phases of development.

—J. Satinover, M.D., Homosexuality and the Politics of Truth (1996) (Grand Rapids,MI: Baker Books).

Byne and Parsons carefully analyzed all the major biological studies of homosexuality. They found none that definitively supported a biological theory of causation.

—W. Byne and B. Parsons, "Human Sexual Orientation: The Biologic Theories Reappraised."Archives of General Psychiatry, Vol. 50, no.3.

Despite recent neurobiological findings suggesting homosexuality is genetically-biologically determined, credible evidence is lacking for a biological model of homosexuality.

—R. Friedman, M.D. and J. Downey, M.D., Journal of Neuropsychiatry, vol. 5, No. 2, Spring 1993.

Virtually all of the evidence argues against there being a determinative physiological causal factor and I know of no researcher who believes that such a determinative factor exists...such factors play a predisposing, not a determinative role . . . I know of no one in the field who argues that homosexuality can be explained without reference to environmental factors.

—S. Goldberg (1994) When Wish Replaces Thought: Why So Much of What You Believe is False (Buffalo, New York: Prometheus Books).

. . . [T]he interaction of genes and environment is much more complicated than the simple "violence genes" and "intelligence genes" touted in the popular press. Indeed, renewed appreciation of environmental factors is one of the chief effects of the increased belief in genetics' effects on behavior. The same data that show the effects of genes also point to the enormous influence of non-genetic factors.

—C. Mann, "Genes and behavior," Science264:1687 (1994), pp. 1686–1689.

"At this point, the most widely held opinion [on causation of homosexuality] is that multiple factors play a role.

'In 1988, PFLAG member Tinkle Hake surveyed a number of well-known figures in the field about their views on homosexuality. She asked: Many observers believe that a person's sexual orientation is determined by one of more of the following factors: genetic, hormonal, psychological, or social. Based on today's state-of-the-art-science, what is your opinion?'

"The answers included the following: 'all of the above in concert' (Alan Bell), 'all of these variables' (Richard Green), 'multiple factors' (Gilbert Herdt), 'a combination of all the factors named' (Evelyn Hooker), 'all of these factors' (Judd Marmor), 'a combination of causes' (Richard Pillard), 'possibly genetic and hormonal, but juvenile sexual rehearsal play is particularly important' (John Money), and 'genetic and hormonal factors, and perhaps also some early childhood experiences' (James Weinrich)." (Page 273)

—Simon LeVay (1996), in Queer
Science published by MIT Press.

AS A PARENT:

Accept your child for who they are, and provide support without judgment Matthew 7:1, 1 Corinthians 4:5 It is your position as a parent to love them, train them, and to keep them safe—no matter what your beliefs are. Speak the truth in love. This is God's command! (Eph, 4:15)

Talk to your child about how hard life is for the LGBT lifestyle. But always remember that a hard life is living a lie every single day!

It can be difficult for a gay person to live openly in society. To allow themselves dignity, they may need to assert themselves. So when a person is bullied about their sexuality, they may find themselves lashing out at people.

What if the child struggling with their sexual identity requests to have a friend spend the night? This is the time to sit down with your teen to have an honest, open discussion. Make sure you are not attacking their sexuality. You must set boundaries with your child whether same-sex or opposite sex and adhere to them.

WHAT DOES THE BIBLE SAY ABOUT BEING LGBT?

According to the Bible, marriage is heterosexual by definition.

The scripture regards homosexuality as falling outside of God's intention in creating man and woman as sexual beings who bear His image as male and female. "From the beginning of creation, God made them male and female. For this cause a man shall leave his father and mother, and shall cleave to his wife, and the two shall become one flesh . . ." (Mark 10:6–8, quoting Genesis 2:24.

Do not practice homosexuality, having sex with another man as with a woman. It is a detestable sin (Lev. 18:22).

"Haven't you read the Scriptures?" Jesus replied. "They record that from the beginning 'God made them male and female.'" And he said, "'this explains why a man leaves his father and mother and is joined to his wife, and the two are united into one.' Since they are no longer two but one, let no one split apart what God has joined together." (Matt. 19:4–6)

In Romans 1:21–32, Paul reveals the inevitable downward spiral of sin. First people reject God, then make up ideas of what God should be like. They will fall into wickedness; from gossip to envy, deception and greed, to malicious acts, quarreling, hate, and murder. Eventually they grow to hate God and encourages others to hate God. When people reject God, he allows them to live as they choose. God allows them to experience the natural consequences of their sin.

That is why God abandoned them to their shameful desires. Even the women turned against the natural way to have sex and instead indulged in sex with each other. And the men, instead of having normal sexual relations with women, burned with lust for each other. Men did shameful things with other men, and as a result of this sin, they suffered within themselves the penalty they deserved (Rom. 1:26–27).

The law is for people who are sexually immoral, or who practice homosexuality, or are slave traders, liars, promise breakers, or who do anything else that contradicts the wholesome teaching (1 Tim. 1:10).

Don't you realize that those who do wrong will not inherit the Kingdom of God? Don't fool yourselves. Those who indulge in sexual sin, or worship idols, commit adultery, are male prostitutes or practice homosexuality, thieves, greedy people, drunkards, abusive people, or those who cheat people – none of these will inherit the Kingdom of God (1 Corinthians 6:9–10).

AS A CHURCH:

Many Christians are hostile toward the LGBT community. It is our responsibility in our Christian walk, to speak the truth in love. This is God's command (Eph. 4:15)!

There is no place for hatred,
hurtful comments,
or other forms of rejection!

TEEN SUICIDE: (ALSO SEE CHAPTER 2, MENTAL HEALTH, SUICIDE SECTION).

Many teens are high-strung and under pressure. They have high expectations of themselves, their parents have high expectations, peer pressure and wanting to do it all!

What teens report they feel puts them over the edge:

- Classes and homework
  - o Some report crying with fear
- School pressure and perfection
  - o Competitive sports and activities
- Parents' hopes and dreams (expectations)
- Friends (competitive)
- Success—especially in hybrid schools
- Use alcohol and/or substances to escape the pressure

  o Some have misused ADD/ADHD medications to increase performance
- Guilt
  o Fear letting people down
  o Not being there for my friends
  o Procrastination

There have been a number of suicides by pact. Teens will pact with a friend to commit suicide together—including copycat suicides. Why does this happen? Obviously, peer pressure is a major culprit of pact and copycat suicides. Bottom line is that teens are prone to compulsive behavior.

People believe conversations about suicide is avoided because of stigma.

According to teen study reported by CDC.gov, suicide is the second leading cause of death for teens.

- 17% have serious considered suicide
- 13.6% have actually planned their suicide
- 8% have actually attempted suicide
- The LGBT admit to attempting suicide one or more times in the last year.
- 2.7% made suicide attempt resulting in medical attention

WARNING SIGNS:

A person may consider suicide when they feel there is no reason or purpose for living, they believe they are worthless. They feel hopelessness and depressed. They may be experiencing extreme guild or a burden to others.

When a person threats suicide, it may be verbally talking about it, texting, writing and/or journaling about it. They may be googling different ways to hurt or kill themselves. Consider this if they are making plans that is out of the ordinary.

Often, you will witness extreme moodiness. They display excessive and persistent rage and uncontrolled anger. You may find your teen seeking revenge.

Your teen may be fearlessly attempting very reckless or risky activities. This may include an increase of alcohol and drug use.

Often, the teen will stop caring about their personal hygiene. They have poor self-esteem. They will withdraw from their friends and family and stop attending/participating at social activities.

Your teen may be giving away special possessions. Another sign that is slow and progressive is anorexia.

WHAT IF YOU ARE THE PERSON THEY TELL?

DON'T over-react with shock or the person will immediately fear judgment and put distance between you.

Don't under-react or minimize the problem. Do something!

Don't lecture him/her about the value of life. They don't care about the value of life right now if they are considering suicide! They will shut you out.

Do not shame them for the way they feel. Unless this person came to you for biblical answers, this is not the time to recite biblical verses at them. If they are so hopeless, they most likely believe God has failed them. They may take the gesture as judgment from you AND God.

Biblical verses are great to share for support—before they get to the point of considering suicide.

Do not ever keep a suicide threat a secret! And don't consider yourself a snitch. Your friend may get angry, or your friend may believe you love them enough to take the risk of them getting angry—to save their life. Always take the threat seriously.

Immediately seek a trusted adult; your parents, their parents, teacher, school nurse, your church leader or pastor. If they are in immediate danger, remove dangerous items and call 911.

GANG ACTIVITY

When someone hears the word *gang*, it raises a number of images for people. For some, a gang is a small group of four or five adolescent troublemakers who loiter on a street corner. For others, the term may actually identify graffiti artists. The gang crime activities generally include guns, burglaries, robbery, theft, property crime, drug and sex trafficking, contraband, extortion, prostitution, gambling, assaults, and murder. Prostitution and the sexual exploitation of juveniles provide a major source of income for many gangs.

Virtually, every crime is a civil wrong against people, business, or the community. As a parent, it is important to understand the perpetrators are civilly liable in damages and/or court injunction.

Gangs are linked to crime in elementary, secondary, high schools, and college campuses. Schools provide fertile grounds for gang recruitment. Approximately 25% of gang members are between the ages of fifteen and seventeen. The average gang member age is between seventeen and eighteen years old.

Gangs target young teens who are vulnerable to trying to fit in and be accepted. Gangs found in schools are a major obstacle for educators, youth service professionals, and law enforcement.

Public schools are widespread with gang activity which includes assaults, robberies, threats, intimidation, drug distribution, and weapons offenses.

Gang members gravitate toward colleges to escape gang life, join college athletic programs, or to acquire advanced skill sets for their gang.

Gangs are not exclusive to minorities or males. Female gangs are on the rise. Female gang members generally support male gang members, serving as drug and weapon mules, and gathering intelligence for their gang. Gangs take advantage of the perceived ability of females to attract less suspicion while participating in illegal activities. However, many are serving as soldiers or co-conspirators. Female gang members are forming their own gangs, committing violent crimes that equally compare to male gangs.

The internet provides a very widespread medium for gang communication, promotion, and recruitment. Social media websites such as Facebook, Instagram, Twitter, YouTube, and others allow gang members to represent their gang affiliation, taunt others, post threats, and to organize and promote gang activities. Social media

JUDITH ISAACS-HERRIG, M.ED, QIDP

increases the potential for violence because it reaches such a large audience.

WHAT DO YOUNG GANG MEMBERS HAVE IN COMMON?

There are a number of commonalities in young gang members. Poverty, learning disabilities, family issues, poor grades, poor self-esteem, behavior problems, and truancy, and may include involvement in property destruction, drug use, and theft.

WHAT ARE THE CONSEQUENCES OF GANG INVOLVEMENT?

Gang involvement is very dangerous and limits opportunities for the future. Some youth believe that gang involvement might provide safety, protection, excitement, and opportunities to earn money. For some, being young, their immature brains believe they are invincible.

Research has shown that youth involved in gangs are more likely to commit crimes, causing them to be arrested and incarcerated. Some become victims of violence. Young girls are especially vulnerable to sexual victimization. Youth involved in gangs tend to not graduate from high school, are less likely to find stable jobs, and are more likely to have alcohol and drug problems.

WHAT PARENTS CAN DO TO PREVENT GANG INVOLVEMENT:

- Spend quality time with your child.
- Get involved in your child's school activities.
- Be a positive role model and set the right example.
- Know your child's friends and their families.
- Encourage good study habits.

- Teach your child how to cope with peer pressure.
- Help your child develop good conflict/resolution skills.
- (See www.safeyouth.org/scri pts/teens/conflict.asp)
- Encourage your child to participate in positive afterschool activities with adult supervision (recreation centers, organized sports, youth groups).
- Take action in your neighborhood (create a neighborhood alliance, report, and remove graffiti).
- Talk with your child about the dangers and consequences of gang involvement. Let your child know that you don't want to see him or her hurt or arrested.
- Get your child involved with a mentor. Research has strong support for the positive influences that mentors have in a child's life.

EXPLAIN TO YOUR CHILD WHAT (S)HE SHOULD NOT DO:

- Associate with gang members.
- Attend parties or social events sponsored by gangs.
- Use hand signs, symbols, or language that is meaningful to gangs.
- Wear clothing including specific colors, which may have meaning to gangs in your area.

Researchers believe gang activity can be reduced with involvement in activities which provide a positive sense of self and identity.

As a community, we all need to get involved—whether you are a parent, youth, or church leaders, social service providers, law enforcement officials, teachers, or a public official together, we can be instrumental in addressing local gang problems. With the different roles within the community, we all have a different and valuable perspective on the problems that gangs pose.

Rally with other parents to keep kids out of gangs. Together, we can make a difference. Let your teen know who their real family is.

WARNING SIGNS THAT YOUR CHILD MAY BE INVOLVED WITH A GANG:

- Admits to "hanging out" with kids in gangs.
- Listening to gang-influenced music and movies.
- Participating in gang-influenced social media.
- Shows an unusual interest in one or two particular colors of clothing or a particular logo.
- Uses unusual hand signals to communicate with friends.
- Has specific drawings or graffiti, gang numbers, or symbols on school books, clothes, walls, or tattoos. Although rare, some young people may self-injure in public or in groups to bond or to show others that they have experienced pain. You can contact your local school resource officer or law enforcement representative to get identifiable information and meanings of symbols or numbers you may see in your area.
- Comes home with unexplained physical injuries (fighting-related bruises, injuries to hand/ knuckles)
- Has unexplained cash or goods, such as clothing or jewelry
- Carries a weapon
- Has been in trouble with the police or overly interested in police activity.
- Exhibits negative changes in behavior such as:
  o Withdrawing from family
  o Declining school attendance, performance, behavior
  o Staying out late without reason
  o Displaying an unusual desire for secrecy
  o Exhibiting signs of drug use
  o Breaking rules consistently
  o Speaking in gang-style slang

WHAT IF MY CHILD IS INVOLVED IN A GANG?

If your child has been threatened or is in immediate danger, call the police immediately.

HOW DOES A PERSON QUIT A GANG?

The author of Helping Gang Youth wrote about his experience as a gang member who has helped others get out of gangs; he says you don't quit by saying you are going to quit. He warns that if you do that, you will experience whatever ritual or hazing the gang has for this. It also means that you really haven't outgrown the gang, you still believe in its logic. He states that all of the former gang members he knows never actually left the gang. He reports that they simply stopped participating in negative and self-destructive activities like violence, drug sales, and theft and remained friends with other gang members.

Often females desire to quit the gang lifestyle once they become pregnant. Becoming a mother forces her to adulthood and often will change in self-worth.

According to Project Gang-Proof Resources, you can get out of a gang. But you need to make some changes. You may need to change your life, activities, and friends. But remember that it could save your life.

Find someone you trust to help you. Whether it is a friend, counselor, parent, or spiritual leader. You should someone you can talk to about your feelings.

MAKE AN EXIT PLAN

- Don't tell other gang members you want to leave as this could put you in danger.
- Stop dressing and acting like a gang members.
- Cover tattoos.

- Change your cell phone number. Do not answer if you know it is a gang member.
- Do not hang with gang member friends. Change your friends. This may take time.
- Think about how you will spend your time differently. Do not spend time alone.
  o Work-out
  o Sports
  o Hobbies and other creative activities
  o Music
  o Join after school activities, community programs or cultural clubs.
- You may need to move to be safe.
- Keep important emergency phone numbers with you.
- What will you say if your gang
  o Calls you to hang out at night?
  o Makes fun of you for changing?
  o Threatens you?
  o Expects you to do something illegal?

HAVE A BACK-UP PLAN:

- Make sure there is an adult or friend you can call in an emergency or if you just need someone to talk to.
- Don't go to the mall, shopping, parties or homes where you may run into a gang member.
- Talk to your teacher/guidance counselor about catching up in school or how to get back into school.
- Keep yourself busy. Get a job, get involved at school, etc.

It is difficult to find conventional success and self-reliance with criminal records, poor education, and liabilities that compiled over the years. But when gang members experience the possibilities of a real life (have a job, a home, a future, and a sense of security), they tend to drop out of the street life. Those who do not outgrow the gang life eventually become addicted to drugs, incarcerated, or end up dead.

ADULT CHILDREN LIVING AT HOME

Some people have their adult children living with them long after they should have left the nest. Parents put up with rudeness and cocky attitudes, their adult child is unwilling to pick up after themselves or help with chores and added expenses.

> "You teach people how to treat you."
> –Dr. Phil

WHY DO PARENTS DO THIS?

I have seen the sadness in parents when their adult children are mixed up in addictions and legal matters. A parent aches for their children when they are hurting even after they have become adults.

Lately, I heard a woman speaking of her adult child who had been involved in a violent robbery causing him several years of time in prison. She was horribly embarrassed because she believed it

JUDITH ISAACS-HERRIG, M.ED, QIDP

would be a reflection on her. When we see our children do well, we feel proud. But when our children don't live up to our expectations, we feel tainted with shame. Bottom line is that she is worried about being judged as a parent.

You don't have to reveal private matters to casual acquaintances. If someone asks you about your children, simply state "name of child is in a tough season of life" and continue discussing your other children or follow up with something positive you are doing. You may want to share this information with those you have a real relationship with for support.

AS A FAMILY MEMBER:

It is crucial to set boundaries and communicate expected behavior and unacceptable behavior. It starts with you as a parent. Whether you are the parent or the child, be honest. We need to know what is appropriate to discuss with our child and understand what age appropriateness. Always be honest (Prov. 12:22).

You should always keep your promises (Rom. 4:21). If you promise to do something, do it. The other person in depending on your promise. It is disheartening to have promises broken.

Parents should always point out the blessings in their lives. Each and every one of them. Good health, good friends, good deeds, a job, a place to live, and so on. Find the blessings in your disappointments. Example: It feels punitive to have to get up early to go to work, but praise God because with the job we have a warm place to sleep and food on the table. We can afford a vacation once in a while. Count your blessings (Psalm 34:1–3).

We need to care about one another's burdens (Gal. 6:2). You can teach your children to bear each other's burdens with specific problems as they arise. Use them as teaching moments. But remember that your children should only bear age appropriate information. Again, never burden children with adult matters. Be available and supportive when your family member has a burden to share. Have a listening ear. Sometimes a person needs to talk things out without the help of being *fixed*.

We must help the weak and look after each other (Acts 20:35).

When we have problems or pain, we need to comfort one another as taught in 1 Thessalonians 4:18.

Nobody is perfect. And when we live together, we learn of each other's imperfections. For personal healing, we need to forgive and forget the mistakes people have made. Forgive and forget (Micah 7:18).

It takes a loving heart to bear kindness and tenderness in this cold, cruel world. As a parent, it should be your goal to leave the legacy of kindness and of being tender hearted. Be kind and tender hearted (Eph. 4:32). Love one another deeply from the heart (1 Peter 1:22).

HONOR YOUR PARENTS

For those who have been abused or neglected by their parents, or a parent that has inflicted the results of their addictions or mental health issues on you and your family, it can be extremely difficult to honor and respect the offending parent. But we need to remember that our Heavenly Father *expects* us to honor our parents, He does not offer exceptions: Honor your father and mother, that you may have a long, good life in the land he Lord your God will give you (Exod. 20:12).

There are people in my family that I have had a hard time forgiving. Unfortunately, when I am angered by something they have done, it brings out the sinful, unforgiving behavior. It takes practice to forgive, but it is what we need to do. Forgive and forget (Micah 7:18.).

SCHOOL POLICIES FOR BULLYING CHECKLIST:

Feel free to copy these questions for future reference.

1. Does the school have a bullying problem?
   - How often does it occur each year?
   - Are records kept and where?
   - How does it compare to other schools in the area?
   - Where and when does the bullying most often occur?
   - What has the school done to prevent this?

2. Does the school have bullying policy? Is it adequate?
   - Does the policy guide teachers and staff in handling bullying incidents?
   - What are the consequences for bullying?
   - Are there consequences for the bystanders?
   - Are the policies applied consistently?
   - Are there posters in place of each classroom, hallway and congregating areas to remind students the school prohibits bullying and what the consequences are?

3. What is done for the victims of bullying?
   - What is being done to further protect the victim?

4. Does the school understand the different types of behavior that constitutes bullying?

5. Is the school aware of the long-term effects of bullying?
   - Can they identify chronic victims and bullies?
   - At what point are the parents brought into the loop?
   - Is the principal included in the loop?
   - Are school counselors included in the loop? Who are they?
   - At what point are social services involved?
   - At what point is law enforcement or a liaison officer involved?

READING RESOURCES:

5 Conversations You Must Have with Your Daughter: Bible Study
5 Conversations You Must Have with Your Son: Bible Study
By Vicki Courtney

The Anger Workbook for Teens: Activities to Help You Deal with
Anger and Frustration
By Raychelle Cassada Lohmann MS LPC

The Anxiety Workbook for Teens: Activities to Help You Deal with
Anxiety and Worry
By Lisa M. Schab, LCSW

Bringing Up Boys Bible Study
Bringing Up Girls Bible Study
By Dr. James Dobson

Bullying: A Spiritual Crisis
By Ronald Hecker Cram

Dare to Discipline Bible Study
By Dr. James Dobson

The Disappearing Girl: Learning the Language of Teenage Depression
By Lisa Machoian

Helping Teens Who Cut: Understanding and Ending Self-Injury
By Michael Hollander

Hoodwinked
By Karen Ehman and Ruth Schwenk

How to Live with Your Parents without Losing Your Mind
By Ken Davis

Missional Motherhood: The Everyday Ministry of Motherhood in the Grand Plan of God
By Gloria Furman

Mom, I Hate My Life!
Becoming Your Daughter's Ally through the Emotional Ups and Downs
By Sharon Hersh

Not My Child
By Frank Lawlis

The PTSD Workbook for Teens: Simple, Effective Skills for Healing Trauma
By Libbi Palmer PsyD

Raising a Princess: 8 Essential Virtues to Teach Your Daughter
By John Croyle

Raising Boys and Girls: The Art of Understanding Their Differences
By Sissy Goff, David Thomas and Melissa Trevathan

Ready to Launch: Jesus-Centered Parenting in a Child-Centered World
By J.D. & Veronica Greear

The Self-Esteem Workbook for Teens: Activities to Help You Build Confidence and Achieve Your Goals
By Lisa M. Schab LCSW

Sensory Smarts: A Book for Kids with ADHD or Autism Spectrum Disorders Struggling with Sensory Integration Problems
By Kathleen A. Chara and Paul J. Chara Jr.

Setting Boundaries with Your Adult Children: Six Steps to Hope and Healing for Struggling Parents

By Allison Bottke

The Sexual Trauma Workbook for Teen Girls: A Guide to Recovery from Sexual Assault and Abuse
By Raychelle Cassada Lohmann MS LPC and Sheela Raja PhD

The Strong-Willed Child Bible Study
By Dr. James Dobson

The Two Minute Drill to Parenting: Molding Your Son into a Man
The Two Minute Drill to Manhood: Becoming the Man God Meant You to Be
By John Croyle

Unashamed: Overcoming the Sins No Girl Wants to Talk About
By Jessie Minassian

What Do I Do When Teenagers Struggle with Eating Disorders?
By Steven Gerali

When Our Grown Up Kids Disappoint Us: Letting Go of Their Problems, Loving Them Anyway, and Getting on with Our Lives

By Jane Adams, Ph.D.
The Volunteer's Guide to Helping Teenagers in Crisis

By Rich Van Pelt and Jim Hancock
Your Boy: Raising a Godly Son in an Ungodly World

Your Girl: Raising a Godly Daughter in an Ungodly World
By Vicki Courtney

QUESTIONS TO PONDER:

1. Do you know anyone raising their grandchildren or some-one else's children?
   What kind of baggage did they come with?
   Did these children learn what they lived?

2. What is the difference between discipline and natural consequences?
   Were you aware of the effects of shaming others?

3. What is the difference between reporting and tattling?

4. What is the difference between sibling rivalry and sibling abuse?

5. List the types of bullying you have witnessed or experienced.
   Were you bullied in school or were you the bully?
   Were you aware of the effects of bullying?

6. What was the most traumatic experience you remember from your childhood?
   In what ways did it affect you?
   Do you still relive the experience?

7. What does the term "Pick your battles" mean to you?
   How will you implement that into your daily life?

8. Are chores a battle in your house?
   What can you change to make chores less problematic?

9. Does your child's self-esteem reflect your self-esteem?

10. Do you believe your friends reflect the kind of person you are?

Are they friends you trust and can be proud of?
Do your children's friends reflect who they are?

11. Have you or someone close to you been molested?
    Were there signs someone should have noticed?
    Was the perpetrator confronted or arrested? What were the consequences?

12. What are you prepared to do if a child tells you he/she was molested?
    What if the perpetrator lived in the child's home?

13. Do you or someone you know have troubled teens?
    Do you recognize any of the behaviors listed?

14. What would you do if your teen came home with bruises?

15. What would you do if you suspected your child was using drugs?
    Would you confront your child?
    Would you search for the drugs?
    What do you do if you *know* your child is using drugs?

16. What would you say and do if your child admits (s)he believes (s)he is gay, lesbian, or bisexual?

17. What symptoms would you look for if you were worried your teen may be suicidal?
    What would you do if your teen reports they feel suicidal?

18. Have you seen signs of gang activity with your teen or someone close?
    If this person wanted to get out of a gang, what would you advise?
    What would your back-up plan be?

19. Do you or someone close to you have an adult child living at home with them?
    What was the reason they moved home?
    Is this adult child living at home because the parent(s) feel guilt? Or fear their adult child's actions?
    Do boundaries need to be set?

20. Was any part of this chapter eye-opening for you?
    Does it motivate you to change anything?

21. What verse or verses are important to you?

CHAPTER TEN

TV, MAGIC, AND OCCULTS

I am extremely careful with what I do in my daily life because I know for a fact that there is a fine line between good and bad spirits—as I have witnessed them both.

Satan is very real!
Never forget that!

In general, we tend to look at some of the magic, meditations, mediums, Ouija board games, horoscopes, chanting, crystals, and the like as rather fun and harmless. We have to understand that the occult is hidden in plain sight all over within our society. We live with new age ideas and need to recognize the weak links in our Christian values. We have to start with our kids while their brains are being molded and shaped. Don't allow your TV to babysit your children.

Some people go as far as believing there are hidden messages in shows as innocent as Disney movies. We see what can be considered hidden messages in our pop-culture movies such as Harry Potter and TV programs such as the television programs Supernatural, The Originals, The Craft, Grimm and Charmed. Some people become obsessed with the schemes of the devil.

According to Reverend, Dr. Brian Connor, anytime someone reaches out to an evil spirit, that spirit puts down roots and will torment and oppress that person. We can still make wrong choices which open doors within us to satanic oppression by dabbling in the occult, attempting to communicate with the dead, using crystals, accepting New Age beliefs, following spirit guides, and participating in rituals.

DEFINITIONS

Look at the listed definitions and compare them to each other.

Definition of magic:

1. a: the use of means (as charms or spells) believed to have supernatural power over natural forces
   b: magic rites or incantations
2. a: an extraordinary power or influence seemingly from a supernatural source
   b: something that seems to cast a spell: enchantment
3. the art of producing illusions by sleight of hand

Definition of witchcraft: Magical things that are done by witches: the use of magical powers obtained especially from evil spirits.

Definition of a witch: a person and especially a woman believed to have magic powers.

1: one that is credited with usually malignant supernatural powers; especially: a woman practicing usually black witchcraft often with the aid of a devil or familiar: sorceress—compare warlock

Used in a sentence: an herbalist and self-proclaimed witch

Definition of occult: of or relating to supernatural powers or practices; occult practices such as magic and fortune-telling.

1. not revealed: secret
2. not easily apprehended or understood: abstruse, mysterious
3. hidden from view: concealed

When you *study* certain aspects of what we do in our daily lives, we need to know the truth about where the devil can sneak into the cracks of our innocent activities. If you are doing any of these activities, I encourage you to research the premise and history of them.

CHANNELING, MEDIUMS, CHAKRA, CRYSTALS, ETC.

Channeling: Channeling can be seen as the modern form of the old mediumship, where the person that does the channeling receives messages from a teaching-spirit, an ascended master from God, or angels. Essentially the results of channeling is through the filter of his own consciousness or Higher Self.

Mediums: Mediums mediate communication between spirits of the dead and living human beings. Some people believe the key role of this sort is played by effect of subjective confirmation. People are predisposed to consider that the information is reliable. Whether the information is a good guess or coincidental, and personally important and significant, it seems to fulfill and answer their personal beliefs.

Spiritualists classify types of mediumship into two main categories: mental and physical. Mental mediums are said to tune in to the spirit world by listening, sensing, or seeing spirits or symbols and physical mediums are believed to produce materialization of spirits, movement of objects, knocking, rapping, bell-ringing, etc.

During séances, mediums are said to go into trances, varying from light to deep, that permit spirits to control their minds. The other non-physical mediumship is a form of channeling in which the medium goes into a trance, or leaves their body allowing a spiritual entity to borrow their body, who then talks through them.

Do not defile yourselves by turning to mediums or to those who consult the spirits of the dead. I am the Lord your God (Lev. 19:31). I will also turn against those who commit spiritual prostitution by putting their trust in mediums or in those who consult the spirits of the dead. I will cut them off from the community (Lev. 20:6).

In the Old Testament, Samuel 28:3–25, the Witch of Endor was a medium who summoned Samuel's spirit per demand of King Saul of the Kingdom of Israel. When Samuel died, he was buried in Ramah. Saul called out to God for wisdom in choosing a course of action against the forces of the Philistines. He received no answer from his dreams or the prophets. Having driven out all mediums and magicians from Israel, Saul searched for a medium while in disguise. His search led him to a woman of Endor, who claimed that she can see the ghost of Samuel rising from the dead. The voice of the prophet's ghost berated Saul for disobeying God, and predicted Saul's downfall. The spirit restates a pre-mortem prophecy by Samuel, adding that Saul will perish with his whole army in battle the next day. Saul is terrified. The next day, his army is defeated as prophesied, and Saul committed suicide.

Chakras: Every thought and experience you've ever had in your life gets filtered through these chakra databases. Each event is recorded into your cells. In some religions, a chakra is thought to be an energy point. It's believed that there are many chakras in the human body, according to the tantric texts, but there are seven major chakras which are aligned in an ascending column from the base of the spine to the top of the head. The function of the chakras is to draw in energy to keep the spiritual, mental, emotional, and physical health of the body in balance.

Crystals healing is a pseudoscientific alternative medicine technique that employs stones and crystals. In one method, the practitioner places crystals on different parts of the body, often corresponding to chakras. Color selection and the placement of stones are done according to the concepts of grounding chakras or energy grids.

Yoga is a physical, mental, and spiritual practice or discipline. There is a wide variety of practices. Yoga is not only physical exercise, it has a meditative and spiritual core.

Meditation: The word meditation carries different meanings in different contexts. It has been practiced as a component of numerous religious traditions and beliefs for centuries. The term "meditation" can refer to the state itself as well as to practices or techniques employed to cultivate the state.

There are proven benefits to meditation. Meditation is often used to clear the mind and ease many health concerns such as high blood pressure, depression, and anxiety. There are rare cases of meditation-induced psychosis, primarily in persons with pre-existing psychotic conditions, and also cases where meditation had adverse effects in individuals without psychiatric history.

Some research has indicated that meditation can have negative effects, often relating to surfacing of pre-existing trauma or depression.

Eastern meditation was a part of the American culture even before the American Revolution through the various sects of European occult Christianity during the era of the transcendentalists between the 1840s and the 1880s. In the late nineteenth century, Theosophists refers to meditation as various spiritual practices drawn from Hinduism, Buddhism, and other Indian religions. In the 1960s, another surge in Western interest in meditative practices began due to a deep spiritual hunger that is not being satisfied in the West.

New Age meditations tend to be influenced by mysticism, yoga, and eastern influences. In the west, during the 1960s and '70s, meditation was rebellion against traditional belief systems as a reaction against the failure of Christianity that was meant to provide spiritual and ethical guidance. New Age meditation as practiced by early hippies used techniques often aided by repetitive chanting of a mantra, or focusing on an object to blank out the mind and release oneself from conscious thinking.

WHAT IS THE CONNECTION?

Although some of these practices may be helpful to people, they are also considered pseudo- effective. The reason it is dangerous to some is that practicing any of them may open your mind allowing Satan an opportunity to fill your mind with deceit.

Worshipping Satan includes opening one's mind and heart to satanic communications, and dabbling in occult type activities to seek spiritual truth—turning away from God.

As Christians, we are told to meditate in prayer at church and throughout the Bible:

Keep this Book of the Law always on your lips; meditate on it day and night, so that you may be careful to do everything written in it. Then you will be prosperous and successful (Josh. 1:8).

Whose delight is in the law of the Lord, and who meditates on his law day and night (Psalm 1:2).

I will consider all your works and meditate on all your mighty deeds (Psalm 77:12).

I will meditate on your majestic, glorious splendor and your wonderful miracles (Psalm 145:5).

Ask yourself what your intent is in meditation. Are you meditating with God or without God? What is your intent?

PAGAN AND OCCULT RELIGIONS

Pagan and occult religions use magic such as Wicca, Thelema, Neopaganism, and occultism that require adherents to meditate in which allows them to perform their magical works. Magic is often thought to require a particular state of mind to make contact with spirits or to focus for long periods of time or to practice a ritual to visualize one's goal in order to see the desired outcome. Meditation practices in these religions involves visualization, absorbing energy from the universe or higher self, directing internal energy, and inducing various trance states. Meditation and magic may overlap as meditation is often seen as a stepping stone to supernatural power.

Paganism has been broadly defined as anyone involved in any religious act, practice, or ceremony which is not Christian. The term pagan is derived from the Latin word paganus, which means a country dweller. The pagan usually has a belief in many gods (polytheistic), but only one is chosen as the one to worship. As Christianity progressed, a pagan became referred to anyone not being a Christian, and paganism denoted a non-Christian belief or religion.

HOW DOES PAGANISM COMPARE WITH CHRISTIANITY?

It is difficult to compare paganism with Christianity since the term pagan can be used to identify many different sects and beliefs. Primarily, Biblical Christianity professes one God, where paganism often teaches many or no god. Biblical Christianity teaches that the Bible contains God's words and message to mankind. It is infallible and inerrant. Paganism does not have one main religious text or set of beliefs to follow. Biblical Christianity teaches that Jesus, God's Son, came to earth as a baby and died on the cross as an adult for the sin of the whole world, and rose to life again. Some pagans believe in Jesus as one of the gods, but do not put significance in Him as Christians do.

A person cannot be a follower of Jesus Christ (a Christian) and a pagan at the same time. Although they claimed to be wise, they became fools and exchanged the glory of the immortal God for images made to look like mortal man and birds and animals and reptiles. Therefore God gave them over in the sinful desires of their hearts to sexual impurity for the degrading of their bodies with one another (Rom. 1:22–24).

Modern Paganism is also known as Contemporary Paganism and Neopaganism. It is a group of New Age religious movements influenced by various historical pagan beliefs of pre-modern Europe. Neopaganism is considered a nature-centered faith.

Prudence Jones and Nigel Pennick in their A History of Pagan Europe (1995) classify pagan religions as characterized by the following traits:

- Polytheism: Pagan religions recognizes a plurality of divine beings, which may or may not be considered aspects of an underlying unity.
- Nature-based: Pagan religions have a concept of the divinity of Nature, which they view as a manifestation of the divine not as the fallen creation.

- Sacred feminine: Pagan religions recognize the female divine principle identified as the Goddess beside or in place of the male divine principle as expressed in the Abrahamic God.

Wicca is a contemporary new age movement with no central authority. It is considered a form of modern Paganism categorized as a nature religion. Their celebrations encompass both the cycles of the moon and the sun, they celebrate season based festivals known as Sabbats and Lesser Sabbats which are of the solstices and the equinoxes.

Its traditional core beliefs, principles, and practices were originally outlined in the 1940s and 1950s in books, secret writings and teachings passed along to new initiates. Wicca typically worships a Goddess and a God. In the 1960s, the Church of Wicca developed a theology rooted in the worship of what they described as one deity, without gender.

According to Rosemary Ellen Guiley, "Demons are not courted or worshipped in contemporary Wicca and Paganism. The existence of negative energies is acknowledged."

Wicca is believed to have many different divine aspects which can in turn be identified with many diverse pagan deities. Many Wiccans believe in magic, a manipulative force exercised through the practice of witchcraft or sorcery. During ritual practices, generally in a sacred circle, Wiccans cast spells or workings intended to bring changes in the physical world. Common Wiccan spells include healing, protection, fertility, or to ward off negative influences.

A common element of Wiccan morality is the Law of Threefold Return which holds a person's actions (positive or negative) will return to that person in triple force or with equal force on the three levels of body, mind, and spirit (aka karma).

As for the afterlife, Wiccans tend to believe that if one makes the most of the present life, then the next life is more (or less) going to benefit from the process, therefore they concentrate on the present. There are Wiccans who do not believe in any form of afterlife.

Many Wiccans do not exclusively follow any single tradition or even are initiated (eclectic Wiccans). They create their own syncretic spiritual paths by adopting and reinventing the beliefs and rituals of a variety of religious traditions connected to Wicca and Paganism.

Most modern pagans believe in the divine character of the natural world and paganism is often described as an Earth religion. Earth-centered religion or nature worship is a system of religion based on the veneration of natural phenomena. It covers religion that worships the earth, nature, or fertility gods and goddesses such as the various forms of goddess worship or matriarchal religion. Earth religions are also formulated to allow one to utilize the knowledge of preserving the earth.

Many earth religions are based on the Gaia principle which is believed that "organisms interact with their inorganic surroundings on Earth to form a synergistic self-regulating, complex system that helps to maintain and perpetuate the conditions for life on the planet" as formulated by scientist James Lovelock.

NEW AGE:

With its highly eclectic nature, the movement typically believes in a holistic form of divinity which imbues all of the universe including human beings themselves. They commonly believe in semi-divine entities such as angels and masters with the ability to communicate with these entities particularly through the form of channeling.

With New Agers, there is a strong focus on healing using forms of alternative medicine. The emphasis is to unite science and spirituality.

To Christians, the most important distinction was whether or not someone worshipped the one true God. Those who did not were outsiders to the Church and considered a pagan.

Many of those who dabble in occults dress dark, Celtic, hippie or gothic, depending on their belief system.

OCCULT PRACTICES

Occult practices are gateways or portals to your soul. Demons know your soul, they take residence in your soul.

When you enter the land the LORD your God is giving you, do not learn to imitate the detestable ways of the nations there. Let no one be found among you who sacrifices their son or daughter in the fire, who practices divination or sorcery, interprets omens, engages in witchcraft, or casts spells, or who is a medium or spiritist or who consults the dead. Anyone who does these things is detestable to the LORD; because of these same detestable practices the LORD your God will drive out those nations before you (Deut. 18:9–12).

Someone may say to you, "Let's ask the mediums and those who consult the spirits of the dead. With their whisperings and mutterings, they will tell us what to do." But shouldn't people ask God for guidance? Should the living seek guidance from the dead (Isa. 8:19)?

Do not give the devil a foothold (Eph. 4:27). Our struggles are against the rulers and the powers of this dark world and against the spiritual forces of evil in the heavenly realms.

Take up the shield of faith, which you can extinguish all the flaming arrows of the evil one (Eph. 6:12-16).

"But cowards, unbelievers, the corrupt, murderers, the immoral, those who practice witchcraft, idol worshipers, and all liars—their fate is in the fiery lake of burning sulfur. This is the second death" (Rev. 21:8).

WHERE IS SATAN?

We don't know because he is hidden in the plain sight. He is everywhere. In books, movies, music, and TV programs. We must educate ourselves so we are able to discern what is deceiving.

Satan himself masquerades as an angel of light. And his servants also masquerade as servants of righteousness. Their end will be what their actions deserve (2 Corinthians 11:14–15).

In Romans 1:21–31, Paul writes how they knew God, but they wouldn't worship him as God or even give him thanks. And they began to think up foolish ideas of what God was like. As a result, their minds became dark and confused. Claiming to be wise, they instead became utter fools. And instead of worshiping the glorious, ever-living God, they worshiped idols made to look like mere people and birds and animals and reptiles.

So God abandoned them to do whatever shameful things their hearts desired. As a result, they did vile and degrading things with each other's bodies. They traded the truth about God for a lie. So they worshiped and served the things God created instead of the Creator himself, who is worthy of eternal praise! Amen. That is why God abandoned them to their shameful desires.

Since they thought it foolish to acknowledge God, he abandoned them to their foolish thinking and let them do things that should never be done. Their lives became full of every kind of wickedness, sin, greed, hate, envy, murder, quarreling, deception, malicious behavior, and gossip. They are backstabbers, haters of God, insolent, proud, and boastful. They invent new ways of sinning, and they disobey their parents. They refuse to understand, break their promises, are heartless, and have no mercy (Rom. 1:21–31).

If someone comes to you and preaches a Jesus other than the Jesus we preached, or if you receive a different spirit from the Spirit you received, or a different gospel from the one you accepted, you put up with it easily enough (2 Cor. 11:4).

Do not let your people practice fortune-telling, or use sorcery, or interpret omens, or engage in witchcraft, or cast spells, or function as mediums or psychics, or call forth the spirits of the dead. Anyone who does these things is detestable to the LORD. It is because the other nations have done these detestable things that the LORD your God will drive them out ahead of you (Deut. 18:10–12).

The Spirit clearly says that in later times some will abandon the faith and follow deceiving spirits and things taught by demons. 1 Timothy 4:1 Do not listen to your false prophets, fortune- tellers, interpreters of dreams, mediums, and sorcerers who say, "The king of Babylon will not conquer you" (Jer. 27:9).

The eye is the lamp of the body. If your eyes are healthy, your whole body will be full of light. But if your eyes are unhealthy, your whole body will be full of darkness. If then the light within you is darkness, how great is that darkness! (Matt. 6:22–23)

My experience shows that those who plant trouble and cultivate evil will harvest the same (Job 4:8). Put on the full armor of God so that you can take your stand against the devil's schemes (Eph. 6:11).

Now this is eternal life: that they know you, the only true God, and Jesus Christ, whom you have sent (John 17:3).

CAN CHRISTIANS HAVE DEMONS?

The devil wants you to think you are inept, incapable, unwanted, unloved, and unworthy. The devil wants you to believe his lies. He is deceiving as we learned from the fall in Genesis.

According to John Eckhardt, "Demons actually help promote the teaching that a Christian cannot have a demon, because they gain strength from staying hidden. They can operate in their destructive ways without being challenged! Some may argue that a believer cannot be possessed. But the dismaying fact remains that born-again Christians, including leaders, are experiencing difficulties that can find no solution in natural infirmities or the endless conflict between the flesh and the Spirit."

He further explains that "every person is made up of three parts: spirit, soul and body. When Jesus comes into a believer's life, He comes into that person's spirit." John 3:6 tells us clearly, "That which is born of the Spirit is spirit." (NKJV). A demon cannot dwell in a Christian's spirit because that is where Jesus and the Holy Spirit dwell. It is the other components that make up a human being—the soul (mind, will and emotions) and the body—that are the targets of demonic attack. Demons can dwell in those areas of a Christian's life."

This man will come to do the work of Satan with counterfeit power and signs and miracles. He will use every kind of evil deception to fool those on their way to destruction, because they refuse to love and accept the truth that would save them. So God will cause them to be greatly deceived, and they will believe these lies. Then they will be condemned for enjoying evil 2 Thessalonians 2:9-12 (NLT).

God knows our hearts. In Revelations 2:18, it refers to Jezebel and her Pagan practices. Because she would not repent, Jesus promises to cast her on a bed of suffering. With that, the churches will know who He is and that He searches their hearts and minds promising to repay each one of them according to their deeds. Those who do not hold to her teaching and have not learned Satan's so-called deep secrets, will not be imposed with any other burden (Rev. 2:23).

Satan will steal your joy!
See the occult for what it really is!!

In Revelations 2:13, Jesus says "I know where you live—where Satan has his throne." The thief comes only to steal and kill and destroy; I have come that they may have life, and have it to the full (John 10:10).

There is total freedom with the Lord. Don't let the devil hold you down. Satan is bondage! The Lord is the Spirit, and where the Spirit of the Lord is, there is freedom (2 Cor. 3:17).

And God raised us up with Christ and seated us with him in the heavenly realms in Christ Jesus (Eph. 2:6).

Jesus Christ is the same yesterday and today and forever (Heb. 13:8).

WARNINGS AGAINST DENYING JESUS IS CHRIST

Dear children, this is the last hour; and as you have heard that the antichrist is coming, even now many antichrists have come. This is how we know it is the last hour. They went out from us, but they did not really belong to us. For if they had belonged to us, they would have remained with us; but their going showed that none of them belonged to us.

But you have an anointing from the Holy One, and all of you know the truth. I do not write to you because you do not know the truth, but because you do know it and because no lie comes from the truth. Who is the liar? It is whoever denies that Jesus is the Christ. Such a person is the antichrist—denying the Father and the Son. No one who denies the Son has the Father; whoever acknowledges the Son has the Father also.

As for you, see that what you have heard from the beginning remains in you. If it does, you also will remain in the Son and in the Father. And this is what he promised us—eternal life.

I am writing these things to you about those who are trying to lead you astray. As for you, the anointing you received from him remains in you, and you do not need anyone to teach you. But as his anointing teaches you about all things and as that anointing is real, not counterfeit—just as it has taught you, remain in him (1 John 2:18–27).

Dear friends, do not believe every spirit, but test the spirits to see whether they are from God because many false prophets have gone out into the world. This is how you can recognize the Spirit of God: Every spirit that acknowledges that Jesus Christ has come in the flesh is from God, but every spirit that does not acknowledge Jesus is not from God. This is the spirit of the antichrist, which you have heard is coming and even now is already in the world.

You, dear children, are from God and have overcome them because the one who is in you is greater than the one who is in the world. They are from the world and therefore speak from the viewpoint of the world, and the world listens to them. We are from God, and whoever knows God listens to us; but whoever is not from God does not listen to us. This is how we recognize the Spirit of truth and the spirit of falsehood (1 John 4:1–6).

WHAT TO SAY TO THOSE WHO DENY GOD

An Atheist or anyone that denies God is a person that is purposely suppressing their knowledge. Paul writes in Romans 1:8 that the wrath of God is revealed from heaven against all ungodliness and unrighteousness of men, who by their unrighteousness suppress the truth.

Where did the world and universe come from? Astrophysicists believe that billions of years ago the universe exploded into being. But if nothing existed then, nothing would exist today.

According to Psalm 19:1, the heavens declare the glory of God and the sky above proclaims his handiwork. We are reminded of God's eternal power and divine nature have been clearly seen, being understood from what has been made so that people are without excuse (Rom. 1:20).

A person cannot technically claim there is not God as there is no scientific evidence to support it. If you are confronted by an atheist or a non-believer, try to reason with them. Always be prepared to have an answer for those who ask the reason for your hope.

But do this with gentleness and respect (1 Peter 3:15).
You can pray for their souls,
but leave their decision for conversion up to God.

PAUL AND SILAS IN PRISON

Once when we were going to the place of prayer, we were met by a female slave who had a spirit by which she predicted the future. She earned a great deal of money for her owners by fortune-telling. She followed Paul and the rest of us shouting, "These men are servants of the Most High God, who are telling you the way to be saved." She kept this up for many days.

Finally, Paul became so annoyed that he turned around and said to the spirit, "In the name of Jesus Christ I command you to come out of her!" At that moment the spirit left her (Acts 16:16–18).

A man in the crowd called out, "Teacher, I beg you to look at my son, for he is my only child. A spirit seizes him and he suddenly screams; it throws him into convulsions so that he foams at the mouth. It scarcely ever leaves him and is destroying him. I begged your disciples to drive it out, but they could not."

"You unbelieving and perverse generation," Jesus replied, "How long shall I stay with you and put up with you? Bring your son here." Even while the boy was coming, the demon threw him to the ground in a convulsion. But Jesus rebuked the impure spirit, healed the boy and gave him back to his father (Luke 9:38–42).

When an impure spirit comes out of a person, it goes through arid places seeking rest and does not find it. Then it says, 'I will return to the house I left.' When it arrives, it finds the house unoccupied, swept clean and put in order. Then it goes and takes with it seven other spirits more wicked than itself, and they go in and live there. And the final condition of that person is worse than the first. That is how it will be with this wicked generation" (Matt. 12:43–45).

THE FALL

Now the serpent was craftier than any of the wild animals God had made. He said to the woman, "Did God really say, 'You must not eat from any tree in the garden?'"

The woman said to the serpent, "We may eat fruit from the trees in the garden, but God did say, 'You must not eat fruit from the tree that is in the middle of the garden, and you must not touch it, or you will die.'"

"You will not certainly die," the serpent said to the woman. "God knows that your eyes will be opened as soon as you eat it, and you will be like God, knowing both good and evil."

The woman was convinced. She saw that the tree was beautiful and its fruit looked delicious, and she wanted the wisdom it would give her. So she took some of the fruit and ate it. Then she gave some to her husband, who was with her, and he ate it, too (Genesis 3:1–6). Then God asked the woman, "What have you done?" "The serpent deceived me," she replied. "That's why I ate it" (Genesis 3:13).

JESUS IS TESTED IN THE WILDERNESS (MATTHEW 4:1–11).

Then Jesus was led by the Spirit into the wilderness to be tempted by the devil. After fasting forty days and forty nights, he was hungry. The tempter came to him and said, "If you are the Son of God, tell these stones to become bread."

Jesus answered, "It is written: 'Man shall not live on bread alone, but on every word that comes from the mouth of God." Then the devil took him to the holy city and had him stand on the highest point of the temple. "If you are the Son of God," he said, "throw yourself down. For it is written: "'He will command his angels concerning you, and they will lift you up in their hands, so that you will not strike your foot against a stone.'"

Jesus answered him, "It is also written: 'Do not put the Lord your God to the test.'"

Again, the devil took him to a very high mountain and showed him all the kingdoms of the world and their splendor. "All this I will give you," he said, "if you will bow down and worship me." Jesus said to him, "Away from me, Satan! For it is written: 'Worship the Lord your God, and serve him only. Then the devil left him, and angels came and attended him.'"

HAVE NO FEAR

*One of the most courageous decisions you'll ever make
is to finally let go of what is hurting your heart and soul.*
–Bridgette Nicole

Nothing can ever separate us from God's Love. Neither death nor life, angels nor demons. Neither our fears for today nor our worries about tomorrow—not even the powers of hell can separate us from God's love. No power in the sky above or in the earth below. Nothing will ever separate us from the love of God that is revealed in Christ Jesus our Lord (Rom. 8:38–39).

So do not fear, for I am with you; do not be dismayed, for I am your God. I will strengthen you and help you; I will uphold you with my righteous right hand (Isa. 41:10).

Use biblical studies and prayer to find strength. The Bible will guide you to find strength, courage and hope in Jesus. You need to have the desire to seek Him. In James 1:5, we are reminded " If any of you lacks wisdom, you should ask God, who gives generously to all without finding fault, and it will be given to you. For the Spirit God gave us does not make us timid, but gives us power, love and self-discipline.

Second Timothy 1:7: Put on the full armor of God, so that you can take your stand against the devil's schemes (Eph. 6:11).

"Yet if you devote your heart to him and stretch out your hands to him, if you put away the sin that is in your hand and allow no evil to dwell in your tent, then, free of fault, you will lift up your face; you will stand firm and without fear" (Job 11:13–15).

READING RESOURCES:

Bondage Breaker
By Dr. Neil Anderson

Cults and the Occult
By Edmond C. Gruss

Comparing Christianity with the Cults; The Spirit of Truth and the
Spirit of Error
By Dillon Burroughs, Keith L. Brooks, Irvine Robertson

Living in Truth: Confident Conversation in a Conflicted Culture
By Mary Jo Sharp

The Reason for God: Belief in an Age of Skepticism
By Timothy Keller

Spiritual Warfare for Your Family Spiritual Warfare for Women
By Leighann McCoy

QUESTIONS TO PONDER

1. Do you agree or disagree with the TV programming being a possible occult problem?
    By reading the definitions, do you understand the connection?

2. What are your thoughts about the different occults and their definitions?
    Does anything you read about them change your beliefs about them?

3. Are you or someone you know pagan?
    What do you understand about paganism?

4. Are you or someone you know Wiccan?
    What do you understand about practicing Wicca?

5. Do you or someone you know practice the occult?
    What kind of occult rituals are you aware of?

6. Do you or someone you know attend a New Age church?
    How is New Age church and traditional Christian church different?

7. Satan is hidden in plain sight and works on ways to get into our heads.
    What areas in your life has Satan been working you over?
    What ways has Satan deceived you?
    How has Satan tested you?

8. Was any part of this chapter eye-opening for you?
    Does it motivate you to change anything?

9. What verse or verses are important to you?

CHAPTER ELEVEN

CHRISTIANS SIN?

You are given the freedom to choose (Gen. 2:15–17).
But you are not free from the consequence
of your choice (Exodus 8:15–19).

Sin is immeasurable. Meaning you cannot put a value on it. A sin is a sin is a sin. I was born a sinner from the moment my mother conceived me (Psalm 51:5). Sin is not a private matter because everything we do affects others. In Romans 14:21, we are reminded that we are to treat others with love, patience, and self-restraint.

BLACK AND WHITE VS. GRAY

Few people are black and white about what is considered sin and what isn't. Most people live by the gray areas where we sinners push the lines of right from wrong. How a Christian should dress is where you will find a multitude of gradations in the gray areas! We need to be careful of the gray areas as they may be justification for our sin. Be mindful of the gray areas and as previously mentioned, be careful of judging other people. Mind your own gray areas! Behave properly as a follower of Christ (Romans 13:13).

SIN VS. GODLY

The Lord shows us how to distinguish right from wrong and discernment. Wisdom and truth will enter the very center of your being filling you with joy. You will be given common sense to avoid going down dark and evil paths (Proverbs 2:6–13).

The devil doesn't come dressed in a red cape and pointy horns.
He comes as everything you've ever wished for.
–Tucker Max

Avoid actions that are forbidden according to scripture. If it is not written clearly biblically, but it gives you an uncomfortable feeling, follow your conscience or your conviction. God is showing you it is wrong for YOU (Rom. 14:23). Satan prowls around like a roaring lion looking for someone to devour. Resist evil and stand firm in your faith (1 Pet 5:8–9).

Be who God says you are, not who your circumstances suggest you are (John 1:12). When you have accepted Jesus Christ as your Savior, you become a member of God's family. Always remember that! That alone should make a person rethink their actions.

When you fail to keep your word, then you have sinned against the Lord. Be assured, your sin will find you out (Num. 32:23). As an ex-smoker, I made all kinds of promises and resolutions to quit smoking. It took promising God in prayer to quit smoking. I haven't smoked in more than twenty years in fear of disappointing God.

We have to remember that Satan will work you over in whatever way he can manipulate you to walk in sin. We can look at what happened to Adam and Eve in the book of Genesis.

- Genesis 3:1: Doubt
- Genesis 3:2–3: Denial
- Genesis 3:4–5: Deception
- Genesis 3:6–7: Disobedience

Sadly, sin introduced division in Adam and Eve's relationship because of blame and self-interest. Isn't that the way the world is in current times?

GUILT VS. SHAME

A lot of people think that guilt and shame share the same meaning. Compare the definition of guilt and shame.

Guilt is a cognitive or an emotional experience that occurs when a person believes or realizes— accurately or not—that he or she has compromised his or her own standards of conduct or has violated a moral standard and bears significant responsibility for that violation.

Paul named guilt *Godly sorrow* because it is the outcome of sin. God uses guilt to bring us to our knees. He wants us to repent.

Shame is associated with genuine dishonor, disgrace, or condemnation. Shame arises when one's defects are exposed to others, and results from the negative evaluation of others.

Shame is worldly sorrow. Shame says you are not good enough.

WHAT THE BIBLE SAYS:

God wanted to be with Adam and Eve but they hid because of their sin (Gen. 3:10).

We need to remember there is no condemnation for those who are in Jesus Christ (Rom. 8:1).

When we sin, God will convict us and guide us back to Him. Christ died for our sins. We do not need to feel ashamed.

> The Son is the image of the invisible God, the firstborn over all creation. For in him, all things were created: things in heaven and on earth, visible and invisible, whether thrones or powers or rulers or authorities; all things have been created through him and for him. He is before all things, and in him all things hold together. And he is the head of the body, the church; he is the beginning and the firstborn from among the dead, so that in everything he might have the supremacy. For God was pleased to have all his fullness dwell in him, and through him to reconcile to himself all things, whether things on earth or things in heaven, by making peace through his blood, shed on the cross. Once you were alienated from God and were enemies in your minds because of your evil behavior. But now he has reconciled you by Christ's physical body through death to present you holy in his sight, without blemish and free from accusation (Col. 1:15–22).

"I, even I, am he who blots out your transgressions, for my own sake, and remembers your sins no more" (Isa. 43:25).

"You will again have compassion on us; you will tread our sins underfoot and hurl all our iniquities into the depths of the sea" (Micah 7:19).

Brothers and sisters, I do not consider myself yet to have taken hold of it. But one thing I do: Forgetting what is behind and straining toward what is ahead (Phil. 3:13).

We need to understand as Christians that the sorrow God wants us to experience leads us away from sin and results in salvation. There's no regret for that kind of sorrow. But worldly sorrow, which lacks repentance results in spiritual death (2 Cor. 7:10).

Jesus said, "Unless you turn from your sins and become like little children, you will never get into the Kingdom of Heaven" (Matt. 18:23).

PATIENCE

Patience is not the ability to wait
but how you act while you are waiting.
–Joyce Meyer

For many, they suffer with anxiety or mental health issues causing great impatience with people and/or situations they cannot control. It can be very difficult for people to control—especially in the public arena. They seem to function well for the most part but lack grace in the patience department. We all know people like that.

Be careful how you live . . .
Your life is a permanent sermon.
(Romans 2:21–24)

SCRIPTURE ON PATIENCE

Whoever has patience has great understanding. A person that is quick tempered is foolish (Prov. 14:29). In contrast of anger and impatience is to display love joy, peace, forbearance, kindness, goodness, faithfulness, gentleness and self-control (Galatians 5:22). Everyone should be quick to listen, slow to speak and slow to become angry (James 1:19).

A great example is what Moses wrote in Exodus 34:6, The Lord is a compassionate and gracious God, slow to anger, abounding in love and faithfulness. This demonstrates God's wisdom in stressful situations. We are being an example to other believers.

If we trust God with our future, it teaches us to wait patiently and confidently (Rom. 8:25).

*You can make many plans,
but the Lord's purpose will prevail (Prov. 19:21).*

God gives us spiritual insight in His ways to respond to conflict with patience (Prov. 19:11).Better to be patient than powerful; better to have self-control than to conquer a city (Prov. 16:32).Faith and patience will inherit the promises (Heb. 6:12).

Make every effort to respond to God's promises. Supplement your faith with a generous provision of moral excellence, and moral excellence with knowledge, and knowledge with self-control, and self-control with patient endurance, and patient endurance with godliness (2 Peter 1:5–6).

It is easy to get impatient and feel hopelessness when my resolve is moving too slowly. Especially when we are close to the situation, it is difficult to see the progress. Joshua teaches us that when we look back, we will see God's hand in it (Joshua 11:18).

And in 1 Samuel 13:11–12, it is recognized how difficult it is to trust God when you feel your resources slipping away. Saul though his time was running out and he became impatient with God's timing, so he substituted a ritual for his faith.

When we are faced with difficulties, we should never allow impatience allowing us excuses to ignore or disobey God. We know God has a plan for us, and often uses delays to test our obedience and impatience. We should never justify our mistakes or sins because of *special circumstances* because God knows our true motives (1 Sam. 13:13).

In Exodus 2:23–25, God promised to bring the Hebrew slaves out of Egypt. The people waited a long time for that promise, but He knew the perfect time to rescue them. God rescues us in His timing, not ours.

Jesus trusted God's timing for His life in ministry according to Luke 3:23. Like Jesus, we need to be patient to receive direction. We need to trust God's timing.

Run the race with patience (Heb. 12:1 and Heb. 10:36).

Patience is the fruit of the Holy Spirit (Gal. 5:22–23).

We can't always see where the road leads, but God promises there's something better up ahead. We just have to trust him (Psalm 56:3).

ACCEPTANCE OF OTHERS

As Christians, we are expected to accept others as they are. Nobody is perfect. In Ephesians 4:1–2, we are shown to live a life worthy of the calling we have received. We are to be humble, gentle, patient, and love one another. We are to aim for harmony in the church and try to build each other up (Rom. 14:19 and James 3:18).

FRIENDS

Show me your friends
and I will show you your future.
–Maurice Clarett
Proverbs 1:8–22, Proverbs 13:20, Proverbs
27:17 and Romans 12:9–10

Don't be misled;
bad company corrupts good character
(1 Cor. 15:33)

We all have baggage and spiritual wounds. As humans, we have a background of sin. None of us had perfect parents. When I was checking into the possibility of doing foster care, I feared being turned down because of the past abuses I had experienced. The wonderful man that came to interview my husband and I warmly smiled and said, "It's not the hand that is dealt you, it's how you play the hand." He has no idea how much I valued that comment. God has a way of using people to heal and restore our lives.

This was an important time for me. It changed me. God was changing me. I have found refuge in being around other Christians who love God and love His word. Not that I would shun non-Christian people, but it is important to maintain my spiritual life.

If you find yourself heading for sin, you need to change your course (Prov. 3:6). Stay on track! Don't compare yourself with others. Your purpose in life here on earth is designed by God differently for each and every one of us (Jer. 29:11).

The Lord has a plan for each and every one of us.
They are plans for good and not for disaster,
to give you a future and hope. (Jer. 29:11)
He knows the secrets of the heart (Psalm 44:21).

The eyes of the Lord are in every place, watching the evil and the good (Prov. 15:3). For the ways of a man are before the eyes of the Lord, and He watches all his paths (Prov. 5:21). Death, hell and man's heart are seen by God (Prov. 15:11).

I like to remind believers how important it is to arm ourselves in the word. We have spent enough time with our sinful nature. We can overcome our sins when we focus on Christ. With leaving sinful behavior, old friends may very well mock you. But they will have to give account for their own behavior (1 Peter 4:1–5).

RESIST TEMPTATION

I have come to terms with the fact that we are all broken. We all find defeating temptation is difficult. We face temptation every day. It is easier to blame others and to make excuses for our actions. But a Christian should accept responsibility for their actions, confess them, and ask God for forgiveness.

Sin does not just happen. It may be a single decision or a gradual process of small poor decisions you justify. Some innocent games of poker and a few drinks with some good buddies becomes an overpowering urge to gamble and/or uncontrollable alcohol problem. An innocent friendship with the opposite sex becomes a sexual attraction. Sounds far-fetched, doesn't it? The devil knows your weaknesses. If faithfulness is a weakness, stay away from being alone with a member of the opposite sex.

If you have addictions in your family, stay away from anything that can cause addiction. I struggle with chronic pain from Lupus and Fibromyalgia. Medications that are addictive are always made available to me, however, I refuse them due to family history of addiction. I take non-addictive medication for pain relief. It is a choice I make to remove myself from possible problems in my future.

People are slaves to whatever has mastered them (2 Pet. 2:19).

Jesus understands trials and resisting temptation because He faced them as a human being (Heb. 2:18). He empathizes us with our weaknesses (Heb. 4:15). If others have overcome the same type of temptation, you can too! God will not allow us to be tempted beyond our ability to resist. In every temptation God will provide you with a way out (1 Cor. 10:13). Remember that the Lord is a loving God. He does not want anyone to perish, but to come to repentance (2 Peter 3:9) Bottom line is that it is still your choice to choose the right path. You may have to live with the consequences of your sin. Think before you act. (Numbers 20:21 and 1 Corinthians 21:13–14).

Mark 9:42–49 and Matthew 8:7–9 warns against temptation and reminds us that we will all be tested.

In James 1:12–15, we are reminded that when we endure trials we are blessed because when we pass the test, we receive the crown of life that God has promised to those who love Him.

If you think for one minute that you can hide your sins, you are only fooling yourself! Nothing is hidden from God. Don't even think about it!

> Every sin is uncovered (Hebrews 4:13).
> The Lord knows my ways (Psalm 139:1–3).
> He knows my thoughts (Matthew 12:25).
> Forgive my hidden sins (Psalm 19:12).

To help resist temptation, you can ask a trusted person to be your accountability partner. It has to be a person you can be forthcoming with. This person should be strong enough to hold you accountable for your actions. It must be someone you cannot fool, manipulate or will appease you. In return, that person should reciprocate with non-judgmental honesty and grace. Make sure your advice does not come from a worldly person, but a Godly person. This person should be someone you are comfortable to pray with. Find someone who will be a prayer warrior for you.

Do not ask God to rescue you from temptation (Psalm 91:11–12). That is using God's power foolishly. You do not want to test God (Deut. 6:16; Luke 4:12; and 1 Cor. 10:9). Instead, pray you will not give in to temptation. Luke 22:40. Jesus warns us that the world tempts people to sin. Temptation is inevitable, Christians (Matt. 18:7)!

If you want to stay away from sin, you need remove yourself from the sin. Protect yourself from influences that are not good (1 Cor. 15:33, Matt. 22:37, Rom. 15:1–7).

REPENT

Repentance is the first step to redemption after committing a sin. It clearly states in 1 John 1:19 "If we confess our sins, He is faithful and just to forgive us our sins and cleans us from all unrighteousness."

What does it mean to repent? To repent is the will to change your mind from sin. You first need to acknowledge that what you are doing is wrong. You cannot rationalize or make excuses for your sin. Stop the sin—and remove yourself from situations that are triggers for you. If you are having an affair, end it immediately.

The NIV dictionary defines the word to repent "to turn from sin and change one's heart and behavior; to feel regret and contrition." The NIV dictionary defines the word repentance "a turning away from sin, disobedience, or rebellion, and turning back to God."

Why should we repent? To cleanse us from a guilty conscience (Heb. 10:22). The Lord wants everyone to come to repentance because he is patient with you and does not want you to perish (2 Pet. 3:9). The kingdom of heaven is near (Mark 1:14-15, and Matthew 3:1-2).

To repent is to confess your sins. Confess to each other and pray for each other so that you may be healed. The earnest prayer of a righteous person has great power and produces wonderful results (James 5:16). If we confess our sins, He is faithful and just and will forgive us our sins and purify us from all unrighteousness (1 John 1:9).

Jesus said "Truly I tell you, the tax collectors and the prostitutes are entering the kingdom of God ahead of you. For John came to you to show you the way of righteousness and you did not believe him., but the tax collectors and the prostitutes did. And even after you saw this, you did not repent and believe him (Matthew 21:31-32).

The way to righteousness is to believe that our Lord Jesus Christ is the son of God born to deliver us from evil. For God so loved the world that he gave his only begotten son. Whosoever believeth in Him shall not perish, but have everlasting life (Jn 3:16).

RECEIVE FORGIVENESS

If we confess our sins, He is faithful and just and will forgive us our sins and purify us from all unrighteousness (1 John 1:9). God is waiting for you to repent. He wants to forgive, cleanse and restore you from your sins. He will release you of shame, pain and regrets.

God wants to give you a clean heart. If you know God has forgiven you, you should be able to forgive yourself. Ask him to manage your sinful nature daily!

Don't talk to several people about your issues. Your sin does not only stain you—it affects the people around you (Exod. 34:7). This is true in many levels.

If you gamble or use drugs, you are hurting and affecting those who love and depend on you. Some people think because they have a job and pay the rent, they are supporting the family financially.

When you have a family, you need to think about how your actions may affect them.

It is not God's will for you to suffer nor to have continued guilt the rest of your life. You have to be willing to forgive yourself as God has. He knows all our flaws and mistakes, yet he sees the best in us. He has delivered us from the domain of darkness and transferred us to the kingdom of his beloved Son, in whom we have redemption, the forgiveness of sins (Col. 1:13–14).

Look for the way to bear it. Pray for God's help and counsel with those who love God and will hold you accountable (1 Cor. 10:13). Don't let the noise of the world keep from hearing the voice of the Lord Jesus (1 Samuel :10). We have to remember, as defense—is prayer and the gospel. Do not give the devil a foothold (Eph. 4:27).

Because Jesus is without sin, Satan has no power over Him. If we obey and follow Jesus, Satan will have no power over us (John 14:30). We are reminded in 2 Timothy 4:18 that the Lord will deliver us from evil. And we should thank God He gives us victory over sin and death through Jesus Christ (1 Cor. 15:57). There is no eternal doom for those who trust Him to save them. But those who don't trust Him have already been tried and condemned for not believing in Jesus Christ (John 3:18). This verse refers to moral darkness. Your justice is eternal and your instructions are perfectly clear (Psalm 119:142).

When we are busy making decisions for ourselves, we need to stop. We need to keep God in our daily activities through prayer and read the Bible daily as our guide. Allow God to guide you and protect you. Because God is a better judge of what is best for us, we need to trust in Him completely in every aspect of our lives (Prov. 3:5). God delights in those who trust him and tries to do his will. He watches over them (Psalm 37:23–24).

Let us approach God's throne of grace with confidence so that we may receive mercy and find grace to help us in our time of need (Hebrews 4:16). And all these blessings shall come upon you and overtake you, because you obey the voice of the Lord (Deut. 28:1–1).

Mature Christians should help new believers with support and encouragement of their new habits that supports their walk with Christ.

In the second letter that Peter wrote to growing Christians; he writes that we are promised grace and peace in abundance through the knowledge of God and of Jesus our Lord. He has given us everything we need to live a godly life. He has given us great and precious promises to escape the corrupt world and evil desires. So make every effort to add to your faith, goodness, knowledge, self-control, perseverance, godliness, mutual affection and love. If you develop these qualities, you will never stumble (2 Peter 1:2–10).

Peter wrote we are to make every effort to be found spotless, blameless, and at peace with Him. He states that Paul has written similar warnings. We are forewarned to be on our guard so that you are not carried away by sin and fall from your position. He warns us to grow in grace and knowledge of our Lord and Savor Jesus Christ. To give Him the glory both now and forever (2 Peter 3:14–18)!

Only wisdom from the Lord can save you from the flattery of prostitutes whose houses lie along the road of death and hell. Men who enter them are doomed and will never be the same. Follow the steps of the Godly instead and stay on the right path for only good men enjoy life fully. Evil men lose the good things in life, destroying themselves (Prov. 2:16–22).

Glorious joy is a result of your faith (1 Peter 1:8).

When we trust in Christ, He takes our sin and makes it right with God (2 Cor. 5:21). He blots out our transgressions for His sake, and remembers your sins no more (Isa. 43:25).

If you are a sinner set free by Jesus, take time to rejoice (Rom. 6:23)!

Now may the God of *hope* fill you with all *joy* and *peace* in believing, that you may *abound in hope* by the power of the Holy Spirit (Rom. 15:13).

> Sin; It will take you where you want to go,
> It keeps you longer than you want to stay,
> And costs you more than you want to pay!
> - Romans 6:23

JOHN WRITES TO US—CHRISTIANS:

This is the message we have heard from him and declare to you: God is light; in him there is no darkness at all. If we claim to have fellowship with him and yet walk in the darkness, we lie and do not live out the truth. But if we walk in the light, as he is in the light, we have fellowship with one another, and the blood of Jesus, his Son, purifies us from all sin.

If we claim to be without sin, we deceive ourselves and the truth is not in us. If we confess our sins, he is faithful and just and will forgive us our sins and purify us from all unrighteousness. If we claim we have not sinned, we make him out to be a liar and his word is not in us (1 John 1:5–2:2).

My dear children, I write this to you so that you will not sin. But if anybody does sin, we have an advocate with the Father—Jesus Christ, the Righteous One. He is the atoning sacrifice for our sins, and not only for ours but also for the sins of the whole world (1 John 2:1).

Everyone who sins is breaking God's law. All sin is contrary to the law of God. Jesus came to take away our sins, so anyone who continues to live in Christ will not sin. Anyone who keeps on sinning does not know or understand who Christ is. Don't let anyone deceive you about this. When people do what is right, it shows that they are righteous. But when people keep sinning, they belong to the devil who has been sinning since the beginning. (1 John 3:4-7)

1 JOHN 5:13–21 CONCLUDING AFFIRMATIONS

I write these things to you who believe in the name of the Son of God so that you may know that you have eternal life. This is the confidence we have in approaching God: that if we ask anything according to his will, he hears us. And if we know that he hears us—whatever we ask—we know that we have what we asked of him.

If you see any brother or sister commit a sin that does not lead to death, you should pray and God will give them life. I refer to those whose sin does not lead to death. There is a sin that leads to death. I am not saying that you should pray about that. All wrongdoing is sin, and there is sin that does not lead to death.

We know that anyone born of God does not continue to sin; the One who was born of God keeps them safe, and the evil one cannot harm them. We know that we are children of God, and that the whole world is under the control of the evil one. We know also that the Son of God has come and has given us understanding, so that we may know him who is true. And we are in him who is true by being in his Son Jesus Christ. He is the true God and eternal life. Dear children, keep yourselves from idols.

MOVING FORWARD

Do not dwell on your wrongs. If you have repented and asked God for His forgiveness, ask God what he wants you to do. Ask Him how you can help others. Many plans are in a man's heart, but the counsel of the Lord will stand (Prov. 19:21).

Remember that God knows our desires. The plans of the heart belong to man, but the answer of the tongue is from the Lord. All the ways of a man are clean in his own sight, but the Lord weighs the motives (Prov. 16:1–2).

There is the expectation to not falter. If you falter in a time of trouble, how small is your strength! Rescue those being led away to death; hold back those staggering toward slaughter. If you say, "But we knew nothing about this," does not he who weighs the heart perceive it? Does not he who guards your life know it? Will he not repay everyone according to what they have done? (Prov. 24:10–12).

The Lord has made everything for its own purpose, even the wicked for the day of evil (Prov. 16:4).

The mind of man plans his way, but the Lord directs his steps (Prov. 16:9). Man's steps are ordained by the Lord. How then can man understand his way? (Prov. 20:24). The Lord will be your confidence and will keep your foot from being caught (Prov. 3:26).

He has made everything beautiful in its time. He has also set eternity in the human heart; yet no one can fathom what God has done from beginning to end (Eccles. 3:11).

But the LORD said to Samuel, "Do not consider his appearance or his height, for I have rejected him. The LORD does not look at the things people look at. People look at the outward appearance, but the LORD looks at the heart" (1 Samuel 16:7).

I cry out to God Most High to God, who vindicates me. He sends from heaven and saves me, rebuking those who hotly pursue me. God sends forth his love and his faithfulness (Psalm 57:2–3).

Nothing in all creation is hidden from God's sight. Everything is uncovered and laid bare before the eyes of him to whom we must give account (Heb. 4:13).

READING RESOURCES:

Counterfeit God: The Empty Promises of Money, Sex, and Power, and the Only Hope that Matters
By Timothy Keller

Defeating Temptation: Biblical Secrets of Self Control
By Doug Britton

Not the Way It's Supposed to Be: A Breviary of Sin
By Cornelius Plantinga Jr.

Moving Forward: Six Steps to Forgiving Yourself and Breaking Free From the Past
By Everett Worthington Jr.

When Godly People Do Ungodly Things: Arming Yourself in the Age of Seduction
By Beth Moore

QUESTIONS TO PONDER

1. Are you a black and white person or a gray area person?
    How does that affect your Christian beliefs?

2. In Genesis, Satan manipulated Adam and Eve.
    How does Satan manipulate you?

3. People are slaves to whatever has mastered them. 2 Peter 2:19
    What are you a slave to?
    What can you do to change that?

4. For many, patience is difficult for them.
    What areas of patience could you work on?
    How does your lack of patience affect other people around you?

5. Do you wish to repent your sins?
    Privately or to a trusted person?
    Do you believe your sins are forgiven?
    Can you forgive yourself?

6. Was any part of this chapter eye opening for you?
    Does it motivate you to change anything?

7. What verse or verses are important to you?

CHAPTER TWELVE

LIFE'S CRISIS PLAN

Give your burdens to the Lord.
He will carry them.
He will never allow the righteous to be shaken.
(Psalm 55:22)

WHAT CAUSES CRISIS?

Crisis are caused for a number of reasons. It is encompassed by forced changes, unexpected circumstances, and painful experiences.

One area of crisis may stem making poor choices such as over-spending, overeating, lying, stealing, and sins that hurt yourself and others.

Illness may cause an instantaneous life change. A person may not be able to care for themselves. Like most Americans who are living paycheck to paycheck, even a short-term illness can cause financial difficulties. Short-term disability or chronic illness can be detrimental to financial stability.

The loss of someone by death can put a person into a whirlwind of grieving and emotional crisis especially with suicide. It can cause financial hardships, legal processes, and time off work.

Adultery is a painful experience and often cannot be reconciled because of distrust and anger.

Broken relationships and divorce is very painful to the person who is not ready to dissolve their relationship. They may find themselves in an emotional crisis while they go through a grieving process. Often divorce and broken relationships can be a financial hardship with legal costs, combined financial ties, and children to consider.

The inability to forgive seldom hurts the person that is not forgiven, but it will always hurt the person that holds on to their anger and pain.

Addiction affects the addict and those who love the addict. The addict tends to make poor choices for themselves, for their family, for their job, and for friendships. They will choose friends that accept and enable their behavior.

When a person lives with any kind of abuse, they suffer with physical and emotional crisis. They tend to not discuss their crisis in fear of the consequences from the abuser.

Hopelessness is a symptom of depression and should be addressed.

Having rebellious children can be heart wrenching for parents. A parent wants the best for their children and find themselves angry and disappointed, questioning their ability as a parent, worried about their child's safety and their salvation.

Often when a family is introduced to the LGBT community, there is a whole gamut of emotions depending on their beliefs. Some Christians and homophobes will disown a LGBT person causing crisis in their relationship. More information is found in the LGBT section.

When a person is going through a mental health crisis, it causes stress on those around them. It can cause financial hardship if the person is hospitalized, and legal ramifications if the person did damage to someone or something. There may be job loss or long bouts of time away from work, and legal fees when involving the court system.

All people handle crisis in different ways. Make sure you can identify the grieving process. Be aware of symptoms of depression, anxiety, and other mental health issues. With understanding the symptoms, you will be able to choose resources most appropriate for the situation.

TOXIC PEOPLE

Why do some people go out of their way to tarnish you or harm you when you work so hard to do right?

Some people suffer with morbid jealousy. They compare notes and cannot celebrate another person's happiness, financial gains, and achievements. They are literally jealous of other people's material possessions.

Some people have personality disorders where they suffer with angry or paranoid thoughts. This could be a symptom of depression. Refer to the mental health section

Research points to the fact that relationships characterized by conflict and turmoil have a negative impact on health. These negative relationships that are referred to as toxic. You need to ask yourself if your relationship is effecting your health.

Here are some classic examples of a toxic relationship:

1. When we spend time together, I feel tired and unfulfilled.
2. I feel bad about myself before, during, and after we spend time together.
3. I feel I have to keep my guard up when we are together.
4. I feel that I am the giver and you are the taker in our relationship.
5. There is always drama, conflict, and anxiety when we are together.
6. You never seem happy in our relationship or appreciate what I do or who I am.

None of this is healthy, uplifting, satisfying, or pleasant. With toxic relationships, set boundaries and follow through with them. You model the expectations. Do not allow toxic behavior. If the toxic person is unwilling to respect the boundaries, or unwilling to change then you need to terminate the relationship. Again, allow me to reiterate Dr. Phil's statement: "You teach others how to treat you."

We are reminded in 1 Peter 3:13–18 that even when we suffer for doing what is right, God will reward you for it. Christ suffered for our sins even though he did not commit the sin. You must keep a clear conscience. We have to remember that it is better to suffer for doing good than to suffer for doing wrong (1 Peter 2:9).

But you, O God, will send the wicked down to the pit of destruction. Murderers and liars will die young, but I am trusting you to save me (Psalm 55:23).

Rescue me, O Lord, from liars and from all deceitful people (Psalm 120:2).

Wrongdoers eagerly listen to gossip; liars pay close attention to slander (Prov. 17:4).

"You must not pass along false rumors. You must not cooperate with evil people by lying on the witness stand (Exod. 23:1).

I WANT TO HELP A FRIEND

Here is what God wants from us: Rejoice with those who rejoice; mourn with those who mourn (Romans 12:15).

Be available and non-judgmental. People want to be heard, not fixed. Not even a single sparrow is forgotten by God and you are worth more than many sparrows. Indeed, even the very hairs on your head are all numbered, so don't be afraid (Luke 12:6–7).

Don't worry about anything; instead pray about everything. Tell God your needs and don't forget to thank Him for His answers. If you do this, you will experience God's peace, which is far more wonderful than the human mind can understand. His peace will keep your thoughts and your hearts quiet and at rest as you trust in Christ Jesus (Phil. 4:6–7).

Don't be afraid to reach out and ask for help from friends, family, pastor or a mental health professional. Wisdom is hearing the lessons learned from pain, either ours or others, and using those lessons to avoid more pain. Listen to pain, it speaks. God can restore what is broken and change it into something amazing. All you need is faith (Joel 2:25).

Do not ask God to guide your footsteps
if you're not willing to move your feet
–Anurag Prakash Ray

I WANT TO MINISTER TO THOSE IN CRISIS. WHAT DO I NEED TO KNOW?

First, you need to equip yourself spiritually with constant prayer. Immerse yourself in the word daily. Have one or two prayer partners to help you through tough times.

Know what your motives are when you are ministering to others. Make sure the reason you are ministering others is not out of self-gratification. The glory needs to be to God (Gal. 1:5–7).

What are your means of being available to others? Can you drive to meet someone or do you need to connect in other ways? Do you have time to minister to others?

What is the environment like—or the venue you intend to use? Is it warm and inviting? Is it too noisy? Will you be able to be discreet with your conversation?

You must always consider confidentiality, except when someone is in danger or is planning to harm themselves or others. You are required by law to report these instances.

Understand what the description of ministering others entails. Who are you ministering to? If you are ministering others through a church, what is their guidelines? Do they have a job description in which you are to follow?

What are your limitations? Are you certified or licensed to counsel? Make sure you know your limitations and stay within those boundaries to prevent legal ramification. If you are only ministering with someone, you are not counseling them. You can listen, but don't diagnose or advise.

Sometimes a person doesn't need to be counseled, but for someone to just listen.

When working with others in crisis, it is important to enforce healthy boundaries. People in crisis can be needy to the point of constant phone calls and unannounced visits. Keep a specific schedule when you are available and stick with it. When making the next appointment, even if you have many open slots, offer only one or two specific time slots.

Practice active listening skills to accurately identify the needs and provide appropriate resources. You may not be the person this person needs. Make sure you have local, online, and Christian resources available. I like to organize my local resources in a portable file box filed by type of resource. I also have an online folder of resources that include online support groups and trainings.

Always listen to their story without judgment. Often, what you hear only scratches the surface of the issue. Ask questions to get beyond that surface layer. Be careful how much you probe as you do not want to appear as interrogating them.

When you are discussing problems, make sure you validate their feelings. Often, the issues may come off distorted or paranoid. Remember that this is their perspective of the issue, it may not be factual. You can still validate their feelings without agreeing with them.

If the person is stuck in their story and cannot move forward, divert them with a question. Do not interpret or analyze them.

When you are ministering with someone, do not make promises. Even under the best of intentions, it can cause great disappointment. Too often, life happens and you are not able to follow through with a promise.

Be careful to not warn a person. Help them make their own conclusions to their actions. Never lecture or argue. This is demeaning and unprofessional.

Be careful in using humor or sarcasm as it may reflect as demeaning. At times, silence may appear as though you are withdrawing from them.

If this person keeps seeking counsel without effort to change, they may not be ready for change. Don't put more time into a person that is unwilling to make changes.

If you are ministering with a group of leaders, make sure each of those leaders are trained.

WHY ME?

When going through a crisis, you cannot help but ask yourself, "Why me?" Trying situations are opportunities for genuine faith to grow stronger.

Those who hope in the LORD will renew their strength. They will soar on wings like eagles; they will run and not grow weary, they will walk and not be faint (Isa. 40:31).

Because of the LORD's great love we are not consumed, for his compassions never fail. They are new every morning; great is your faithfulness (Lam. 3:22–23).

Your difficulties are used by the Father to produce Christ-like character. For we are God's handiwork, created in Christ Jesus to do good works, which God prepared in advance for us to do (Eph. 2:10).

Jesus looked at them and said, "With man this is impossible, but with God all things are possible" (Matt. 19:26).

Be joyful in hope, patient in affliction, be faithful in prayer (Rom. 12:12).

God will walk with you through all trials. The Lord stood at my side and gave me strength, so that through me the message might be fully proclaimed and all the Gentiles might hear it. And I was delivered from the lion's mouth (2 Tim. 4:17).

The Holy Spirit will enable you not only to survive but also to come out a conqueror. We glory in our sufferings because we know that suffering produces perseverance (Rom. 5:3).

If you are really struggling with the question, "Why me?" I recommend you to read the book: *Why Do Bad Things Happen to Good People* by Pastor David Arnold. Though we live in an imperfect world, there is always hope through our Lord Jesus Christ. In *Why*

Do Bad Things Happen to Good People, Pastor Arnold's words help you to understand our fallen world and the comfort and hope found in Christ.

IT IS NEVER TOO LATE TO START OVER.

Sometimes, we have to start over to start healing.

We can get our lives back when we give away our broken life in exchange for grace (Mark 8:35).

You can clear the memories of the past and start over with God and with others. God created people in his image for eternal fellowship (Genesis 1:26–28).

You must remain faithful to what you have been taught. If you do, you will remain in fellowship with the Son and the Father. In this fellowship, we enjoy the eternal life he promised us (1 John 2:24–25).

If we rely on the Holy Spirit, he will teach you everything. I (Jesus) am leaving you with a gift—peace of mind and heart. And the peace I give is a gift the world cannot give, so don't be troubled or afraid (John 14: 26–27).

COMFORT AND SUFFERING?

When you endure extreme pressure with unexplainable peace and joy, the Lord will demonstrate His sustaining power to the world. God is our merciful Father and the source of all comfort. He comforts us in all our troubles so that we can comfort others (2 Cor. 1:3–4).

Intentions do not bring results, but actions do. No matter what your intentions are, if you don't do it, it won't happen. We need to have a plan for all disasters and crisis. But have you ever thought about having a plan to guide you from allowing crisis and disasters from destroying your spiritual life?

You can make many plans,
but the Lord's purpose will prevail (Proverbs 19:21).

You are *not* in control! God is in control of the timing and intensity of your trial and will not allow it to go beyond His plan (Exod. 2:23–25). He has a purpose for your suffering which you may not understand until it is over (1 Pet. 3:13–18). "I have told you all this so that you may have peace in me. Here on earth you will have many trials and sorrows. But take heart, because I have overcome the world." (John 16:33) Submit to God and trust Him through it (Psalm 62:8).

But when I am afraid, I will put my trust in you (Psalm 56:3).

The number one reason for fear is rejection. People who fear rejection have a strong need for acceptance. They have a hard time standing their ground because they thrive on approval.

If you fear that something traumatic might happen again, understand that this is a natural reaction following a traumatic event. Be patient with yourself. Understand there is rational fear and irrational fear. It is considered a rational fear when you react to a real threat to protect yourself.

With an irrational fear, you are afraid even though there is not a direct threat. If you were injured with your traumatic event, it's normal to have fears (even somewhat irrational) until you're feeling better.

Seasons don't last forever (Eccles. 3:1–13).

3:1 For everything there is a season,
a time for every activity under heaven.
2 A time to be born and a time to die.
A time to plant and a time to harvest.
3 A time to kill and a time to heal.
A time to tear down and a time to build up.
4 A time to cry and a time to laugh.
A time to grieve and a time to dance.
5 A time to scatter stones and a time to gather stones.
A time to embrace and a time to turn away.
6 A time to search and a time to quit searching.
A time to keep and a time to throw away.

[7] A time to tear and a time to mend.

A time to be quiet and a time to speak.

[8] A time to love and a time to hate.

A time for war and a time for peace.

[9] What do people really get for all their hard work?

[10] I have seen the burden God has placed on us all.

[11] Yet God has made everything beautiful for its own time. He has planted eternity in the human heart, but even so, people cannot see the whole scope of God's work from beginning to end.

[12] So I concluded there is nothing better than to be happy and enjoy ourselves as long as we can.

[13] And people should eat and drink and enjoy the fruits of their labor, for these are gifts from God (Ecclesiastes 3:1–13).

Often we don't appreciate the small things in life until we lose them. Without sacrifice, there is no value (Mark 8:36–37).

The Holy Spirit will help us in our weakness. We know that God causes everything to work together for the good of those who love God. If God is for us, who can be against us (Rom. 8:26–31)?

Are we going to allow a hardship to separate us from Christ? Does it mean he no longer loves us when we are going through trouble or calamity, hungry, destitute or in imminent danger? No, despite all these things, overwhelming victory is ours through Christ who loved us (Rom. 8:35–37).

OUR HEAVENLY FATHER WANTS US TO LIVE IN CONFIDENCE!

Can anything ever separate us from Christ's love? Does it mean he no longer loves us if we have trouble or calamity, or are persecuted, or hungry, or destitute, or in danger, or threatened with death? No, despite all these things, overwhelming victory is ours through Christ, who loved us. And I am convinced that nothing can ever separate us from God's love. Neither death nor life, neither angels nor demons, neither our fears for today nor our worries about tomorrow—not even the powers of hell can separate us from God's love (Romans 8:35, 37–38).

And now, dear children, remain in fellowship with Christ so that when he returns, you will be full of courage and not shrink back from him in shame (1 John 2:28).

IF I COULD HAVE...

Could have, would have, should have . . .

Stop! Don't get stuck in that kind of negative thinking!

You cannot change what has already happened. Allow yourself to find a lesson in everything. Sometimes you have to swallow your pride to grow from a bad experience. But it is worth it.

For everything there is a season. Ecclesiastes 3:1 What is happening now has happened before and what will happen in the future has happened before because God makes things happen over and over again (Eccles. 3:15).

People have ups and downs (yes, even Christians). As I mentioned before, this does not mean you are depressed. So what can you do to work your way through this slump?

Get out and do something! Get some sun, have coffee with a friend. Engage in social activities and try new activities. Take time out from your busy schedule to laugh and play!

Make sure you are paying attention to your body's needs. Get enough rest, try to eat healthier, and get some exercise. Make sure to take care of your appearance. How often do you skip the haircuts and snip here and there to save time? Take time to take care of yourself. When you look good, you feel good.

Are you fulfilling your spiritual needs? Spend quiet time in prayer and reading God's word. Work through things by journaling. Make an effort to maintain positive thinking and have a heart of gratitude.

WHAT DO YOU DO WHEN YOU ARE FEELING OVERLOADED?

First, search what it is that may be causing you to feel overloaded. You may have to remove yourself from your triggers—at least for a short amount of time. Often it makes an immense difference just to get a little help, delegate what you can. Spend your time and energy on what is important and let go of things that can wait until you are feeling less overwhelmed. Sometimes looking at the big picture is overwhelming. For example; the house is trashed and it is going to be a huge ordeal to get it cleaned up. That is where you find someone that you can delegate things to. Start with clearing and cleaning one small area at a time. Accomplish little jobs and before you know it, the whole thing will be done.

Don't overwhelm yourself by extending yourself too much. Learn to say no when you need to. If you are working full time with little children to care for, you will be pretty stretched already. So volunteering at the church might not be a wise decision at the time. You might ask yourself what God has called you to do that no one else can do? Remember that your children need your time too.

I found a saying that makes a lot of sense to me, "God doesn't give us what we can handle, God helps us handle what we are given."—Unknown.

Sometimes, it is the people in our everyday lives that cause us great stress. It is vital to understand that you teach people by what you allow, what you stop, and what you reinforce. You have to set boundaries. Danielle Koepke wrote and I quote, "You don't ever have to feel guilty about removing toxic people from your life. It doesn't matter if someone is a relative, romantic interest, employer, childhood friend, or a new acquaintance. You don't have to make room for people who cause you pain or make you feel small. It's one thing if a person owns up to their behavior and makes an effort to change. But if a person disregards your feelings, ignores your boundaries, and continues to treat you in a harmful way, they need to go."

"Do not be afraid" is written in the Bible 365 times. God wants us to live every day of the year without fear. For I know the plans I have for you. They are plans for good and not disaster to give you hope and a future (Jer. 29:11).

Trust in the Lord with all your heart. Do not depend on your own understanding. Seek His will in all you do and He will show you which path to take (Prov. 3:5–6).

MONEY—BLESSING OR BURDEN?

Have you ever heard about those people who have won huge jackpots and lotteries or had a great aunt leave a bundle of money of inheritance to someone who later regretted they ever received money? They report they have new family members appearing on their doorsteps and unfavorable people claiming to be their new found BFF aka *frien-emy*!

Don't store up treasures here on earth because they can be taken away. Look at how many of those lost millions when terrorists crashed into the Twin Towers. Your treasure should be heaven. Whatever your treasure is, the desires of your heart will be. No one can serve both God and money (Matt. 6:19–24).

With money comes responsibility. People who are rich fall into temptation and are trapped by foolish desires that lead them to ruin and destruction. Some people that have craved money have wandered from their faith and live with many sorrows (1 Tim. 6:9–10). With that being said, should you be blessed with wealth, thank God and use it generously to help those in need (Prov. 31:20).

God gives wisdom and joy to those who please him. But when a sinner becomes wealthy, God will take the wealth away and gives it to one that pleases him (Eccles. 2:26).

Help the needy (Matt. 6:2, Acts 20:35; Eph. 4:28; and Titus 3:14).

Tithes are to pay or give 10% of your earnings as an offering. You are a hypocrite when you do not tithe (Matt. 23:23). Do not neglect others just because you tithe. (Luke 11:42).Pleasures are from the hand of God (Eccles. 2:24–25).

SELF-DISCIPLINE

It is not easy to follow through with the busyness of our daily lives. When we commit to something, we need to be disciplined and follow through. There is reward in self-discipline, and there are consequences for laziness.

"You don't drown by falling in water;
you drown by staying there."
-Edwin Louis Cole

For God has not given us a spirit of fear and timidity, but of power, love, and self-discipline (2 Tim. 1:7).

A hard worker has plenty of food, but a person who chases fantasies has no sense (Prov. 12:11). Wise words bring many benefits, and hard work brings rewards (Prov. 12:14). Work hard and become a leader; be lazy and become a slave (Prov. 12:24). Lazy people want much but get little, but those who work hard will prosper (Prov. 13:4). Good planning and hard work lead to prosperity, but hasty shortcuts lead to poverty (Prov. 21:5). Despite their desires, the lazy will come to ruin, for their hands refuse to work (Prov. 21:25).

DOES GOD DISCIPLINE?

Yes. The Lord disciplines those he loves and punishes each one he accepts as his child. As you endure divine discipline, remember that God is treating you as his own child (Heb. 12:6-7). Our earthly father disciplined us for a few years, as best as he knew how. But God disciplines us so that we might share in his holiness. No discipline is enjoyable while it is happening, but there is a peaceful harvest of right living for those who are trained in this way (Heb. 12:10–11).

Know that it will not be like this forever. God cares about you! Cast all your cares upon God, for He cares for you (1 Peter 5:7).

Come to me all you who are weary and burdened and I will give you rest (Matt. 11:28–30).

The Lord your God is with you, He is mighty to save. He will take great delight in you. He will quiet you with his love and will rejoice over you with singing (Zeph. 3:17).

Neither life or death, angels or demons, present nor future, or any powers, height or depth, or anything else in all creation will be able to separate us from the love of God that is in Christ Jesus, our Lord (Rom. 8:38–39).

We suffer, so when others suffer, we can meet their needs (2 Cor. 1:6–7).

When you pass through the waters, I will be with you; and through the rivers, they shall not overwhelm you. When you walk through fire, you shall not be burned, and the flame shall not consume you (Isa. 43:2).

He will cover you with his feathers, under his wings you find refuge; His faithfulness will be your shield and rampart (Psalm 91:14).

And our hope for you is firm because we know that just as you share in our suffering, so also you share in our comfort (2 Cor. 1:17).

May your unfailing love rest upon us, O Lord, even as we put our hope in you (Psalm 33:22).

Be joyful in hope, patient in affliction, and faithful in prayer (Romans 12:2).

Rejoice in hope (Romans 5:2).

When you do survive a moment of crisis, know that there is a reason. Stop stressing and focus on your blessings. My brethren, count it all joy when you fall into various trials, knowing that the testing of your faith produces patience (James 1:2–3).

Wisdom has its own reward. If you scorn it, you hurt yourself (Prov. 9:12).

He is our teacher (1 John 2:27).

He teaches discernment (Prov. 2:9).

He grants wisdom, good sense (Prov. 2:7–8).

The wisdom that comes from heaven is all pure and full of quiet gentleness (James 3:17).

WHAT CAN I DO TO BE STRONG?

First look at what you perceive to be a strong person. What are the traits you look for or admire? What do they say and do that impresses you? You need to distinguish what you like and what you don't like. You may like that they stand up for themselves but not like their approach or their tone. Are you willing to work on those skills? When you emulate those traits, you too will become strong.

What are some of the common traits of a strong person? A strong person is kind, fair and will speak up for themselves and others. They don't worry about pleasing other people. They are able to say no.

No is a good word. Say no to things that take away life.

Say yes to things that is positive, encouraging and builds you up!

A strong person does not need to be around people to escape loneliness. They appreciate alone time.

They don't dwell on the past because it is a waste of time to feel sorry for yourself. They accept responsibility for their mistakes and don't repeat them. And they don't allow others to steal their joy.

They are willing to work hard to succeed and don't feel the world owes them anything. They are able to tolerate discomfort and replace negative thoughts with productive thoughts.

They think productively, using their mental energy wisely. They evaluate their core beliefs and stand by them. They will reflect on their progress daily and will consider their achievements and goals.

A strong person will do what they can to stay happy, they refrain from complaining. They tend to be patient, not expecting immediate results.

They don't waste energy on things they cannot control. They embrace change and challenges. They will weigh out risks and benefits and will usually take calculated risks. They are willing to fail using the experience as a teaching moment. They don't allow negative things to control them.

A strong person is able to celebrate success, and celebrate other people's success without resentment and jealousy.

LOVE YOUR LIFE

Sometimes, God closes doors for you because you will not change otherwise. For some, whey will not make a change unless it has been forced on them. Remember He opens doors for us.

Time heals most everything, but you have to give yourself permission to make peace with your past. Move forward to the present. You are in charge of your happiness. And the Bible provides us with tools to help you.

Don't worry about what others think of you, God is on your side! Don't compare your life to other people. Not only lusting what others have, but judging others.

The eye has not seen nor ear has heard, neither have entered into the heart even imagined what wonderful things God has ready for those who love the Lord (1 Cor. 2:9).

If you want to know what God wants you to do, ask Him and He will tell you (James 1:5).

His life is the light that shines through the (mental) darkness and the darkness can never extinguish it (John 1:5)

Don't think too hard about getting answers for everything. Trust that the answers will come to you. He makes all things beautiful in His time (Eccles. 3:11).

LOVE YOUR SELF

We are all designed unique from each other, and we are designed by God (Eph. 2:10).

To acquire wisdom is to love yourself; people who cherish understanding will prosper (Prov. 19:8). This does not mean to be conceited or selfish. It is saying to love yourself enough to care for yourself.

And you must love the Lord your God with all your heart, all your soul, all your mind, and all your strength. "The second is equally important: 'Love your neighbor as yourself.' No other commandment is greater than these" (Mark 12: 30–31).

Women, you need to dress modestly, wear decent and appropriate clothing. Do not draw attention to yourself with showy hairstyles and expensive clothes and jewelry. Women who are devoted to God should make themselves attractive by the good things they do (1 Timothy 2:9).

CHOOSE HAPPINESS

God wants us to be happy. But some people with mental health issues, may need to make a conscious effort to be happy. That is what is meant by choosing happiness.

A joyful heart makes a cheerful face, but when the heart is sad, the spirit is broken (Prov. 15:13).

We can find happiness in wisdom and understanding (Prov. 3:13–18).

We can find happiness in hope and disappointment with false expectations. The hope of the righteous is gladness, but the expectation of the wicked perishes (Prov. 10:28).

May the God of hope fill you with all joy and peace in believing, so that by the power of the Holy Spirit you may abound in hope (Rom. 15:13).

There is joy in helping others.

Blessed are the merciful, for they shall receive mercy (Matt. 5:7). Jesus tells us "What you do for others, you do for me" (Matt. 25:40). Happy is he who is gracious to the poor and needy (Prov. 14:21).

Blessed are the peacemakers for they shall be called the Sons of God (Matt. 5:9).

GOD'S PROMISES

First of all, we need to remind ourselves that God is there for us. He will protect you (Gen. 15:1). He will protect you from harm (Prov. 19:23). He promises good things (Joshua 23:15)

Study scripture that pertains to your specific problem. Scripture is inspired by God and is used to teach us truth and correction in our lives. He uses it to prepare and equip people to do good work (2 Tim. 3:16–17). Study this book of instruction. (Joshua 1:8) The Bible should be our road map as we travel through life. The Bible will point out safe routes, obstacles to avoid and our final destination (Psalm 119:19).

You may need to forgive yourself and others. Forgive, and you will be forgiven (Luke 6:37).

Avoid negative thinking. In Philippians 4:8, 9 Paul tells us to fix your thoughts on what is true, right, honorable, pure, lovely, and admirable. Think about what is worthy of praise. Practice what we have learned and the God of peace will be with you. In Matthew 5:22–24, Jesus reminds us that if you are angry, you are subject to judgment. And to curse someone puts you in danger of the fires of hell. Jesus want us to reconcile with anyone that has something against you before you come to the altar.

Talk to God openly about what bothers or hurts you. You may need help to overcome painful parts of your past and create new coping skills you can live with. Always remember to thank God for your blessings (Psalm 92:1). A thankful heart is a glad heart. Paul tells us in 1 Thessalonians 5:16–18, Always be joyful. Never stop praying. Be thankful in all circumstances for this is God's will for you who belong to Jesus Christ.

Let all that I am praise the Lord; may I never forget the good things he does for me (Psalm 103:2).

David wrote in his song of thanksgiving to give thanks to the Lord and proclaim His greatness. Let the whole world know what he has done for us (2 Chron. 16:8). The Lord is my deliverer, rescuer and comforter. He reached down from on high and took hold of me. He drew me out of deep waters (2 Samuel 22:17).

Be who God says you are, not who your circumstances suggest you are (John 1:12). As he thinks within himself, so he is (Prov. 23:7). I am leaving you with a gift of peace of mind and heart. The peace I give isn't fragile like the peace the world gives. So don't be troubled or afraid (John 14:27).

You were not created by God to be depressed, defeated, feel guilty, condemned, ashamed, or unworthy. Jesus says to not worry because you are more valuable to Him than many sparrows (Matt. 10:31).

God, renew my energy when I am tired.
(Psalms 103:5)

His life is the light that shines through the darkness and the darkness can never extinguish it (John 1:5). The word darkness refers to mental darkness. Jesus said, "My light will shine out for you just a while longer. Walk in it while you can and where you want before the darkness falls, so you will find your way. While you are in the light, you are children of the light (John 12:35–36).

Search me, Oh God, and know my heart; test me and know my anxious thoughts, and lead me in the way everlasting (Psalms 139:23–24). When I say I feel so empty, God says, "I created you with a longing in your heart that only I can fill (Psalm 90:14). For which cause we faint not; but though our outward man perish, yet the inward man is renewed day by day (2 Cor. 4:16).

Be strong and courageous. Do not be afraid or discouraged for the Lord your God will be with you wherever you go (Joshua 1:9). For God hath not given us the spirit of fear; but of power, and of love, and of a sound mind (2 Tim. 1:7). He that over-cometh shall inherit all things; and I will be his God and he shall be my son (Rev. 21:7). Consider it all joy when you encounter trials knowing that the testing of your faith produces endurance (James 1:2–3). We are troubled on every side, yet not distressed; we are perplexed, but not in despair (2 Cor. 4:8).

Blessed are those that don't doubt me (Matt. 11:6). I can do all things through Christ which strengthens me (Phil. 4:13).

He heals the broken hearted, and binds up their wounds. (Psalm 147:3) Come, and let us return unto the LORD: for the hath torn, and he will heal us; he hath smitten, and he will bind us up (Hosea 6:1).

These things I have spoken unto you, that in me ye might have peace. In the world ye shall have tribulation: but be of good cheer; I have overcome the world (John 16:33).

MY DAILY PRAYER

Today, Father, I want to pray for a number of people on my heart who face struggles of all kinds. Some are family members and friends, some are faithful servants of your Kingdom doing your work in hard places. Some are grieving, facing tough times, hard decisions, and family struggles. Some have opportunities they don't want to miss. And some are overcoming addictions. And there are many others. Please hear my prayer for them today.

In Jesus name, Amen.

Rephrased from "All for God's Glory."

GROWING CHRISTIANS

We are reminded throughout the Bible not to follow the worldly. To let God transform you into a new person. Learn to know God's will which is good, and pleasing, and perfect (Romans 12:2)

Ask anything in my name and I will do it (John 14:14) When Jesus says to ask for anything, we need to remember it must be asked in His name. We cannot expect magic or use the requests to fulfill selfish desires.

And this I pray; that your love may abound more and more (Phil. 1:9).

Oh God, help me to never tell a lie. Give me neither power nor riches. Give me just enough to satisfy my needs because if I am rich, I may deny you and if I am poor, I may steal and insult your holy name (Prov. 30:8–9).

O Lord, I have come to you for protection; don't let me be disgraced. Save me and rescue me for you do what is right (Psalm 71:1–2).

Don't keep thinking about the same questions over and over, days on end.

Reach out! Ask someone to help guide you.

ARE YOU TEACHABLE?

We should always be open to learning from one another. Do you accept training or constructive criticism from others? In Proverbs 27:17, we are reminded: "As iron sharpens iron, so a friend sharpens a friend." NLT further explains, "Mental sharpness comes from being around good people. And a meeting of minds can help people see their ideas with new clarity, refine them, and shape them into brilliant insights. This requires partners who can challenge one another and stimulate thought—people who focus on the idea without involving their egos in the discussion; people who know how to attack the thought and not the thinker. Two friends who bring their ideas together can help each other become sharper."

Hebrews 13:1–5, NLT, "Real love for others produces tangible actions: Hospitality to strangers, empathy for those who are in prison, and those who have been mistreated, respect for your marriage vows, and contentment with what you have. Make sure that love runs deep enough to affect hospitality, empathy, fidelity, and contentment."

In Joshua 24:14–15, we are to fear the Lord and serve him wholeheartedly. Put away all idols and serve the Lord alone. The choice is yours. Will it be God or will it be a substitute? If you chose God, then reaffirm your choice daily. It is important that we take a stand for the Lord regardless of what others think, say or do. "As for me and my family, we will serve the Lord." The way we live reflects the strength of our commitment to serve the Lord.

Where there is strife, there is pride, but wisdom is found in those who take advice (Prov. 13:10).

JUDGING OTHER CHRISTIANS:

Some people refuse to attend church because the gossip runs rampant and the politics are oppressive. The politics are awful! "They only want money." Or they have been judged harshly for a sin they committed or someone in their family has committed. Sadly, I have been severely hurt by Christian people!

> "It is not for you to judge the journey of
> another's soul. (2 Chron. 19:6)
> "It is for you to decide who YOU are,
> not who another has been or has failed to be."
> –Neale Donald Walsch

Here's a perfect example (I am going to breeze over this because it could be a novel in itself): My husband and I were removed from a *Minnesota nice* Baptist church membership over something other family members did.

Another example: At an Assembly of God church we attended, a couple made the choice to get a divorce. Some of the elders of the church decided they would take it upon themselves to move the furniture out of their house for the person they were siding with. Then they revoked the family's church membership. Whatever happened to hate the sin, love the sinner? (Jude 1:23). The entire family suffered—including the grade school aged children. We decided to leave the church in fear of harsh judgment for something one of our own teen children or foster children may do.

First Corinthians 4:4–5 is so important! My conscience is clear, but that doesn't prove I am right. It is the Lord himself who will examine me and decide. So don't make judgments about anyone ahead of time—before the Lord returns. He will bring our darkest secrets to light and will reveal our private motives. Then God will give to each one whatever praise is due.

Bless those who curse you and pray for those who hurt you (Luke 6:28). Welcome those who are weak in faith, but do not argue with them about their personal opinions (Romans 14:1). Do not judge so that you will not be judged (Matthew 7:1, Luke 6:37). Therefore you have no excuse, O man, every one of you who judges. For in passing judgment on another you condemn yourself, because you, the judge, practice the very same things. We know that the judgment of God rightly falls on those who practice such things. Do you suppose, O man—you who judge those who practice such things and yet do them yourself—that you will escape the judgment of God? (Romans 2:1–3).

Do not judge or look down upon our brothers or do anything to cause a fellow Christian to stumble or fall spiritually (Romans 14:10).

DISCERN FALSE PROPHECIES

In 2 Timothy 2:14–16, Paul explains how false teachers will use trivial arguments that cause strife and division. To know if their teaching is true, we have to study scripture so we understand what it means. We are instructed to build our lives on scripture because the Bible tells us how to live for Him and to serve Him. We are to study the Word regularly or we will find ourselves neglecting God and our true purpose for living. Hebrews 2:1 tells us to pay close attention to the truth so we don't fall prey to false teachings. We must not neglect our salvation.

In Acts 1:11, Paul wrote about people who teach wrong doctrines and lead others astray. Some are misguided or confused, and some are evil. Acts 17:11 says we can verify teachings by comparing them from scripture. Anyone who teaches God's word will never contradict the Bible. According to NLT, "You can recognize false teachers because they will (1) focus more attention on themselves than on Christ, (2) ask you to do something that will compromise or dilute your faith, (3) de-emphasize the divine nature of Christ or the inspiration of the Bible, or (4) urge believers to make decisions based more on human judgment than on prayer and biblical guidelines."

ABOUT PRAYER

Many people report they have a problem with staying focused because they are too busy or side tracked. Electronic devices are a huge time thief. It's no longer just the TV and phone calls. We have computers and laptops, smartphones, iPhones, iPads, readers, and mini-tablets. Americans waste a huge amount of time on their electronic devices!

If having a prayer life is truly a strong desire, set a designated time and place to devote time to prayer and reading your Bible. Spending time daily with God is as important as a workout schedule or an event. Perhaps you can forfeit a TV program, gaming, or Facebook time. Remove yourself from electronic distractions. Using my iPad with an electronic Bible can be too distracting for me as it is too easy to flip to Pinterest, Sudoku, and Boggle.

Make sure to have a specific Bible study to work on and a prayer list to keep you on task. A quiet and comfortable place with no distractions will help you to stay focused. I like to keep a notepad next to me when I pray so that if I am distracted I can write down what is jogging my memory and go back to praying. When I lay down, I will pray. My husband shared that he likes to talk to God while he is driving to work because he is usually too tired when he goes to bed.

In Luke 11:1–4 and Matthew 6:9–13, Jesus told his disciples how to pray. These are exemplary examples for family prayer.

> Our Father which art in heaven. Praise God by keeping his name holy (Matt. 6:9 and Luke 11:2).
>
> May your kingdom come soon. May your will be done on earth as it is in heaven (Matt. 6:10 and Luke 11:2).
>
> Each day, give us the food we need (Matt. 6:11).
>
> Forgive us for our sins as we are to forgive those who sin against us (Matt. 6:12 and Luke 11:4).
>
> Keep us from temptation and rescue us from the evil one (Matt. 6:13, Matt. 26:41 and Luke 11:4).

Open prayer with praise and worship. Reading the book of Psalms will help you through this.

Sometimes, people have a hard time praying in front of others. Or just find it difficult to pray. They cannot find the words, or feel inadequate in prayer. When you pray, your prayers should be private and sincere (Matthew 6:5-6). God is not concerned with the length of your prayers or the trendy wording we always hear; only your faith and the depth of your sincerity.

Jesus says to not pray like hypocrites who pray publicly for everyone to see. And not to babble on repeating words again and again (Matt. 6:7). I had a discussion with an elderly gentleman that shared that he only likes to hear the old hymns at church. He says the newer church music repeats itself over and over Matthew. 6:7 would prove his point. I explained that the verses of the songs are meant to guide people toward intimate prayer.

The Father knows what you need before you even ask him (Matt. 6:5–8). The Spirit helps us in our weakness. We do not know what we ought to pray, but the Spirit himself intercedes for us with groaning too deep for words (Romans 8:26).

It is wise to ask God to guide you Galatians 5:16, or to work on you. You should always ask for God's hand in change. Whether it be a personal change, job change, or spiritual change. Change me, Lord (Titus 2:14, 3:4–5).

Prayer is a privilege (Heb. 10:32, Matt.6:9, Romans 8:15, Gal. 4:6).

Often we are frustrated and impatient when we don't get answers for our prayers. However, in 1 Thessalonians 5:17, Paul reminds us to never stop praying. God answers prayer at will: The eyes of the Lord watch over those who do right and his ears are open to their prayers (1Peter 3:12). Pray with perseverance (Luke 18:1-8 and 1:11, Luke 11:1–13 and 1 Kings 18:41–46).

Prayer should be two-way communication. Remember, no prayer goes unanswered, so make sure to set aside time to pray and hear Him. Draw close to God and He will draw close to you (James 4:8). Prayer is a partnership with God. Romans 8:26-27. We hear God's voice when we pray (John 10:27). The prize is the relationship with God (Matt. 6:6).

If you want something, keep asking (Matt. 7:7–11). God will supply all my needs (Phil. 4:19). But remember that you may not get answers if you don't expect results (Psalm 145:13–19).

Sometimes it is difficult to forgive someone. This is when we need to pray for them. It may not change them, but it will make a difference for yourself. Whenever you stand praying, forgive if you have anything against anyone so that your Father in heaven may also forgive your sin (Mark 11:25). If you forgive those who sin against you, your heavenly Father will forgive you. If you refuse to forgive others, your father will not forgive your sins (Matt. 6:14–15).

Be careful with repetitive, rehearsed prayer as they can become meaningless. Prayer can be powerful! If you have a friend that asks you for prayer, it is important to follow through with that prayer. God answers prayer! Always pray in the Spirit for everyone and everything (Eph. 6:18). Find like-minded believers and form a prayer team. Be prepared to be surprised by the power of your prayers. Spur one another on toward love and good deeds (Heb. 10:24).

God rewarded Job for being prayerful for others. When Job prayed for his friends, the Lord not only restored his fortunes, but gave him twice as much as before (Job 42:8–10).

Keep a prayer journal to visualize the power of God through answered prayer. Pray God's agenda (Matt 6:9–13). If you desire to learn to have a deeper relationship with the Heavenly Father, make sure to seek Him by reading your Bible, prayer, and talking with your pastor or minister. Often, people learn the deepest information through Bible group studies.

READING RESOURCES:

A New Kind of Normal
By Carol Kent

A Scarlet Cord of Hope
Sheryl Griffin

A Woman's Guide to Hearing God's Voice
By Leighann McCoy

Are You Here? Finding God During Times of Pain, Despair, and Crisis
By Ron Wagley

Creating a Haven of Peace
By Joanne Fairchild Miller

From Pain to Purpose: Learning to Thrive Not Just Survive the Challenges of Crisis
By Chris McQuay

Hope: For Troubled Hearts, Those Who Lost Loved Ones, Those Who Grieve, Those Facing Crisis, Single People, Failing Marriages, Prodigal Children
By Greg Laurie

Me, Myself & Lies: A Thought Closet Makeover
By Jennifer Rothschild

More than Enough: How Jesus Meets Our Deepest Needs
By Jeff Lorg

Setting Boundaries with Difficult People: Six Steps to Sanity for Challenging Relationships

By Allison Bottke

Stronger: Finding Hope in Fragile Places
By Angela Thomas

Unanswered: Lasting Truth for Trending Questions
By Jeremiah J. Johnston

Victory Over the Darkness: Realize the Power of Your Identity in Christ
By Neil T. Anderson.

Walking With God through Pain and Suffering
By Timothy Keller

You Make Me Crazy
By Rick Warren

QUESTIONS TO PONDER:

1. If you are ministering with others, are you in compliance with the law?
    If you are ministering through a church, do you have a job description to follow?

2. Do you have or plan to have a local resource system?
    Do you have Christian resources on hand?
    Do you have online resources on hand?
    Do you have training resources available?
    How will you access and keep all of this information accessible?

3. What boundaries are important to you? Why?

4. Does this chapter entice you to learn more about ministering to others?

5. Does this chapter entice you to prepare personal goals?

6. Do you feel your prayer life is a standard acceptable to God?
    What will you do to improve your prayer life?

7. Was any part of this chapter eye-opening for you?
    Was any part of this chapter motivating for you?

8. What verse or verses are important to you?

REFERENCES AND RESOURCES

REFERENCES:

Abels, Vicki; Director, Race to Nowhere documentary. www.racetonowhere.com

Addiction; Rehab-International.org, myaddiction. com, techaddiction.ca, techaddiction.ca,

psychiatryadvisor.com

Alliance of Hope; wwwalliaceofhope.org

Alzheimers.net Alzheimer's (by state): http:// www.alzheimers.net/resources/

American Psychological Association, APA.org, Understanding Compulsive Sexual Behavior

October 2003, Vol 34, No. 9, Print version: page 20

Anxiety and Depression Association of America (ADAA), Posttraumatic Stress Disorder; www.adaa.org/ understanding-anxiety/posttraumatic-stress-disorder-ptsd

Barrick, Audrey; Christian Post

http://www.christianpost.com/news/ survey-christians-worldwide-too-busy-for-god-28677/

Blueletterbible.org

Brain and Spinal Cord; Emotional Stages of Recovery for Traumatic Brain Injury (TBI), http://www. brainandspinalcord.org/emotional-stages-tbi/

Breen, Sophia; Less Stress, More Living, Huffington Post. http://www.huffingtonpost.com/2013/03/27/ mental-health-benefits-exercise_n_2956099.html

Bressert, Steve PhD; PsychCentral, Body Dysmorphia Disorder Symptoms, http://psychcentral.com/ disorders/body-dysmorphic-disorder-symptoms/

Camp Recovery Center http://www.crchealth.com/

Campbell, Ross M.D.: How to Really Love Your Teenager. Victor Books, Wheaton Illinois

Caruso, Kevin; Suicide is NOT a sin. www.suicide.org

Center on Addiction; List of Street Names for Drugs, centeronaddiction.org

Chapman, Gary; www.5lovelanguages.com

Chaucie's Place, Statistics on child sexual abuse. chauciesplace.org

Christ Unlimited; Answers, http://christunlimited. com/answers/awar.html

Christians and Mental Illness, http://www.internetmonk. com/archive/the-christian-and-mentalillness- iv-is-there-mental-illness-in-the-bible

Collard Miller, Kathy. The Useful Proverbs, World Publishing, Grand Rapids Michigan

Community Oriented Policing Services (COPS): Gangs and Bullying in Schools http://www. cops.usdoj.gov/default.asp?item=1309

Chaucie's Place, Statistics on child sexual abuse. chauciesplace.org

Connor, Rev. Dr. Brian N., Good Shepherd Institute, Spiritual Warfare

Davis, Ken. How to Live with Your Parents without Losing Your Mind Zondervan Publishing House, Grand Rapids Michigan

Dobbins, Richard. Your Feelings… Friend or Foe? Biblical Guidelines for Managing Your Emotions, Totally Alive Publications, Akron Ohio

Drug Abuse; Addiction Library, drugabuse.com

Drug Free World: www.drugfreeworld

Eckhart, John; Why a Christian can have a Demon, Charisma Magazine, 1/20/2015

Food and Drug Administration (FDA)

FBI National Gang Report: 2013 https://www.fbi.gov/stats-services/publications/national-gang-report-2013

Gang Prevention: An Overview of Research and Programs. www.ncjrs.gov

Hancock, Jim. Raising Adults, Getting Kids Ready for the Real World. Pinon Press, Colorado Springs, Colorado

Help Guide; Helpguide.org

Helping Gang Youth: Most Frequently Asked Questions About Gangs http://www.helpinggangyouth.com/faqs.html

Henderson, Dr. E. Harold, Overcomer's Adult Sunday School Baptist Publishing House, Texarkana, TX

Hybels, Bill. Who You Are When No One's Looking, Choosing Consistency, Resisting Compromise, InterVarsity Press, Downers Grove Illinois

International Helpline for Abortion Recovery; Internationalhelpline.org

Ken Baird Studios, http://kenlairdstudios.hubpages.com/hub/Mental-Illness-in-the-Bible-Part-II KidsHealth.org

Knauss, Brandon http://www.viprecovery.com/suspect-your-child-is-using-drugs-tips-for-parents

Kushner, S. Harold, When Bad Things Happen to
    Good People. Avon Books, New York, NY

Lohmann, Raychelle Cassada, M.S., LPC, GCDF:
    Teen Gangstas, How Can You Protect

Your Teen From Gangs? https://www.psychologytoday.
    com/blog/teen-angst/201010/teen-gangstas

Mayo Clinic, Post-Traumatic Stress Disorder

Mayo Clinic, Self Injury/Cutting

MCHA, Medica Member Assistance Program:
    Don't Let Stress Get the Best of You

Mental Health and the Church: www.
    mentalhealthandthechurch.com

Mental Help; www.mentalhelp.net

Miller, Bud and Betty, Pastors; War and
    Rumors of War: What the Bible

Says about War, http://bibleresources.org/war/

MN ASAP Family Voices, Spring 2006. Claudia and Bart Fletcher,

Parents of ten children through adoption.

Motivating Caregivers: An Applied Approach,
    March 2012. Janet Yeats, MA LMFT

National Alliance on Mental Illness (NAMI): www.nami.org

National Center for PTSD: www.ptsd.va.gov/public/index.asp

National Coalition for Homeless Veterans:

http://nchv.org/index.php/help/help/step-by-step/

National Gang Center: Parents Guide to Gangs

https://www.nationalgangcenter.gov/Parents-Guide-to-Gangs

National Institute on Drug Abuse (NIDA)

National Institute of Health; On the Self-Stigma of Mental
    Illness: Stages, Disclosure, and Strategies for Change; http://
    www.ncbi.nlm.nih.gov/pmc/articles/PMC3610943/

National Institute of Mental Health, NIMH: www.nimh.nih.gov

NIMH National Institute of Mental Health.
Transforming the understanding

and treatment of mental illnesses. http://www.
nimh.nih.gov/index.shtml

National Mental Health Association Information
Center: www.nmha.org

National Network to End Domestic Violence www.nnedv.org

National Sleep Research Project: The survey was
overseen by Professor Ron Grunstein, Dr

David Joffe and Dr Bruce Thompson of the
Australasian Sleep Association.

http://www.abc.net.au/science/sleep/facts.htm

Nolte, Dorothy Law and Rachel Harris, Children Learn
What They Live. Workman Publishing, NY

NRMA Research Center, Home and Auto
Insurance www.nrma.com

Omartian, Stormie. The Power of a Praying Parent
Harvest House Publishers, Eugene Oregon

Project Gang-Proof Resource: Getting out of Street
Gangs http://www.gov.mb.ca/justice/safe/
gangproof/pdf/interventionsheet.pdf

Saddleback Church Mental Health Conference March 2014,
"Troubled Families: Support for Loved Ones Affected
by Mental Illness" with Amy Simpson. Speaker/Author
of Troubled Minds: Mental Illness and the Church's
Mission (InterVarsity Press) - See more at: http://
amysimpsononline.com/books/#sthash.vMHswXhn.dpuf

Tartakovsky, Margarita M.S.; PsychCentral,
Demystifying Treatment for Body Dysmorphic
Disorder http://psychcentral.com/lib/
demystifying-treatment-for-body-dysmorphic- disorder/4/

Tennessee Suicide Prevention Network; tspn.
org/myths-about-suicide

US Department of Veterans Affairs; Spirituality and Trauma:
Professionals Working Together. http://www.ptsd.va.gov/
professional/provider-type/community/fs-spirituality.asp

Veterans Crisis Line: Veterans and Suicide,
veterancrisisline.net WebMD

Weir, Kirsten, Journalist, Minneapolis, MN; APA.
org. Is Pornography Addictive?

April 2014, Vol 45, No. 4, Print version: page 46

WKRN Town Hall Meeting; Heroin at Home with
Bob Mueller at Belmont University.

Workforce Fatigue Raises Concerns, July 2014.
Provider Magazine / Human Resources

Wrenn, Glenda, MD; Research of Behavioral Health,
Satcher Health Leadership Institute

RESOURCES:

Autism: "The Autism Answer" by Dr. Frank Lawlis

"The Everyday Advocate; Standing Up For Your
Autistic Child" by Areva Martin

A Place For Mom: Senior care near you. Free
referrals. www.aplaceformom.com

Adult Bullying; http://www.bandbacktogether.
com/adult-bullying-resources/

Bible Study Verses by Topic: www.
biblestudytools.com/topical-verses/

Bullying Help: http://www.bullyingstatistics.
org/category/bullying-help

Connected Families: www.connectedfamilies.org

Drug-Free America 1-800- 662-4357

Eating Disorders: www.psychcentral.com

Focus on the Family Counseling 855-771-HELP
(4357) www.focusonthefamily.com

Family and Marriage; worksheets and videos.
www.5lovelanguages.com

Family First Aid: Troubled Teens First Aid
http://www.familyfirstaid.org/

Focus on Recovery Helpline: A 24-hour national
alcohol and drug abuse addition and treatment
hotline: 1-800-374-2800 or 1-800-234-1253

Helpguide.org

International Helpline for Abortion Recovery;
www.internationalhelpline.org

KidsHealth.org

Local Mental Health Resources: Dial 2-1-1

National Suicide Prevention Hotline: Call 1-800-273-TALK (8255)

National Action Alliance for Suicide Prevention:
www.actionallianceforsuicideprevention.org

National AIDS Hotline: Talk to someone who knows
about HIV/AIDS and can tell you about AIDS
services in your city or state: 1-800-CDC-INFO

NAMI National Alliance on Mental Illness
Helpline: 1-800-950-6264

National Military Family Association; http://
www.militaryfamily.org/

National Suicide Support Number:1-888-784-2433
(1-888-SUICIDE)

Project Gang-Proof Resource Line: 1-800-691-4264

PTSD http://www.ptsd.va.gov/public/PTSD-overview/
reintegration/gen_deployment_stress_families.

Sober Recovery www.soberrecovery.com

Strength of the Moment for Caregivers Call 888-806-4784 for 24 hour support and resources.

Veterans Crisis Line: 1-800-273-8255 (press 1)

Violence Prevention;

http://www.cdc.gov/ViolencePrevention/intimatepartnerviolence/teen_dating_violence.html

http://www.cdc.gov/ViolencePrevention/DatingMatters/index.html

WebMD has great information for researching medical and psychological information

ABOUT THE AUTHOR

Judith Isaacs-Herrig, M.Ed, QIDP

Judith Isaacs-Herrig, a.k.a. Judy Herrig is married to the love of her life, Gordy. Although they lived most of their lives in Minnesota, they moved to the beautiful state of Tennessee in 2013 where they found a church and Bible study worth moving for!

Judy and Gordy have two hardworking, intelligent daughters, both married and living in Minnesota. They have four grandchildren they adore, and two Husky grand-dogs. Judy is a lover of Pomeranians and would be one of those "dog ladies" if it were up to her.

Judy and Gordy love to go camping and fishing together, and play cards and games with friends and family. She also likes to read, write, paint, craft and quilt.

Judy has almost thirty years of human services experience: from Direct Care Staff to corporate level management. She also owned and operated a residential facility for women with dual diagnosis of physical, developmental and mental health challenges. She is a consultant for those seeking guardianship, opening and operating foster and waivered group homes, facilitates trainings and consults staff as well as assist with licensing related issues.

Judy worked closely with Child Protection Services (CPS), family court and law enforcement as a Guardian ad Litem and a Custody Resolution Specialist. She passed the CPS Social Services Merit Exams in the State of Minnesota.

She is a member of Toastmaster's, Word Girls and Christian Women in Ministry (CWIMA) and is a recent graduate of Christian Communicators. She has recently attended Christian conferences and seminars including You Lead, Business Boutique with Dave Ramsey, Patsy (Clairmont) on the Porch, Speak-Up, Love Life Women's Conference, etc.

With her education and experience, she has the desire to teach the many facets of the human services field. And her heart is to reach out to those in crisis—the tough stuff.

For more information about this author, visit Judy Herrig at her ABLE website. www.abetterlivingexperience.com

CPSIA information can be obtained
at www.ICGtesting.com
Printed in the USA
LVHW02s1029010618
579197LV00005B/5/P